ZUNIGA

ecologic architecture

ecologic architecture

richard l. crowther, faia

Butterworth Architecture
Boston London Oxford Singapore Sydney Toronto Wellington

Butterworth Architecture is an imprint of Butterworth–Heinemann

Library of Congress Cataloging-in-Publication Data

Crowther, Richard L.
  Ecologic architecture / Richard L. Crowther.
    p. 297 cm.
  Includes bibliographical references (p. 273) and index.
  ISBN 0-7506-9171-9 (case bound)
  1. Architecture—Environmental aspects. 2. Architecture, Organic.
I. Title.
NA2542.35.C78   1992
720′.47—dc20   91–36482
                                        CIP

British Library Cataloguing-in-Publication Data

  Crowther, Richard L.
    Ecologic architecture.
    I. Title
    712

    ISBN 0750691719

Butterworth–Heinemann
80 Montvale Avenue
Stoneham, MA 02180

10 9 8 7 6 5 4 3 2 1

Printed in the United States of America

Contents

Foreword

Within the necessity to sustain vital planetary systems for Life on Earth and our own well-being, this book is written. Architecture is the central theme within an ecologic context of urban planning, architecture, interiors, landscaping, products, and system design.

The four sections of *Ecologic Architecture* are:

- NECESSITY OF ECOLOGIC DESIGN
- ECOLOGIC DESIGN CONCEPTS, STRATEGIES, AND PROCESS
- HOLISTIC ECOLOGIC ARCHITECTURE/CASE STUDIES
- ECOLOGIC DESIGN GUIDELINES

Our assertive American technologic ingenuity is roughshod in ecologic deprecation and disregard of biologic risk. The mentality of more space, more amenities, more devotion to sybaritic escapism pyramids the illusion of gratifying attainment and myth of the American Dream.

Frugality and constraint are virtually dead issues. Opulence of architecture and interiors by the affluent is far from benign. It places not only an excessive demand on nonrenewable resources and energy, but collectively we all undermine the critical path of Nature and our own sustainability.

In addition to the inordinate demand upon materials and energy, the petro-energies that pollute our great outdoors, indoor air pollution is further compounded by toxic, particulate, electromagnetic, and in some buildings radioactive emissions. "Tight" homes and buildings tend to be bio-antagonistic in light of most often used materials, products, and systems.

The ecologic responsibility is to ourselves and the global legacy of human habitation. *Every choice made from concept, to design, to realization is a demand that results in ecologic and biologic consequence.*

Environmental illness is increasing and the supportive and healing attributes of Nature are decreasing. The necessity is double edged in the express need for ecologic and biologic well-being. Both the "natural" and "synthetic" of our techno-culture of architecture, products, and systems can have physiologic, psychoneural, and ecologic benefits or cause distress and degrees of illness.

A *"purist ecologic ethic"* is most desirable. But in our techno-world design, architecture, and specification are crucially compromised by our built environs and infrastructure; nonavailability of materials and products that are ecologically and biologically compatible; and often in a lack of familiarity and experience with their use.

Within the planning, design, and specification of each project trade-offs are inevitable. Meeting objectives of the criteria, adhering to the limitations of zoning and building codes, minimizing adverse ecologic and biologic effects, and staying within budget requires a *holistic comprehension* based on the best of relevant trade-offs.

The *Necessity of Ecologic Design* section examines our present technologic architecture in light of societal, biologic, and holistic ecologic design. A pressing necessity for change to an ecologic paradigm is imperative. Our separation from rather than coherence with the ecologic forces of our planet is graphically set forth in the context of perception, aesthetics, social responsibility, opportunity, science, and technology.

The *Ecologic Design Strategies* section centers on holistic ecologic design and the multiple concepts, strategies, and processes we can use in gaining freedom from the ecologic and biologic burdens of techno- and petro-energies. Natural systems, techniques, and pertinent considerations for urban planning, residential and commercial architecture, and interiors are evaluated as strategic elements of ecologic/biologic design.

Case Studies embody completed projects by the architect/author. Earlier designs are presented as more simply meeting physical and psychoneural needs, ecologic coherence, solar and climatic orientation, and frugality in the use of materials and construction than the extravagant spaces, materials, construction, and maintenance common today. Two ecologically designed commercial projects are included, as well as a more detailed account of the author's 1980 research facility and an adjoining project just completed.

The *Ecologic Design Guidelines* section categorically covers the specifics to be addressed in the ecologic/biologic concept, design, and planning of any project. The urban infrastructure, architecture, landscaping, interiors, products, and systems acquire an integrated relevancy in use of the guidelines. This guideline is a compelling base for education, programming, research, discussions, conferences, and seminars, as well as for the practice of ecologic design and architecture.

The strategy, case study, and guidelines sections of the book are most applicable to locations with temperate to cold with hot seasonal climates. But it can still serve as a general guide in evaluation and strategies for other site-specific climatic conditions.

Acknowledgments

Gratefully acknowledged are reviews of the manuscript by architect Malcolm Wells, leader in the field of underground architecture, and by Jack Kremers, professor at the School of Architecture at Kent State University in Ohio for their constructive insights and evaluations.

Acknowledgment and special appreciation to Robert F. Steimle, AICP, urban planner, for his multifold role in computer programming and processing, delineation of meticulously executed graphics and plan drawings, and evaluative editing.

For finely crafted delineations of perspective renderings and sectional drawings, an appreciative thank you is given to artist and architect James Day.

ecologic architecture

necessity of ecologic design

Architecture and Context

Architecture is a reflection of our society in attitude, customs, desires, needs, and technology. In our society it is an expectation that runs counter to ecologic coherence and sustainability.

Architecture shapes and conditions our attitudes, our habits, and the relationship of people with people. It instigates networks. The urban fabric is a network of streets, utilities, and of architecture with architecture.

Architecture is the protector from sun, vagaries of climate, people, and roaming animals. It is the protector of self, possessions, and activities.

Architecture bears a relationship to community and to the built environment and its attendant infrastructure. All of the foregoing attributes rest within the conventions and traditions of architecture. But a new inspiration is needed to accord with the natural ecologic forces and regenerative vigor of our planet.

Architecture is a technologic assemblage. Its parts, its pieces, and its entirety are given structure, systems, forms, and finish by characteristics from low to high technology. In the time of less than a century, Life has dramatically changed. The advent of labor-saving and comforting technologic conveniences has displaced a less energy-intensive lifestyle.

Architecture has become more technologic in design and construction. It has become more energy intensive. Energy intensity bears a relationship to air pollution and environmental denigration. Our architecture is largely an "artificial environs" isolated from the natural forces of the sun, air, earth, and water. These *in situ* energies are largely ignored in concept, planning, and design, except as to exclude them from the architectural equation.

Architecture is also configured and formed by the requirements of zoning, building codes, and the penchant of designers and builders. The accepted norms of planning, design, specification, and construction have a dominant influence on the resolution of siting, architecture, urban connections, and concepts of functional space planning. Zoning needs to be structured with greater concern for solar access, daylighting, and the use of natural energies. For the most part, greater flexibility from imposed regulations and conventions is needed to equate with ecologic design.

There is a tendency to overlook singular and compounded effects upon the vitality and health of occupants in the architectural and interior environs. In one indoor environs or another people spend most of their time.

Indoor air pollution prevails not only from the architecture, contents, furnishings,

A venturi fireplace with large black hood provided inductive ventilation as desired and served periodically for cooking. The natural cork floor over slab-on-grade unreinforced concrete was the basic surface for interior furniture and lamps designed by the author.

Efficient high-voltage discharge illumination was used for the kitchen and indirect illumination for the living room and bedroom. The space planning worked with consummate adaptability.

The architect/owner's first designed and built passive solar and climate-responsive home was in 1946 near Balboa Park in San Diego. It was a passive solar direct gain system with dark tile covered thermal mass floor. Cooling was by its siting into a hill and a mist spray patio fountain.

Humboldt St. Passive Solar Residence

A Baubiologie type house was designed and built by the author for his family residence in 1952. It was constructed of unpainted low fired hollow clay tile block, exposed resawn wood beams, and exposed interior wood roof decking and was built as a duplex around a south solar exterior court with white marble chips to enhance daylighting and winter solar gain. With full south and east glazing, a projecting eave of the flat roof shaded in summer, and a mist head fountain pool in the courtyard provided evaporative cooling. Deciduous trees to the south provided summer shade.

We spend 90% of our time indoors. The holistic design of the interior, site, and architecture was the generator of form through ergometric planning and carefully considered climate response. The southside roof of the living room had tilted glass and a skydome, daylighting interior plants set in the earth. They provided an intimate contact with the sky, trees, and exciting changes in weather.

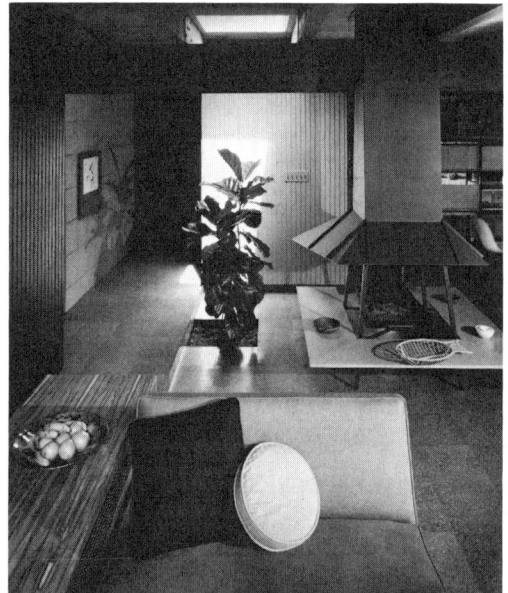

devices, and equipment but also from people and what people do. Biophysical well-being is also at risk due to pervasive electromagnetic fields present in homes and buildings, as well as from radionuclides that may be present. Local and global ecosystems suffer in degree as to the planning and design of the site, architecture, interior, and as to occupant activities and networks that serve the architecture.

The private ownership of property, location, site-specific characteristics, the scale and energy intensities (initial and life-cycle) are pertinent to effectual, efficient, and ecologic resolution and design. Architecture within a locale can be in harmony or disharmony to neighboring architecture, the setting, and general characteristics of a community. But to design within a literal and stylistic context of existing architecture is likely to ignore a disharmony with Nature's ecologic and ecosystemic well-being. Every site and every project is unique as to the diversity and possibilities of holistic context in microclimatic optimization, effectual and efficient realizations, and satisfaction of human well-being and purpose.

An *ecologic context* embodies not only that of Nature but also of ourselves. Our present technologic, artificial environs are counter to Nature. Our encumbering impact upon and mutilation and defilement of Nature's ecosystems has been an affair of unconstrained and rapid attrition. The exponential demand on energy, rate of technologic obsolescence, pyramiding waste, lavish expecta-

tions, rate of societal change, new paradigms of energy-intensive industry and business, invasion of computers, and adroit marketing leave their critical impact upon our society. As the structure of society changes, so does architecture.

New relationships in information, transactions, communication, processes, systems, and economics are shaping a new world with some ecologic advantages and some disadvantages. A new order is bound to arrive out of practical and economic necessity. To what extent it will be ecologic is the pressing question. Our commercial world is in many sectors outpaced by foreign competition. A tightening in American business and industry seeks to lessen internal costs to gain a competitive edge. Employment at middle management and at the lower echelons of labor is subject to reduction and technologic displacement.

The need to move bodies to a place of work is becoming less of a necessity with computer technologies, fax machines, and other technologic sophistication in information and communication. Large office buildings with "pools" of workers can well be displaced by individuals working either at home or at secondary workplaces in which they would not have to travel to a central place of business.

This profile fits well with sociologic factors of single-parent families, ability to provide labor in the most appropriate time periods, to avoid the traffic hassle, parking, and all the effort and cost expended to "get to work" and the cost to provide and maintain a primary place for work. Air pollution in accordance would also be reduced with any traffic reduction.

Every type of business bears a relationship to architecture. It is clear that homes should be reasonably zoned to work functions and to encourage cultural activities such as studios of art, music, craft, dance, tutoring, home industry, research, invention, and of architecture. The more that specific communities are developed (or redeveloped from older ones) with such aspects directed to creativity and the intellect, the greater can we develop intuitive and constructive ways of life.

Co-housing and integrated communities in which people can share ideas, activities, assistance, and skills hark back to the colonial and communal religious communities of America. The difference would be in the high level as well as appropriate low levels of technology, actions, and engagements in harmony and coherence with Nature's ecology and our own need of "holistic" vitality and health.

Our coming age of the year 2000 and beyond will fail in terms of constructive social meaning, sustainability, and vitality unless a revolutionary restructuring is brought into being. Time is against us as our present sociologic, ecologic, and psycho-physiologic form and environs must be replanned to be coherent with sustained global habitability.

Architecture will have to be viewed from an entirely new perspective consistent with ecologic and societal values and equity. Our own expanding population and that of our planet is a provocative and prime problem. Unless we can soon develop heroic measures to stabilize our global population, our prospects of a less livable world will dramatically increase. Nature's ecosystems have considerable resiliency and ability to recover from our years of gross intrusion, depletion, and defilement. But our society and its institutions of commerce, education, recreation, architecture, health, and government will be impaired if they do not practically and spiritually meet the cataclysmic evolutionary realities of today.

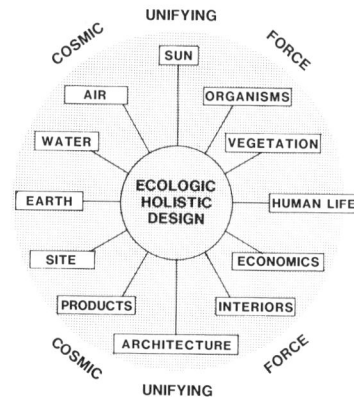

Cosmic unifying force that flows through our planet's dynamic, systemic order with ecologic balance has made us what we are. Our being within the provisional miracle of life has sustained us. But our divisive minds and sophisticated technologies have and continue to deplete the life-giving and sustaining ecosystems and abundance of our planet's resources and energies. We threaten ourselves within how we think, design, specify, and act.

Aesthetics, Architecture, Vitality

The sensory delight of our human spirit is of consummate importance to our vitality of mind and body. Aesthetics fulfill this role. Aesthetics is an art of being stimulated and vitalized by what we behold and experience. Every sense comes into play as we experience our ever-changing environs. Space, light, and form of *how* architecture, its setting, and its interior are composed leave a visual and sensory imprint upon our physiologic and psychoneural being.

The sky, the sun, the earth, the moon, the stars, the wind and its calm all lie within the province of the architect, designer, and planner. The changing of the seasons and all of Nature's dynamic are an aesthetic with which design can fortuitously accord.

Architecture can be with or within Nature or assertively dominate over Nature. In any guise, it can entrance our senses. In the outdoor setting architecture bears a relationship to the all that we can see and sense. The architecture of indoors (where we spend most of our time) encloses about us. Within its visual and biosensory openings of inner to outer space, we respond.

In the aesthetic of our techno-society we live, work, and play within the containment of "artificial environs." It is a far cry from our primitive antecedents of rudimentary natural structures. We are stimulated by high-tech or other aesthetic sophistication. This conjuration aligns with our perceptions of "progress."

Exterior aesthetic stylistic impressions rule the day. The drive-up appearance is an attempt at beguilement. "Luxury" too often making a maudlin farce of "good taste" is a watermark of much of today's architecture and interiors. Imitations and aesthetic overload abound at every hand.

How concerns, sensitivities, and imagination can join architecture and urban environs with the cosmic unifying forces of Nature is critical to our well-being and survival.

Architecture at its best always remains an intuition of the spirit. It is the most fixed element of the dynamic equation. It should be coherent to Nature's ecologic processes and our own biologic well-being. How it can of its whole and of its parts abide with the changing ambience and energies of the day and season lies within the province of solar and climate-responsive ecologic design.

Ancient peoples felt the power of Nature and gave subservience to the mysteries that empowered life. The propitious forces of nature that provided food, shelter, and relieved maladies were given a spiritual accord. Sacred architecture was located coherent to phenomenal geomagnetic forces of the earth. Sun, earth, air, fire, and water gave forth their energies for Life. To quote from the ancient *Essene Gospel of Peace*:

> Thy Earthly Mother is in thee, and thou in her. She bore thee; she giveth thee life. And to her shalt thou one day give it back again. Happy art thou when thou comest to know her and her kingdom.

This ancient aesthetic was of and with Nature. The techniques and technologies of the time posed little interference with the workings of Nature. But by the time of the Christian Era the Mediterranean basin had been extensively denuded of trees for construction, boat building, firewood, and to make way for agriculture and proliferation of cities. Henceforth, nascent technologies circumscribed and demeaned more and more of Nature. *Now technology and techno-habitat and habits are exponentially undermining global habitability*.

As architecture can acquire its vitality from the sky, the sun, the earth, air, and water, so can it transmit this vitality to Life. We are part of Life, although as architect, designer, and planner we play "god" in the creative process. *How to remain faithful to the cosmic powers above us and empower Nature are primal challenges*.

So far our technologies have kept us both adrift and prejudicial to their benefit as we make them part and whole of our "design." The ingenuity invested in techno-materials, systems, constructions, and energies is beguiling and vast in scope. The high-tech look, the practicality of chemicalized synthetics, articulate devices that substitute for labor, and circuitry that does our bidding have become part of us. They become a form of our addiction.

What is made easier, what extends our physical and mental limitations, what extends our sphere of territory and possessions is compelling. We become loyal addicts to these dimensions of our "self" and "being." It is hard to question that which augments our spirit, enhances our sense of self, and gives us a greater sphere of control over the disparate and uncertain conditions of Life.

But the *time has come* to think of ways in which the "vitality of the aesthetic" can mesh with Mother Nature rather than in a substantial measure be counter to her life-giving and life-sustaining forces. The isolation of architecture and ourselves in large degree from Nature is not conducive to our well-being. The aesthetic of Life is that within every moment of existence.

There is no implication herein that we should be of necessity contained within walls of *visible* wood, stone, or earth. But rather that our architectural aesthetic can have meaning and accord with ambient phenomena of the sky, verdancy of the earth, the advent of sun and night, and visible Life of people and creatures. We are biologic receptors of light, imagery, form, and substance. Incessant change within either a natural or artificial environs has its constant effect upon us.

Of notable effect is how space is occupied by people, things, or whatever. We perceive holistically. Our psychoneural receptivity is always in a state of change, but we are forced to adapt, to escape from, or otherwise change the conditions of our environs to our perceptions, conceptions, and desires. We seek out our own vitalities. We are on one hand something like the cat that moves to a warmer place in the sun. But on the other hand, we may preempt this physiologic response to move to another place that fits better with reading a book or any other pursuit. We can and do pick and choose.

So what do we choose to do with architecture, with interior design, and with land planning? At present some of what we do may not offend Nature's ecology and ecosystemic processes. But it is obvious that *in the main* our conceptions, choice of materials, systems, processes, and procedures are out of line with and deprecating to Nature's ecologic regenerative and sustaining powers.

An ecologic conscience, an ecologic understanding, and analytic view of what we have been doing in design and what we *can* be doing in design are critical to our human destiny and ultimate survival. *As we create habitat, how much do we destroy the habitability of our wondrous and life-providing planet? Is not our personal, collective, and social responsibility clear?*

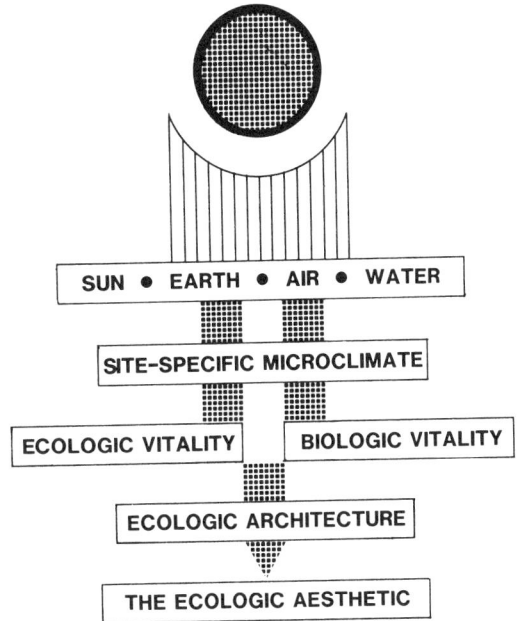

SUN ● EARTH ● AIR ● WATER

SITE-SPECIFIC MICROCLIMATE

ECOLOGIC VITALITY   BIOLOGIC VITALITY

ECOLOGIC ARCHITECTURE

THE ECOLOGIC AESTHETIC

As the site-specific energies of sun, earth, air, and water are optimized and the site and architecture are climate responsive, an ecologic design accord and aesthetic are circumscribed.

As ecologic and biologic vitality are the focal ecologic design intent, architectural ecologic design develops as a coherent architectural aesthetic.

Life and Ecologic Design

Our American paradigm is that every human life has inestimable value. Every heroic attempt is made to save life. Emergency facilities abound. The design of laws and regulations is to protect us. From birth to death we are in the hands of a social order intent on keeping us alive.

Nature is also intent upon keeping us alive. Our organic being through millennia of evolution has a vitality, immune response, and a will to live. We live in a world oscillating between what is supportive and what is hostile to our vigor and well-being.

On the one hand, Nature nurtures us and on the other, imposes threatening and dire circumstance upon us. The forces of Nature inherent in sun, earth, air, water, and fire give life but can take it away. Our remarkable sensory system (created by Nature) keeps us alert to the anomalies of Nature or other events that threaten our lives.

From our earliest human beginnings we learned to use the materials and province of Nature to sustain us. Clothing, shelter, and artifacts conducive to our existence paralleled our resourcefulness in gathering and cultivating food. Our species to date has survived the grand experiment of Life.

But along the way we have created new thresholds of Life between Nature's design and that of our human origin. Through centuries it has sometimes been "nip and tuck" as to whether our provocative conceptions would sustain us or lead us to failure in Nature's scheme of things.

Our mastery over the abundant and wondrous energies of our Earth combined with ever-expanding population and expectation are not without penalty. Nature has limits of resiliency and the sustainability for Life on our global home travelling through space. The regenerative, recuperative, healing, and vitalizing energies of Nature's ecosystemic design have dwindled, been outflanked, or have been overpowered by our intransigent expectations. Science, technology, architecture, transportation, and production provide what we mainly possess.

All design we originate of product, system, process, transport, and construction by means of fossil fuel, toxic chemicals, and nuclear energies is counter to ecologic viability. The origination and life-cycle use of most of what we have and/or the channels of handling and transport have a degree of adverse impact upon Nature's Design. The trail of pollution and environmental havoc from source to place of use and factors of use bear a *pollution quotient*. Every substance, product, and construction should be so measured.

As designers are inspired, conceive, and create, they do so with petro-energy and materials, equipment, and devices of industry. There is no global or national ecologic resource and energy policy that dictates (for the most part) what type, amount, or what processes may attend manufacturing, distribution, and the use of manufactured products. Wild elephant tusks as a resource may be on the verboten list and certain other materials may not be exported or imported. But in the main there is no lid on oil or coal as principal culprits of acid rain, stratospheric ozone depletion, global warming, and health-depleting urban smog.

Agencies of government were designed to protect us. They promulgate national regulations and controls over products we eat and drink. There is literally little protection over what we may breathe. But what we breathe can be as much or more troublesome to our health than what we ingest.

Within the closed environs of homes and buildings we spend our time continually breathing. But within the indoor environment we are surrounded by the toxic chemicals of floor coverings and other materials and surfaces of architecture and interior furniture, equipment, appliances, furnishings, and other contents. Within a medley of poisonous and particulate detractors from health at home or at work or shopping we spend most of our time.

Workplace, industrial, store, educational, other environs, and travelling to and from them in enclosed vehicles make up our

"artificial habitat." Our technologic society has ever added new dimensions to the indoor assault and insult to our physiologic and psychoneural vitality. The multiple stresses are not only from polluted air, but also fields of adverse electromagnetism, radioactivity, and prevalence of noise. Fatigue and other symptoms of distress prevail in our discordant society.

Design is best not as a casual exercise in space planning, aesthetics, structure, and mechanical and electrical systems, but within an ecologic and humanistic perspective. As we have set ourselves apart from Nature, our existence within our artificial environs largely excludes Nature's intemperate moods but also remains out of sync with the vitalizing and calming aspects of Nature.

Life and time move on. Our tendency to fixed-state enclosure, lighting, and mechanical systems and most often of space planning is counter to our own dynamics of thinking, articulation, and mobility. Our bodies need physiologic exercise and challenge as does our mind. Fluctuations within reasonable parameters of comfort contribute to our vital attunement.

Buildings and homes might be thought of as to prudent adaptability. Design of site, architecture, and interior most amenable to an eloquent alignment with the microclimatic and site-specific physical aspects of Nature and diversity of human conduct and activity tends to be conducive to our biologic vitality. Exercise of body and mind by our migration and mobility within our environs and Nature's harmonic flux upon our sensory systems is salutary to our electro-organic physiology.

A factor mainly unnoticed and a usual issue of design are the electromagnetic energies of the Earth. The Earth has strong positive and negative magnetic fields related to geologic formations and underground water courses. A statistical preponderance of bio-dysfunctions is in evidence in locations where the Earth's geopathic fields are present. There is also a Hartmann field that with regularity encircles our globe and a Curry field rather large and diagonal to the points of the compass. There is a probability that adverse magnetic fields from power lines, transformers, house wiring, and wired equipment may coincide with the Earth's geopathic fields, increasing an adverse biologic effect.

Be that as it may, our bodies are complex. We are electro-organic creatures subject to both that which is visible and to the invisible that can harm us. We are a sophisticated ecologic end-product of Nature with extraordinary capabilities to form and alter our environs.

Our primary question of today is, *how we can perceive the wisdom of virtually restructuring our entire concepts of resource and energy use?* We have gone so far with our science, technology, and actions of Life antithetical to Nature a further question is, *have we the time to repent, to reorder our thinking, to create global resource and energy policies consistent with ecosystemic vitality and our human habitation of the Earth?*

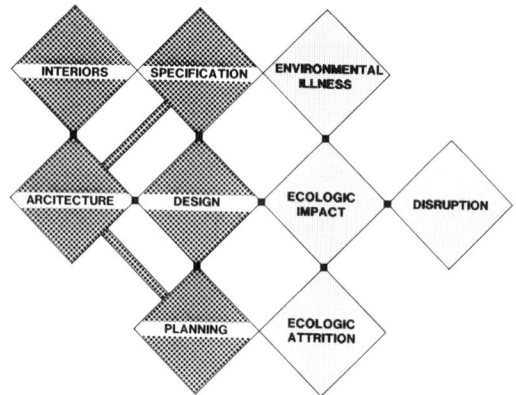

An ecologic-disruptive design, technology, architecture, interior, and infrastructure result in ecologic impact, attrition, and a condition of biologic harm and environmental illness.

Planning, design, and specification are keys to sustained ecologic and biologic vitality. Our unmindful society is exploiting finite resources and seriously disrupting our planet's ecosystemic coherence.

Habitability

Global habitability is at risk from architecture, vehicles, technology, lifestyles, and the development and networks that serve them. The burden of this technologic erosion of Nature, petro-energy denigration of our global atmosphere and living systems, unbridled chemistry, and electromagnetic and radioactive ecologic assaults is a continuum for catastrophe.

No one likes to hear the "bad news," but we are all part of it. If our human destiny is worth a "plugged nickel," we are not giving destiny its value.

Sun, climate, and ecology follow Nature's functions. The *form of life* follows Nature's regenerative, sustaining, and vitalizing powers. Architecture has traditionally followed the form of shelter, protection, culture, space need, desire, and to beguile the ego and "manipulate" people.

"Form follows function" was the tenet of contemporary architecture. At present architectural form follows nostalgia, technology, lifestyles, hyper expectations, marketing, convenience, sinful comfort, and personal aggrandizement. The cost in ecologic terms is not presently weighed. For the most part in choice, purchase, and possession environmental cost is not part of the equation, and further is seldom part of the operational, maintenance, and other life-cycle costs occurring from what is acquired.

All of us are manipulated by the form of architecture, vehicles, and machines. How they are designed and how we perceive our role and position in society program us within illusions of self-will. We believe we determine choice and our fate. But in reality with our techno-culture, conditioned societal responses, and exercised options, we are more pawns than masters of decision and of our destiny.

We live in the "land of the free." To be certain, the oppressions we suffer are not blatantly visible. But corporate power that brings us the goods, visions of the "good life," and expectations in progress for the "best" of what resources can give us is apt to favor corporate rather than ecologic and human well-being. As we are an indivisible part of Nature's ecosystems, what does not sustain Nature's ecology cannot as a bottom line sustain us.

Architecture is a major element of human life. It is a major concern, a major purchase, and has a major effect upon our lives. We spend over 90 percent of our time indoors. In the main our present techno-logic archetype of architecture is a composite of materials, energy, and systems synergistically counter to human vitality and health. Airborne toxic gases, noxious particulates, anti-biologic chemicals, electromagnetism, and radioactivity are dominant in our environs of home, workplace, marketing, and places of learning, entertainment, and relaxation.

No one "drops dead" instantly from the multifarious and multi-level assault upon our sensitivities, the integrity of our immune system, and general biologic fortitude. But the attrition is there and most visible in persons who suffer symptoms and maladies from their environs. All of us are subject to probability of physiologic and psychoneural disturbance, discomfort, or dysfunction from our compound exposure to and risk from ever-present environmental sources.

"Form follows function." Our own evolutionary biologic form is not so adaptable and well tuned to meet the multi-levelled concentrations of aberrant stressors that exist in our "developed" (?) society. Every sense that we possess is under duress. Our environs are loaded with noise and hyper sound and overloaded with visual impressions and stressors that intrude upon our composure. Television and other media, population densities, and our vying for space compromise biologic well-being.

As form follows function in Nature, so should architecture follow, or at least notably align with, the natural resource and energy systems of our planet. Whether we like it or not, we must become responsible stewards of our local and global environment. Our wayward course that has largely ignored Nature's regenerative and life-sustaining atmosphere and dynamic planetary balance of interdependent ecosystems is bringing us close to the brink of disaster.

Design is the primary key in our worldly realm of energy and matter. Nature has no sacred vow nor responsibility to preserve us above all other species, nor to preserve us at all. From primal origins Nature's ecologic and ecosystemic design has kept our species provided and sustained. Our pre-emption *over* Nature has cause to haunt the providence of our species.

Our dominion *over* Nature has not only brought us to the "brink," but also our contrived minds and misapplied ingenuity with unconstrained libidos threaten the world with ever-escalating numbers of people. People require homes, buildings, transport, and the goods and services essential to life. More and more of our global land mass is being devitalized and made less habitable by expanding population.

To save ourselves from ourselves may yet be possible. But our ingrained desires and expectations that translate into per capita decimation of global habitability are critical threats to the probability of ecologic vitality and our concomitant survival.

PER CAPITA ENERGY CONSUMPTION

Canada	
United States	
Netherlands	
West Germany	
United Kingdom	
Japan	
France	
Italy	
U.S.S.R.	
Czechoslovakia	
Poland	
Mexico	
Brazil	
China	
Indonesia	
India	

0   50   100   150   200   250   300   350

Million Btu's per Person per Year

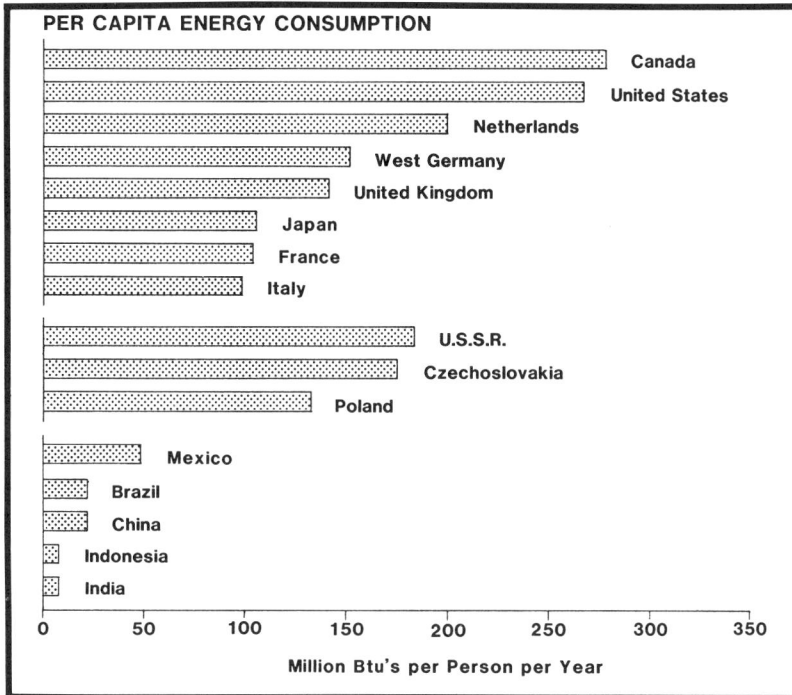

Relevant per capita energy consumption for various nations underscores our profligate demand. Our consumerism (literally consuming our planet's irreplaceable resources and energy), wasteful habits, inefficient systems, and energy-intensive and polluting gadgets, vehicles, products, and architecture can be spelled out as societal arrogance and ecologic neglect.

As other nations strive for and succeed in copying our malfeasant ways, the natural sustainability of our planet will be further compromised. The rapidly expanding populations of developing nations, coupled with technology transfer and a tide of expectations, provide a picture of exponential environmental depletion.

The fate of our worldly habitat lies within the province of our global perceptions, concerns, attitudes, and actions to amend and end our wayward resource and energy exploitation.

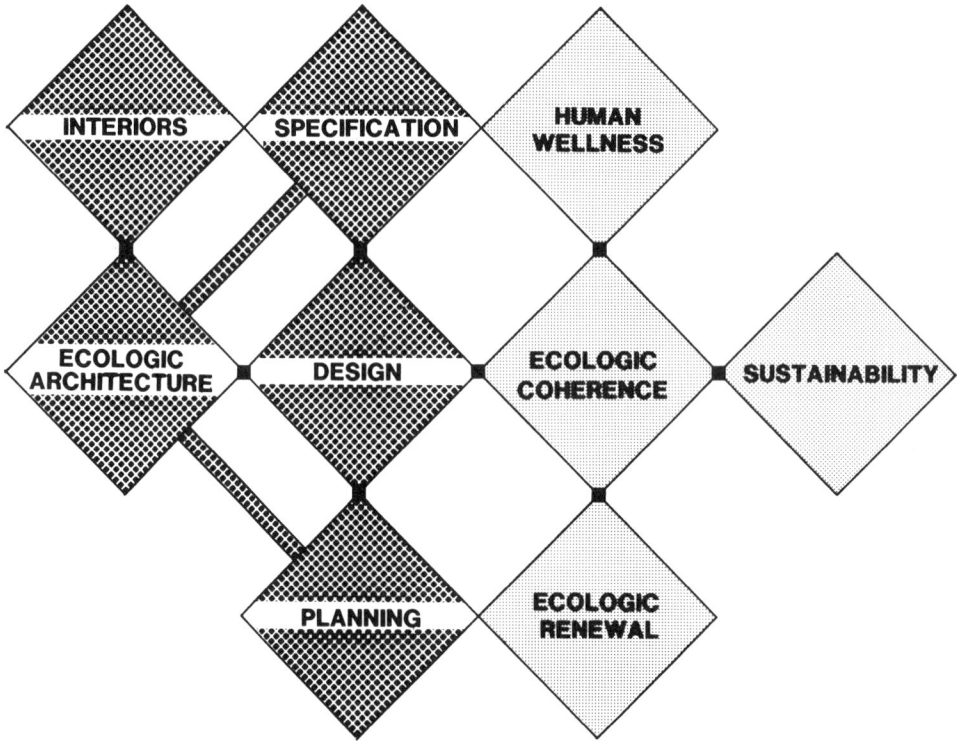

The ecologic necessity translates to ecologic coherence in design of architecture, its products, and its systems. Global systems sustainability and ecologic renewal are principal to our planet's habitability. Concept, planning, design, and specification of architecture, interiors, and all elements of the site and urban infrastructure are critical to ecologic and biologic viability and vitality.

Information, Perception, and Design

Our minds are constantly assaulted with a deluge of information. Imagery and voice of the media, illustrations and text of periodicals, books on every subject, the complex environs of place, sophisticated lifestyles, technologic products, and transient ways of life leave us exposed to multiple and concentrated levels of information. Our sensory system is overloaded.

Added to the inescapable intrusive loads of advertising are the self-imposed loads of computers. The base of information has vastly expanded and keeps proliferating. There is no "top" to where it can go.

We tend to selectively discriminate in what our vision and other senses encounter. For the most part, what our eye and mind selectively see and what our ears hear are what we tuck away in memory and sensation. How confused or relevant our perception is shapes the scenario of our world.

We seek order and security in finding relevancy. But information is not perceived as order. It is mostly disassociated snapshots of sensory arousal and visual impressions. Most of our other senses translate into visual impressions. It is our human penchant to transform impressions in designing the form and nuances of our environs. *We imagine, conceive, and design.*

From our font of information, "what and how we design" is drawn. We perceive needs. We cater to desires. We design within this context. We are conditioned by our experience and by our encounter with information. Each of us is unique. We are genetically one of a kind and one of a kind in experience. But meanwhile the media, our technologic orientation, technologic conditioning, and technologic immersion capture our minds, saturate our soul, and inaugurate our direction.

Nature has no media voice, no representation, except as an isolation from or a supplement to architecture, design, and planning. Nature has not been viewed as *the* dominant force of Life but has rather been regarded as an object for control and subservience. We talk of architecture as a shelter (shelter from Nature), as functional (as a useful separation from Nature), as an aesthetic (aside from the beauty of Nature).

We do not admire Nature any less. The sky, the vegetation, the hills, valleys, forests, plains, mountains, and waterways refresh our spirit. *But the less noticed powers of Nature by which we are nourished, restored, and vitalized are less evident.* The furies of Nature in storms, hurricanes, etc., are most visible as her hostile moods and attributes.

Human dominance over Nature has been perceived as the safeguard of our well-being and survival, and indeed from the periodic violence of Nature we do need protection. The reality is that Life and our survival lie in an interplay among diverse and opposite elements.

While Nature can be a threat to Life, it is essential to the sustenance of Life. As expressed in my first book, *Sun/Earth*, published in 1974:

> The forces of nature are regenerative, deriving their impetus from the sun and universe. To ensure man's survival, the fragmented, isolated systems and constructions of man need to acquire the elegant holistic inter-dependence of nature's resources and systems. Nature remains as the most sophisticated designer of the cosmic and world environment. Man's systems need to be made fully regenerative in concert with natural forces and nature's bounteous provisions.

As we may listen to Nature's information about Life and existence and her powers invested in planetary sustainability, we can secure a clearer picture of how to perceive, conceive, design, and realize. Coherence with the powers of the sky, sun, earth, air, and water is neither an easy task nor without some obscurity. *We need more information about the full spectrum of primal cosmic forces that are expressed through Nature in our global habitat.*

Science seeks the truth. Technology uses and often exploits favorably or unfavorably the information from science. Shortcomings occur as science in probing for the "truths"

of Nature seeks it in increments separate from the whole or misconstrues the information that Nature contains. Proponents of technology are always eagerly waiting in the side wings to pick up a new idea that can be made and sold.

Information, perception, and design isolated and separated from Nature's life-sustaining integrity are fraught with pyramiding hazard and consequential peril. Only by a total scope of information, perception, and design within which Nature and cosmic forces are inseparable can we responsibly create. Our role as architects, designers, and planners depends upon holistic perception that finds no separation among all facets of design nor any exclusion in the optimization of natural site-specific energies of sun, earth, air, and water.

More questions than answers prevail as to perception and design:

- How can we escape from our misdirection in technology and lifestyle?

- How can we acquire the most credible informational and responsive relationship with Nature?

- How can we find values and satisfactions that conserve and sustain Nature and assure our future?

- How can we establish an ecological ethic?

- How can we design for health and vitality?

- How can holism free us from separational errors and inefficiencies?

- How can we assure the credibility of our information base?

- How can our global environment remain vital and habitable?

More questions than answers prevail as to fundamental information needed for holistic ecologic design. The following are areas where information is needed:

- *site-specific* daily and seasonal microclimatic projections (temperature, humidity, precipitation)

- *site-specific* angles of daily and seasonal solar access and solar flux

- *site-specific* wind patterns and velocities for wind rose development for large projects

- *site-specific* influence of neighboring structures and properties

- *site-specific* topographic land survey, covenants, and zoning and building code regulations

- *site-specific* road access, automotive emissions, and projected effect upon outdoor and indoor space

- *criteria* for the project and how it may be conceived and developed to fulfill needs and desires with ecologic accord

- plan and volumetric consideration that addresses all of the above and the concordant influence upon the local and global atmosphere

- most efficient, energy-conserving, non-polluting earth handling, earth placement, land forming, berms, and embankments

- value of topsoil, prevailing trees, and other vegetation to be saved

- projected land forming and landscaping to make the site-specific microclimate more gentle, outdoor spaces useful, and with the least unwanted climatic impacts upon the architecture

- data pertinent to the optimization of sky, sun, earth, air, and water energies

- field testing information from power line and other adverse electromagnetic sources

- track-etch radon, soil bearing, and other test data pertinent to the project

- *in situ* local availability and suitability of materials and methods for construction (the greater the distance from source to use, the greater the trail of pollution)

- evaluation of singular and multiple factors that could be contrary to health, vitality, and well-being

- appropriate manner in which to handle wastes and recycling

- planning and arrangements best aligned with tasks, functions, and interactions

- aesthetic most appropriate to psycho-neural and biophysical well-being

- short-term versus long-term flexibility and suitability for project modification and renovation

- initial and life-cycle cost-benefit evaluations

- long-term ecologic effects and ultimate disposition of the architecture, contents, and systems

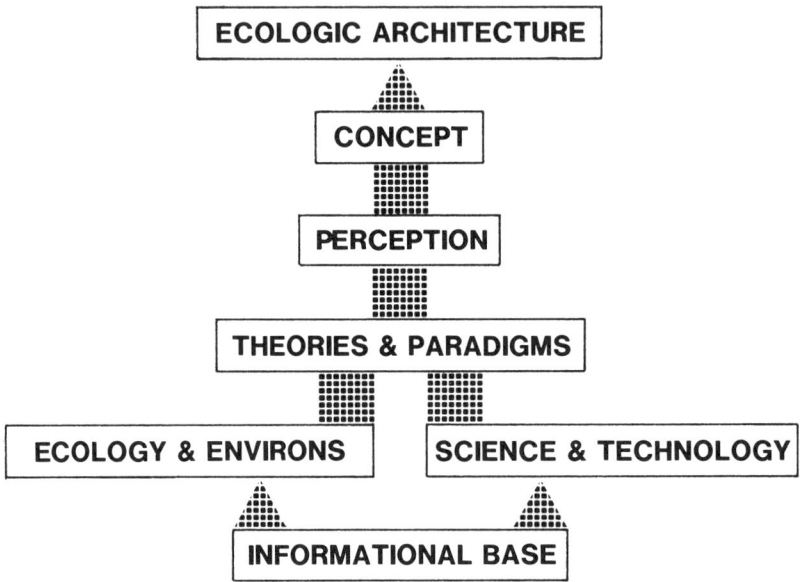

```
                    ┌──────────────────────────┐
                    │  ECOLOGIC ARCHITECTURE   │
                    └──────────────────────────┘
                              ▲
                       ┌──────────────┐
                       │   CONCEPT    │
                       └──────────────┘
                              ▲
                       ┌──────────────┐
                       │  PERCEPTION  │
                       └──────────────┘
                              ▲
                    ┌──────────────────────┐
                    │ THEORIES & PARADIGMS │
                    └──────────────────────┘
                       ▲              ▲
        ┌──────────────────────┐  ┌─────────────────────────┐
        │  ECOLOGY & ENVIRONS  │  │  SCIENCE & TECHNOLOGY   │
        └──────────────────────┘  └─────────────────────────┘
                       ▲              ▲
                    ┌──────────────────────┐
                    │  INFORMATIONAL BASE  │
                    └──────────────────────┘
```

From origination to final realization, architecture, interiors, products, systems, supportive infrastructure, and local and global impacts rest upon perception, concept, and decision. The knowledge we acquire through experience and inquiry and the *sensitivity* with which we perceive and design are critical. Without a sound informational base the ecologic intent is compromised.

Architecture and Social Responsibility

As architects, designers, and planners, our role as shapers of the habitat calls for social responsibility. How can the power of design be most effectively used in a social context?

Traditionally architecture provides the edifices of government, commerce, education, religion, recreation, and places for dwelling. "Urban" planning serves the networks, spaces, and setting for architecture. Interior design provides the indoor environs.

All of these lie within our social responsibility. But usually they are not in a prime design coherence with Nature's *in situ* and local influences on the global ecology. Nature's ecosystemic vitality and sustainability suffer at this neglect.

As the resources and energies invested in architecture, urban planning, and interior design are planned and specified, our global ecosystemic well-being and habitability are being undermined and put at serious risk. *How can we redeem our neglect is an essential responsibility and an a priori question.*

Various inquiries are essential to the urgent criticalities of environmental degradation within the sphere of design. Whether of materials, means, methods, systems, or programs for built or renovated projects, concept, planning, design, and specification, *information* is critical to Nature's ecologic well-being and vitality. *Only as Nature can sustain Life can our designs for habitat and ourselves be part of Nature's planetary continuum.*

Every choice and option we exercise should be regarded in *holistic ecologic terms* if we acknowledge and accept our role as guardians of the environment. For the most part, criteria, regulatory statutes, accepted concepts, and modelling give form and articulation to design.

Ecologic design questions are:

- Where is the site and what is its setting?

- What are the *in situ* factors of sun, earth, air, water?

- What of Nature's ecology and ecosystemic vitality prevails?

- What are likely to be the local and global impacts attributable to development?

- How can we disrupt the site the least in project planning?

- How can the land planning and architectural project have the least negative ecologic impact?

- What is the ecologic, climatic, and solar microclimate of surrounding properties?

- How can the site-specific interface between natural and architectural forces be best equated?

- How can we optimize functional and energy self-sufficiency?

- How can the project most effectively serve the criteria of place and people?

- How can we synthesize the total project within an ecologic, vitalizing, and monetary economic?

- How can we prioritize the use of *in situ* and local materials and energies?

- What choices of materials, methods, and processes are the least energy intensive?

- How can we protect and preserve the on-site vegetation and topsoil with its teeming microorganisms?

- How can exterior and interior planning be most climate responsive?

- How can we optimize indoor and outdoor space use?

- How can we avoid and control auto and other fumes and noise from nearby or on-site sources?

- How can we optimize solar and daylighting orientation and utilization?

- How can we control diurnal and seasonal wind patterns?

- How can we optimize land forming with landscaping to control sun and wind and climatize the site for architectural indoor and outdoor space use benefit?

- How do we provide privacy and coherence with pedestrian and automotive access?

- How can the architectural envelope and forms of the site be most effective to climatic and occupant thermal response?

- How can the total project favorably affect migrational, psychoneural, and biophysical responses?

- How can interdependencies and space use isolation be best accomplished?

- How can adaptability to initial and future functions best be accommodated?

- How can functional efficiency, effectual space use, and personal effectiveness be best realized?

- How can we provide the most biologically invigorating environs with concordant flux in thermal and lighting systems?

- How do we create the most healthful, fulfilling, and satisfying environs for people and purpose?

- How can we effectively use centrifugal and centripetal people planning and inter-reactive arrangements?

- How can we avoid or attenuate the fields of 60-cycle and other anti-biologic electro-magnetic energies?

- How can we test for radon and control it in the indoor environs?

- How do we plan and design to accord favorably with the earth's geomagnetic forces?

- How can we be coincident with daylight-ing for minimal artificial lighting use?

- How can we use form, color, texture, details, furnishings, and interior openings for visual correspondence, people inter-reaction, borrowed light, and visual and thermal comfort?

- How do we best use the tactile and acoustical properties of floors, walls, and ceilings?

- How can we best connect outdoors with indoors and indoors with outdoors?

- How can we use plants outdoors and indoors for CO_2 absorption and oxygena-tion and thermal control (such as by evaporation)?

- In planning and design, how can we minimize construction waste?

- How do we best reuse or recycle all waste from demolition, construction, and life-cycle occupancy?

- How can we maximize food supply with organic gardens and fruit-bearing trees?

- What trees and flowering plants most likely to cause allergies should be avoided?

- How can we best avoid contraindicative allergenic and electro-biologic reactions to materials, processes, systems, procedures, equipment, and devices?

- How can we choose task lighting systems compatible with visual and psychoneural well-being?

- How can we prioritize natural energy thermal systems and minimize mechanical supplementation?

- How do we keep all energy forces in a dynamic flux that vitalizes us by sequential stimulation and relaxation (stress and stress release)?

- How do we design an ecologically sensi-tive environment with respect to short- and long-term objectives?

- How can we design and develop inspiring public and private places as well as being ecologically vital?

- How can we keep Nature vital so that we can be vital?

• How can we best plan and design relative to the sum total of initial and life-cycle investment in land, architecture, services, networks, energy, and resources?

Every urban place and work of architecture is unique and site specific. As all persons are individually unique, so is every spot on Earth. Within this uniqueness, *only* within a holistic perspective and ecologic regard of design can a project represent a notable degree of social responsibility.

Regional architecture addresses terrestrial and climatic and cultural commonalities. *But holistic microclimatic architecture within a context of the ecologic site-specific location addresses the reality.*

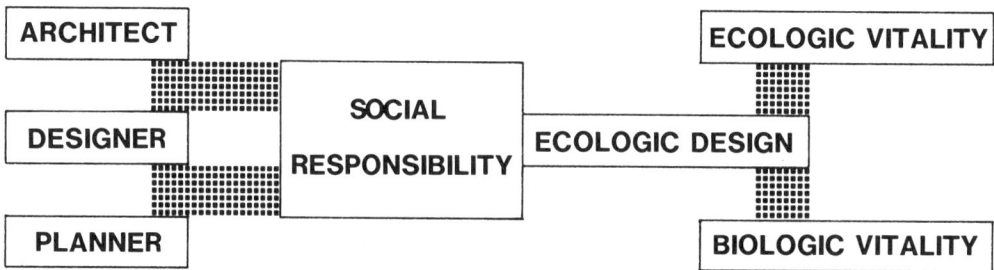

ARCHITECT		ECOLOGIC VITALITY
DESIGNER	SOCIAL RESPONSIBILITY ECOLOGIC DESIGN	
PLANNER		BIOLOGIC VITALITY

Humans are *part* of the ecologic equation. Nature's ecosystemic vitality, renewability, and sustainability can provide for us as we design in concern and coherence with the natural forces of our planet.

Social responsibility is basic to our fragile species and to our habitat and societal systems. In our concepts, design, and our realizations a holistic societal relevance is much needed within a holistic ecologic harmony. Violence, strife, and war eat at the heart of ecologic viability and demean our human value.

A Problem is an Opportunity

When there is a problem, there is an opportunity to eliminate, lessen, or otherwise solve it. Our number-one problem is: "As we technologically and in lifestyle keep threatening our habitat and all of the systems that support Life, can we survive?"

The depth of peril is not perceived by most people, or we would be doing more about it. There are numerous activists and a lesser number of environmental whistle blowers who express an abiding concern. Environmentalists have benefitted the environment to an extent that belies their number and means. Business and industry have not always demonstrated in the assurance of profit an environmental responsibility. But business and industry are showing greater concern about the environmental and health effects of what they make and market. Assurance of market share and litigation avoidance are concerns within a growing public environmental consciousness. Makers, purveyors, and promoters of materials, products, and processes are in a "catch-22" position. If they do not proceed to market that which is not harmful, they can lose in the marketplace. If they proceed to design, make, and sell that which is not harmful, they can face litigation for all that they have made which is harmful. To bridge this dilemma, a marketing and promotional initiative can focus on "ecologic design."

The architect, designer, and planner can provide a relief service, alternatives, and other perspectives of environmental concept and design to benefit a business, residential, or other category of client. There is a coincidence among frugality, saving energy, providing a more healthful building, and the well-being and profit of any firm, and savings and well-being for a home owner.

The beginning of frugal design is in orientation. Climate-responsive architecture and urban planning with optimal *site-specific* use of sky, sun, earth, air, and water energies. Minimal earth handling for maximum site use and optimal earth placement, climatic buffering, solar gain, shading advantages, effectual vegetation, and architecture that aligns with the *in situ* ecology can make the microclimate more gentle and in accord with energy frugality and biologic well-being. Frugality in construction tends to the least energy-intensive materials, methods, and construction planning. Initial frugality in construction dwells in structure, materials, and enclosing systems that have the least initial energy demand. Efficiency and effectiveness of heating, cooling, ventilating, and equipment systems should include initial and life-cycle frugality. Durability and other factors that minimize maintenance, operational, and repair costs are part of a frugal package. Initial cost may be higher on some items that save energy and money in the long run.

A step beyond initial frugality lies in the effectiveness of any home or building to serve its intended purpose. Architecture planned with a sense of the present but with an eye to the future can remain economically and energy-wise more adaptive. Possible and probable shortcomings may be averted when viewed as a problem prone to happen. Foresight aligns with extended-term frugal practicalities and avoidance of waste. Meaningless stylisms that provide no effectual function can be costly and wasteful of construction energy and often are an affectation (but sometimes a delight).

Architecture is an art. The spirit invested by design within a project has a psychoneural and bioneural effect. Thus every resolution to "rock-bottom" cost and construction is not necessarily the best investment in human terms. Nor is it in ecologic terms when it may demean ecologic vitality. An ideal is when projects can be most frugal in cost and environmental terms. Reasonable judgment can tell us when the environment and ourselves may be better served by some departures from "rock-bottom" cost and construction.

It is impossible to avoid environmental deprecation with whatever we build or do in architecture and urban development. But what may become problems inherent in most of today's conventional design approaches, a new view and overview are needed that encompass the site-specific, local, and global energy and resource impacts, Nature's ecology, ecosystems, and our own health and survival.

Herein lies the opportunity for the design professions. All of Nature's processes and systems are a design. *Design (our design) is critical in its relationship with and inter-effect upon Nature.*

Not only can architecture, the interior, and urban design be more correspondent to the prevailing daily and seasonal flux and advantage in use of natural energies. But also the *sustained vitality of Nature assures our own sustained vitality*.

Our species originated and prospered in the natural environment. As electromagnetic beings, we accord with the resonant (Schumann) electromagnetic field between the earth and ionosphere. We accord with the sun, daylight, air movement, and earth energies and find our connection with oceans and other bodies of water. These potent forces are attenuated or excluded by our enclosure within homes and buildings (where we spend most of our time).

Our vital being needs connection to, not exclusion from, primal cosmic and global energies. Everything is energy. We are a dynamic portion of energy. All of Life and even inanimate substances are endowed with their own properties and characteristics of form and energy. We cannot afford to keep looking at parts irrespective of the whole. Only by a holistic view, holistic frugality, ecologic interconnection, and economics based on global habitability and vitality with *in situ* habitability in concordance can we provide such opportunity through design. Through such opportunities, we provide employment for ourselves and opportunities for others.

There is a horde of ecologic, ecosystemic, biophysical, spiritual, and economic problems. All of these can be viewed as a storehouse of design opportunity.

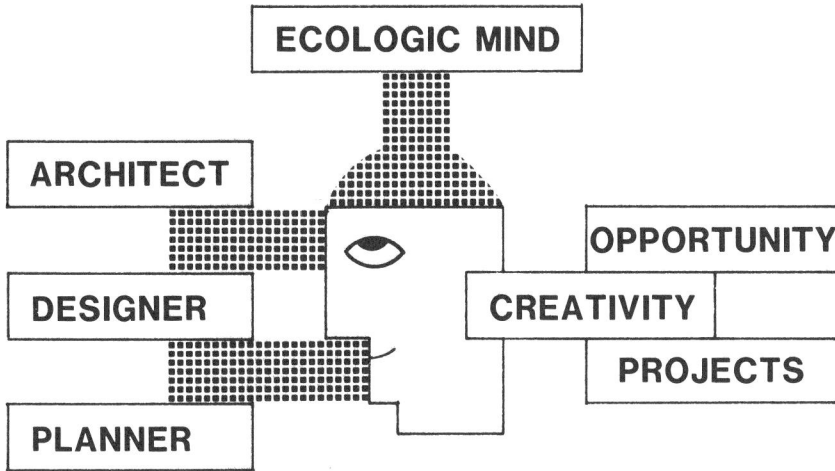

ECOLOGIC MIND

ARCHITECT

DESIGNER

PLANNER

OPPORTUNITY

CREATIVITY

PROJECTS

Within an ecologic perspective, creativity in concert with the sun and natural systems can open the door to new project opportunities. Ecologic design is not only a social necessity but also an effectual precept and commitment to new work opportunities.

Architecture and Science

From historic beginnings science has sought to unravel the mysteries and secrets of Nature. Underlying properties and behavior of matter and energy have stimulated scientific curiosity and reasoning through the ages.

Ideas become theory, then a premise, an exploration, a structuring, and a test within the province of order and logic. Fortunate accidents, mishandling, or purposeful research can lead to discoveries. Building upon information and knowledge in the light of inquiry and leaps of insight further the process and development from theory to resolution. Laboratory and clinical studies and statistical evidence are the testing ground of practicality. Science connects to the everyday world through technology and through social response and behavior.

Architecture purports to be an art, not a science. But parallels can be drawn. Architecture acts on the properties and behavior of matter and energy. Both science and architecture deal with physics, biophysics, and human responses. Both science and architecture evolve from and have a significant effect upon planetary ecosystems. Both architecture and science rely on experimentation, the work of peers, and what can be labelled as "case studies." Architecture has been shaped and formed by science and technology, its handmaidens.

But with architecture and science there has been less than a reciprocity with Nature. Science and architecture both extract from our planet's finite and nonrenewable fossil fuel, chemical, and nuclear energies to serve our ingenuity. But the resolutions of our manipulative mind, whether of science or architecture, for the most part have left critical ecologic and ecosystemic effects out of the equation. Misguided imagination, spirited conceptualization, adroit development, and compelling products of gratification are in principle upon origin and upon life-cycle demands counter to Nature's vitality and sustainability.

Each one of us lives an instant of celestial time. It is both impressive and calamitous how from the days of colonial settlement, pristine wonderment and ecologic resources have been overridden by science, technology, urbanization, architecture, and networks. How the ingenious inventions of architecture and science with technology have transformed the wonderment of wilderness would be mind-boggling to a reincarnated colonist today.

The question today is not a matter of how it happened, but rather, "How can we prudently save Nature's ecosystemic viability as well as ourselves?". Our historic transformation of Nature's resources and energies within our myopic self-serving purpose has obscured our incessant decimation of global habitability. In creating habitat and the "good things of life," we have been destroying Nature's global habitat that keeps us alive. *As Nature fails, so do we fail.*

How do we extract ourselves from the dilemma we have created? Our conventions, societal habits, concepts of "progress," and gross national product more clearly translate into measures of environmental destruction than of laudable coherence with the living and regenerative systems of our planet.

We have no responsible sustainable resource and energy policy of science nor of architecture. We have no national coherent energy policy that should not only be national but global. Our society of today is inexorably linked on a global scale. But while the global interlocking of communication, resources, energy, industrialization, distribution, and transactions forms an interdependent fabric, in our petro-fuel, chemical, and nuclear economy, the greater the distance from *source to use*, the greater is the negative impact upon global well-being and the survival probabilities of Life.

Every decision we make at any level be it personal, group, corporate, or otherwise has an agreeable or contrary effect upon ecologic and human continuity of Life. According to John Page, Emeritus Professor of the University of Sheffield, in respect to architecture: "Energy use in buildings currently probably accounts for 2/3 of the global warming risks." This is only one risk in the diverse, multiple, and compounding risks that attend what we conceive, develop, and realize through science and architecture.

Professor Page further states:

"... clean renewable energy, like the substitution of passive solar heating for the 'dirty' combustion of fossil fuels for heating, simultaneously providing effective ventilation to keep the environment biologically clean, can make important contributions to the health both of individuals and of the global ecosystem, as well as contributing to the energy economy."

As matters stand, the greater our urban development, our product lines, proliferation of vehicles, and the greater our GNP, the greater is the making of our debacle.

Architecture, the urban setting, and networks that serve them are derived from science and technology. Of particular note are materials, structural, mechanical, and electrical systems, control methods, and devices. But how many of these elements are coherent with Nature's ecosystemic sustainability and ecologic vitality, of which we are a part?

We need to reexamine the Second Law of Thermodynamics. Namely, not to dwell on the concept of entropy in which energy is rendered less useful, but rather that small energy inputs discretely applied can result in large, more favorable and productive outputs. We have Prigogine to thank for this perception.

As matters stand, all of the regenerative powers of Nature from seed to developed structures of Life reinforce this perception. The computer with small energy inputs provides vast amounts of information. However, despite its revolution of Life and process, the computer on a personal basis generates anti-biologic magnetic fields and has a screen that has a preponderance of positive ions converse to well-being, drawing airborne bacteria into the vicinity of our breathing and stressing our vision. We need greater care in how we subtly or otherwise threaten our psychoneural and physiologic integrity.

And so it is with architecture. Often the subtle and seemingly innocuous considerations, decisions, and actions we take can have as "small energy inputs" monumental adverse and sometimes catastrophic outputs. But the more science and architecture align, keep aligned, and are concerned and caring for Mother Nature, the better her lot and that of ourselves.

A new direction in thought and responsibility within our processes, designs, and realizations is at the ultimate critical edge of our immediate and future human destiny. As we flub it *now* it can be hopefully minor, but it takes very little to scuttle the state of Life, our wondrous world, and ourselves.

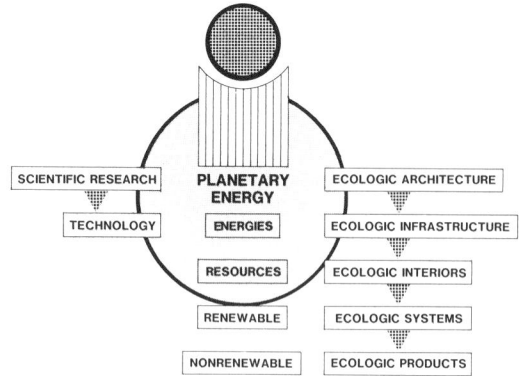

Everything is energy. Elemental matter and renewable and nonrenewable materializations of our planet are theorized, scrutinized, and structured by science. Within the dominant weight of our science, extensive technologies, and energy-intensive society, the counterweight of ecologic design is prudent and essential. Energy and design within higher levels of science and responsible technologies are the key to our near and extendable future. Phasing out nonrenewable in favor of renewable energies and biologic and electromagnetic strategies is becoming more evident and will predominate in science, technology, architecture, and other societal facets.

Technologic Dilemma/Ecologic Necessity

Business and industry depend upon science and technology for basic concepts in assessment of market potential. Business and industry are predicated upon what can be conceived, designed, and sold to make a profit. In the face of changing market attitudes, competition, governmental regulations, the flux in capital availability, interest rates, and capital deployment, business and industry maintain a perspective of effort and organizational capability for financial return. Not a small ecologic issue is executive as well as all levels of occupational employment.

In the face of escalating public awareness and concerns about ecologic and biologic well-being, the marketing challenge is invading the executive mind and motivating an environmental attitude. Design and specification by the architect and designer can be the life or death knell of any specific business or industry. Ecologic design in organizational and financial business and industrial terms can be evolutionary or revolutionary. A significant number of businesses and industries are and more will be predictably switching to nontoxic, environmentally oriented materials, products, and systems. However, promotional and advertising environmental and health claims require a cogent degree of scrutiny as to purported environmental and health benefits.

Certain industries are "cleaning up" their more strident toxic and noxious means and methods and are producing more ecologically compatible products but often fail to address *the total factors*. The rate of change to an ecologic ethic across the board, however, is too little, too slow, and often too ineffectual.

Corporate profits and dividends to stockholders are essential to the survival of the corporate structure. Small businesses of wholesaling, distribution, and retailing also are vulnerable to marketing fluctuations and change. Our entire economic system is petro-based and dependent upon the synthetics of production.

Business and industry are caught in the web of capitalized investment, internal organization, established lines, and connections of distribution. Litigation also rears its ugly head. Changing from a product or system that can or does result in biologic distress or illness to one that is devoid of such consequence creates a tenuous situation. If the business or industry declaims its former product it can open the door for legal suit. Furthermore, the issue of a "free" replacement of part or an entire product can also become a serious financial setback. An ever-growing number of businesses are being caught in this web, including utilities in the health effects of electromagnetic fields they produce.

But as architects, designers, and businesses subscribe to an ecologic conscience and paradigm, responsive change in the commercial sector will occur, not only materials, products, and systems but also commercial architecture itself. *Revolutionary rather than evolutionary changes are most needed in our society.* Our deprecation upon global habitability is too great. Technologic reform to an ecologic conscience is too slow at this point in time. Our technologies are beyond our current Band-Aid fixes and recycling binge.

Recycling can be applauded, but for a true ecologic ethic a persistent inspection and evaluation of what we design, make, and buy is of vastly greater importance. How we use what we may buy, how we may in some way use it when its initial use is terminated, or how it may be recycled or become a resource instead of waste should be part of the ecologic design, business, and industrial responsibility.

Ecologic economics is the key to environmental preservation and renewability. But it has to be a complete, manageable, holistic economics relevant to a vital ecologic continuity. The technologic dilemma is great because it has preempted ecologic sustainability by its persistent magnitude and multileveled environmental exploitations through too many decades.

The technologic dilemma has in-depth facets and synergistic dimensions that exacerbate an ecologic and biologic impact. Individuals who might succumb to one technologic insult can be overwhelmed by a synergistic assault. While ecologic and biologic risk can be significant from "low" tech, the risk can be further compounded by high tech concepts. The sophistications of business and industry have an ongoing experience with the performance of materials, products, and systems and the processes and procedures that accompany their realization and their marketing and profit potential. "Low tech" and "high tech" ecologically compatible technologies can have their individualistic niche among potential users.

Ecologic design often tends toward the low-tech viewpoint, but high tech can often meet the necessity and the total aspects of architectural, product, and systemic order and the activities, work tasks, and other propensities of human action and interaction.

Energy-intensive activities of home and workplace have been displaced by technologic devisements. Cases in point are too numerous to be mentioned. How would our society function without mechanical refrigeration, electric illumination, the motor car, machine-produced items, the ubiquitous telephone, the computer, and now the fax machine?

Our overwhelming urban populations are caught in the web of industrial and technologic sustenance. Short-sighted policies constrain long-term ecologic design benefits. Despite the technologic dilemma, our creative ingenuity, fluidity of information, and adaption to necessity make possible an ecologic public mind. Nascent beginnings are gathering with more assurance towards a predominant ecologic conscience.

Architects, designers, and principals of commercial enterprise despite formidable institutionalized deprecating technologies are on the forefront of design and its place in our society. *The ecologic precept and necessity are inescapable.*

Laws are made to purportedly protect health and ensure safety. As more knowledge about consequences of our environs and their contents is evident, more regulations come into being. The Environmental Protection Agency has a broadening agenda. But government is contradictory. While regulating commercial enterprise within some limits, it opens the door to continued environmental exploitation in others. Political expediency allows corporate power to produce less than efficient and optimally conserving products.

On the positive side, a substantive portion of new, cutting edge high-tech research, visionary concepts, technologic breakthroughs, and market potential with relative ecologic coherence is close to realization. New efficiencies in energy conversion and resource use and alternative strategies in concept, design, and use will make obsolete less efficient and more cumbersome techniques and production. Micro-miniaturization that conserves space and requires a frac-

tional use of resources and energy is taking place.

Small discrete energy impacts can result in larger collateral energy outputs. High-tech, high-temperature ceramic vehicular motors and more efficient drive trains will likely become common in a few years.

Waste is becoming a more important resource. Vortexian mechanics and beneficial electro-fields are likely to play a major role in our energetic future. Noninvasive diagnosis is possible beyond the present definition of today's electromagnetic resonance imaging. Limited access surgery is already in use and a shift is increasing towards holistic medical practice.

Architecture is changing within its internal attributes as technology offers more attractive design and specification options. Conventions of client desire stand more in the way in residential architecture than in commercial architecture.

Even minor conditions and changes can be disruptive and erosive of organization and profit. But the vast to cataclysmic changes in some business and industrial enterprises pose a contemplative dilemma in the course of business success and survival. Our collective survival needs ecologic precedence. The ecologic necessity becomes more technologically essential with every moment of time. Vacillation is a great ecologic enemy.

Holistic ecologic coherent design is friendly to our well-being, wellness, and vitality.

ecologic design concepts, strategies, and process

Holistic Ecologic Architecture

Ecologic concepts, strategies, and process are individualistic to each site. The sustained vitalities of Nature's ecosystems are in *site-specific* terms of solar radiation, seasonal microclimatic energies, and energies of earth, air, and water. Ecologic coherence is essential within ecologic design.

An ecologic mind is principal to disciplines of ecologic architecture. Concepts, strategies, and process require a sensitivity, awareness, and discipline within ecologic design specification and construction. Only by a *holistic ecologic perspective* can the equated form and economic division of space and openings be best ordered within the ecologic planning and design of architecture and its landscaping, systems, products, and natural energies of the site.

Ecologic architecture takes its *inner form* from efficient and healthful interior solar and climatic space planning. It acquires its *outer form* from its interface with the radiation of the sun and the daily and seasonal microclimate. The site can be ecologically designed to attenuate climatic extremes, extend seasonal use of outdoor space, reduce traffic and other external noise, and provide ecologic coherence with the architecture.

Surrounding properties and community have their effect upon the ecologic factors of the project. Holistic ecologic design is inclusive of all ecologic elements of architectural and site needs. The greater the energy sufficiency and sustainability within the project, the greater is its conservation of utility energy. Each project has its own ecologic and economic profile.

A core of the *ecologic equation* is ourselves. We are endowed within Nature's ecosystems with remarkable creative powers and adaptive ingenuity. But our brain power and technologic feats threaten our existence within our defilement of Nature's resilience and planetary habitability. We are creatures of the earth. But have forgotten our own fragility in our technologic but illusory Utopia of material possessions and our needed connection with the energies of our planet Earth.

Experiential as well as functional factors are part of Life and meaning. Architecture as an element *within* rather than *dominant over* Nature's ecosystems and ecology equates with the vitality and sustainability of our wondrous planet as a place for human habitation.

Our technology has largely *separated* us from rather than sustained us *within* our planet's ecologic reality. Isolation from Nature's life-giving, sustaining, and healing powers is at odds with our own vitality. We spend most of our time *within* architecture. How we elect to design reflects upon our state of health and wellness. Our concepts, strategies, and processes of design reveal our level of ecologic and human concern.

We are living within a societal and technologic *revolution* rather than evolution. Sustainable communities, energy-efficient "smart buildings," energy-efficient and "healthy" homes, effectual co-housing (integrated group housing with shared tasks), ecologic products, and conservation systems are directional towards the global ecologic necessity. But the scope is short of the need.

New societal, business, and economic order is changing the needs and character of architecture. Looking ahead is better than looking back. Our concepts, strategies, and processes of design aligned with and preserving Nature's vital systems are critical. *Architecture in meeting new societal paradigms should not lack the critical ecologic connection with holistic insights, strategies, and processes in design.*

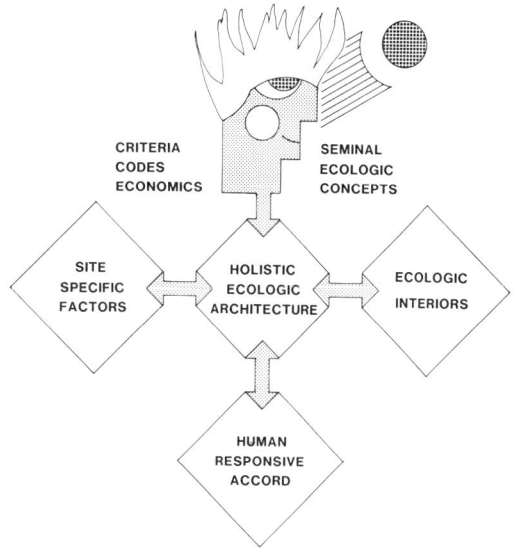

Holistic ecologic seminal concepts depend upon an in-depth comprehension, experience, and focus on the integration of the site-specific and architectural criteria and the bio-harmonic interior. An interface between human dynamics of the interior and site with the sun, ecosystems, and microclimate becomes the architectural envelope with its responsive form and openings. The aesthetic is a function of these interresponsive design elements.

Architectural Materials, Products, and Systems

Architects are specifying more energy-efficient materials, products, and systems. Energy-conscious attitudes within the building industry, codes and regulations, and in the buyers of homes and managers of businesses have led to more energy-efficient and conserving materials, products, and systems with better energy performance. Most of these materials, products, and systems, however, have varying degrees of environmental impact, energy intensity in their extraction of resources, and a trail of pollution from source to final place of use.

Conservation and energy efficiency are highly commendable within the architectural design and specification. But on an *ecologic scale of value* materials, products, and systems fall short in answer to the following questions and matters of human vitality, well-being, and health, which are ecologic factors seldom adequately regarded in the design and selection process.

In ecologic design and selection can it be determined as:

- most ecologically appropriate
- nontoxic and nonallergenic
- a local resource
- renewable and sustainable
- recyclable
- energy efficient
- meeting more than one functional purpose
- synthetic versus natural

- energy conservation manufacture
- distance of transport
- durable and long lasting
- to useful expectancy
- to function without utility energy demand
- easy to maintain and repair or its components being reused in the future
- to its ultimate disposition

This basic ecologic criteria sounds like a tall order relative to the materials, products, and systems available. But without a definitive *yardstick of ecologic values* it is difficult to assess our best options and choices. Some of the most energy-conserving products in use can be some of the most energy intensive in extraction of resource, manufacturing, transportation, and being nonreclaimable in the environment. The more that the site, the architecture, and its interior perform through all seasons as a holistic, interrelevant, self-sustaining system, the less demand may be made on the environment and utilities.

Without a representative number of ecologically equated materials, products, and systems, let alone a predominant number, the selection is apt to be narrow. Within the experiential, functional, ecologic, constructive, daylight and thermal, total materials, systems, maintenance, and operational factors of design, ideal selections can be constrained by budget as well as by lack of ideal ecologic choice.

Much research, investigation, evaluation, and substantiation is needed to confirm in *all* categories of materials, products, and systems those that either somewhat or greatly denigrate our global environment. Architectural journals in measure are addressing air quality and other environmental issues. A fortuitous "Environmental Resource Guide" of the American Institute of Architects has been prepared for architects, engineers, and builders to make environmental assessments during the design and construction process. It is a reference tool covering the environmental aspects of products and building materials.

Time keeps marching on. Meanwhile, more attention has been given in architectural education, practice, and polarity to design stylism. Trends that more responsibly embrace environmentalism in significance to human wellness and ecologic vitality will inevitably blossom anew in education and practice. The strong solar, conservation, and environmental systemic design within the architectural profession of the late 1970s and early 1980s should be reevaluated in the light of today. In some respects we tend to reinvent the wheel.

All materials, products, and systems have an experiential, psychoneural, and usually an aesthetic factor derived from design and specification. There are vast visual and tactile differences in experience among the exposed surfaces of materials, with products that are handled, and with systems that affect our senses. The impressionable difference in tactile, olfactory, and visual response to flooring materials can be subtle or unmistakable. The toxic outgassing of flooring materials may or may not be perceived. As the sun may heat a thermal mass floor, the temperature difference relative to other types of surfaces can be notable. Hard, soft, cold, and hot floor surfaces transmit their messages to our body.

Energy-intensive materials such as steel, aluminum, brick, ceramics, and glass can have properties of durability, strength, or appropriateness not easily duplicated by other materials. Renewable materials like wood, bamboo, and reeds; plentiful earth, sand, and gravel that require little or no processing; and nonreinforced concrete mainly of sand, gravel, and cement have a relatively low energy demand. Poured-in-place concrete systems have a relative in-place permanence. Depending upon the amount of structural steel reinforcement needed, they become more energy intensive, as well as for possible future removal. Concrete has a broad range of uses in which it can be ideal as a formative product.

Steel is an energy-intensive material. It can be recoverable from construction. But its bioelectromagnetic effects need more investigation. Glass becomes more brittle with age. Aluminum is more energy intensive than steel but is more readily recycled.

As soils conditions might permit, the author in every type of climate has used nonreinforced and wire mesh reinforced poured-in-place concrete for on-grade and sub-grade slabs in preference to crawl spaces. The economic simplicity, elimination of more involved wood construction and necessity of crawl space ventilation, added thermal mass to the interior and for passive solar use, and time-saving construction are the multiple advantages. Insulation is an easier matter, and radon can be easily sealed off or as advisable vented from under the slab.

Simplicity of systems in construction as appropriate to each specific project and site conditions can save time and cost. "Trouble-free" architectural systems and details are an important economic and ecologic objective. Details can be critical.

Prevailing methodologies that accompany such matters as excavation, earth hauling, extraction, processing, and transport of materials and products pyramid their effect. We are not simply dealing with materials per se, but also within *each project its total demand* upon our local and global environment. The heavier the demand on energy-intensive materials, products, systems, and equipment, the greater the increment of air pollution.

Wisdom and foresight in design as to concept, strategies, and project realization are essential to an ecologic paradigm. Standards are needed that can be clearly equated with ecologic and biologic vitality and sustainability. Congress in the Clean Air Act of 1990 and the EPA have laid the

base for what can become standards for toxic control. Major polluters are being targeted. The EPA is currently focusing on 17 chemicals identified as posing the greatest threats to human health: benzene; cadmium and its compounds; carbon tetrachloride; chloroform; chromium and its compounds; cyanides; dichloromethane; lead and its compounds; mercury and its compounds; methyl ethyl ketone; methyl isobutyl ketone; nickel and its compounds; tetrachloroethylene; toluene; 1,1,1-trichloroethane; trichloroethylene; and xylenes. Government enactments and enforceable actions are usually too slow in facing reality.

RECYCLED MATERIALS AND PRODUCTS

So many recycled products are made from discarded printed materials or other salvageable materials that the biologic effect of these reconstituted materials cannot be ignored. Saving the environment should reasonably include saving one's health.

Recycling methodologies have become more extensive in reclamation of wastes and more intensively promoted. As the biologic consequence of a material or product becomes more evident, the demand will be for a retrieval and processing concern to be biologically as well as ecologically acceptable.

For either recycled or newly made materials and products that may be known, suspected of, or are questionable as to their effect on health, *interception means* can be used to act as a containment of and barrier to pathogenic chemistry and particulates. Natural as well as synthetic materials and products that have an allergenic or pathogenic effect upon environmentally sensitive individuals (and likely all of us who may be less aware) can be attenuated or isolated by an appropriate interceptor.

Interceptors should themselves have no counter-biologic effect. Furthermore, the most appropriate interception substance should also include instructions for the most effectual method of application.

Recycled, reconditioned, or remanufactured products are likely to become more economic and more broadly specified within ecologic concerns of the architect and designer.

Ecologic Systems

Although in ecologic design the architecture becomes the "system," subsystems should be examined. Although the holistic integration of systems is critical to ecologic architecture, every system within the "*system*" has its ecologic advantage or disadvantage.

SOLAR SYSTEMS

The sun's energy is intermittent and not equably distributed across the continental U.S. But despite the variant available radiation by cloud cover, smog, and fog, it is the most direct ecologic energy that we can employ as an architectural system. The most efficient use of solar energy requires study of each individual project. Passive and hybrid solar systems are most applicable to residential projects for space heating and air tempering. Every glazed opening that receives direct solar radiation is a passive solar receiver. How thermal mass may be located, its characteristics of solar gain and retention, and its size relative to the area of glazing affect indoor comfort levels and systemic time-frame thermal sustainability.

In commercial and residential architecture the building envelope itself can be regarded in concept as an effective solar receiver that can be designed to be the principal heating, air tempering, cooling, and daylighting system of the building. The outer "skin" and roof can be formed and detailed to optimize the building response to diurnal and seasonal solar and climatic energies.

PASSIVE SOLAR

In architecture, *passive solar* can be most effectively used for space heating by means of south glazing, sunspaces, solar galleries, atria, and attached greenhouses. A thermal mass can avoid direct solar gain overheating and provide a time-period retention of solar heat. The thermal mass may consist of dark concrete, brick, stone, marble, gravel, tile, eutectic salts, or water. Eutectic salts are materials that can acquire increased energy at a phase-change temperature. Due south solar exposure is most effective. The type, location, configuration, and amount of thermal mass most appropriate and effective to the solar incidence and use of space is specific to each project. Passive solar systemic design covers a broad scope of applications and possibilities.

The sun's energy can be effectively used to temper outdoor intake air for ventilation through a sunspace and to exhaust indoor air by the inductive stack action of a solar chimney. Sunspaces closed off from occupied space can act as a thermal buffer for the outgassing (with separate sunspace ventilation) of materials and items before bringing them into an occupied space and also as an intervention against intruders.

Crestmoor Passive Solar Homes

Five contemporary passive solar demonstration homes were designed, built, and sold by the author in 1950. The intent was to promote the concept of contemporary solar design. South sections of full glazing, thermal mass slab-on-grade floors, low-pitched roofs (retain winter snow as a thermal advantage) that minimized construction and labor, and monolithic brick fireplace walls, overhangs for summer shade and minimal west and north glazing were within environmentally conscious design.

Ergometric planning optimized space use and the simplistic treatment of all details with contemporary flush surfaces minimized cleaning. It should be noted that front carports protected from north winter winds and driving snow have been haphazardly enclosed, tastelessly defacing the architecture.

It is interesting to note that comparative resale value of these homes 30 years after they were built was higher than neighboring traditional homes of the same size and vintage. Today, however, with an anti-ecologic reversion to "ersatz" traditional residential designs, the buyer's sense of "value" is open to question. Stylism has something to do with perception of personal identity and feelings of comfortable security. But most often in new residential and commercial architecture the "eye wash" effect of glorified central staircases, marble prominently displayed, a galore of traditional details in architecture and cabinetry, and sometimes chandeliers requiring more energy in cleaning than they give in light pamper mind-sets out of phase with an ecologic economic.

On the other side of the coin, some ancient and historic ways of building, daylighting interiors, and adroitly using natural materials embraced an ecologic paradigm.

Roof overhangs, canopies, awnings, recessed windows, and other exterior and interior shading devices can provide appropriate diurnal and seasonal shade. Vertical south glazing avoids problematic angled glass, clear-sky energy loss, overheating, and direct radiant annoyance. Otherwise unheated airlocked and enclosed commercial and residential entries can be solar heated.

Depending upon assured direct solar radiation during cold winter months (considering the low angle of the winter sun), architectural openings and outdoor spaces can benefit by the sun's radiation. Passive solar subsystems should be appropriate to the use and comfort of space. Site-specific solar and climate-responsive space planning is basic to ecologic architecture.

Interior residential spaces that lend best to direct gain passive solar are unoccupied and part-time occupied sunspaces, greenhouses, atria, and galleries. Direct passive solar radiation to breakfast nooks and dining rooms (with furniture that does not significantly interfere with thermal mass or is harmed by radiation) are generally better candidates than living and bedrooms that can interfere and be subject to the fading and solar injury of surfaces and materials.

Thermal mass slab-on-grade floors are inexpensive and practical. Thermal mass objects and furniture within the space can be receptors of solar gain. Thermal mass elements such as dark masonry bulkheads,

water containers, eutectic salt arrays, and concrete forms can be located close to exterior glazing to allow greater space for any interior purpose. Thermal window treatments, such as insulated coverings when solar radiation is not received, can reduce interior re-radiant and convective energy loss.

HYBRID SOLAR

But the closer that the thermal mass is to the glazing, the greater is the re-radiant loss from the mass through the glazing to cooler temperatures outside. Instead of a thermal mass intercepting direct solar radiation, an intercepting dark initial blind or other surface can quickly convert the sun's radiation to heat the air. The heated air can then be distributed by a blower (preferably powered by photovoltaic cells) and duct system to interior space or a remote thermal mass. Centralization of the hybrid thermal benefit by relocation to other interior spaces of greater need can make more efficient use of solar gains. Such relocation of solar energy can improve effective efficiency by as much as 50 percent.

Hybrid solar systems consist of usually a direct interception and transfer of solar-heated air to a location remote from the place of interception. A forced air duct or plenum system is generally used for relocating the solar gain for the most effective use. The intent may be for immediate space heating or for retained thermal mass storage. Almost all of such systems will use a blower that is best powered by photovoltaic cells.

ACTIVE SOLAR

Active systems make use of air or liquid type solar collectors. These are usually a flat-plate type of insulated metal casing with a black chrome (lower emissivity) or other surface adsorber plate with preferably a low-iron glass cover (greater solar transmissivity). They are commonly roof mounted at an angle to the south, calculated as the latitude plus 15 degrees for space heating in winter and latitude plus 5 degrees for year-round hot water heating for domestic purposes, a hot spa, a swimming pool, or any number of commercial and industrial uses (such as a car wash, laundry, or wherever year-round large amounts of hot water are needed).

Active air systems can serve well for air tempering for commercial, institutional, and other uses when cold outdoor air needs to be preheated for ventilation. Active concentrating collectors can also consist of some highly reflective surface in a parabolic concentrating form. They can be trough-like with the apogee of reflection upon a horizontal glass tube or can be dish-like or deep-well parabolas that concentrate the sun's reflected energy to a point. A fluid receives the solar concentration and the heated fluid is either used or stored for use. The uses can be for any purpose to which the solar fluid temperatures would apply. Air systems typically use gravel bed thermal storage. The energy from fluid solar collectors can be in thermal water storage.

In cold climates freezing of the collector fluid has to be guarded against. Drain-back water systems in which water is pumped to the collectors only when solar preheating is adequate are effective. Other active systems require a nonfreezing fluid (often achieved with additives).

A drawback of any mechanical system is the power requirement and maintenance service. Passive systems avoid such necessities but may be less appropriate to need.

Active concentrating-type parabolic trough collectors are being used directly to purify water by means of the sun's ultraviolet spectral radiation. Brackish or contaminated water is fed through the system and the result is clear and potable. Industry can well expand upon this concept in meeting water purification needs.

Central power generation using solar concentrating parabolic field collectors focused to a receiving tower is already in operation in southern California. Systems of this type are essentially in a prototype stage. Location, insolation, and relative energy efficiency are principal to the installation of solar field collectors.

DIVERSE USES

Other large-scale solar projects most likely to become realized are biofuels from

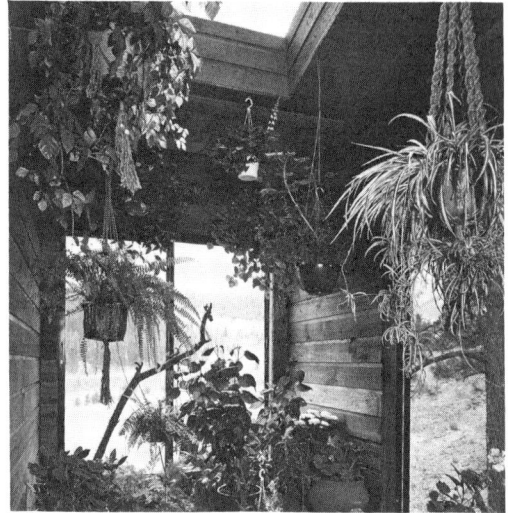

Mountain Retreat Solar Residence

Active air-type vertical solar collectors with rock bin storage system serve this two-level home with a passive solar greenhouse. Nestled into the trees for wind protection, an exterior patio deck to the west is also protected from the sun. The stairway between levels is located behind the vertical solar collectors shown in the photograph. It is ventilated by a roof wind turbine. It is also the principal entry from the southeast.

Living areas are on the main level with bedrooms above. The compact and minimal exterior surface to interior volume ratio and simple span four-foot increment planning minimized construction materials and labor. It is a very energy-efficient ecologic and economic design.

biomass and desalinization of sea water for coastal cities. A biospheric research self-sustaining project is being developed in Arizona. Mini-scale biogenic residential and commercial ecologic sunspaces and green-houses can *in situ* provide oxygen, absorb CO_2, filter the air, and act as a solar thermal receiver. Molecular adsorbers can inhibit the proliferation of mold from plants. Soils bacteria can convert gaseous air pollutants to less harmful gases. The electrophoresis effect is conducive to plant growth and air quality.

As part of the architecture of residential, commercial, and institutional projects, the inventive use of the sun's energy is limited only by practicality and cost. The sun's energy, used directly or indirectly stored, can be effective for industrial processes and agricultural uses (such as food and crop drying).

Solar ponds, aquaculture, water pumping for irrigation, useful gravity energy from storage, electrolysis in production of hydrogen and oxygen from water, and solar steam-gener-ated power for many uses are all either feasible or have been practically used or demonstrated.

Solar energy can also be used for humidifi-cation; dehumidification; distillation of water for homes, buildings, and industrial process-es; dehydration of foods and other items; various forms of bioconversion; bacterial sterilization; outgassing of toxic chemicals; photochromic, photosynthetic, and photo-

disassociation processes; photoelectric controls (as for architectural interior and exterior lighting); and other applications using thermal or photon energy.

Therapeutic uses can be for controlled ultraviolet light exposure, heat for therapy and swimming pools, solar saunas, sunspace furniture designed to hold heat to relieve sore muscles, or other purposes and other portable devices that can employ the sun's radiative energy.

Photovoltaics are becoming more efficient and less costly, providing electrical energy at 16 watts per square foot or more. More efficient batteries and fuel cells need to be developed to provide available solar electric power when the sun's radiation is not avail-able.

Residential, commercial, practical, and economical use of photovoltaics to power electric vehicles is in a nascent stage. Remote power applications are increasing, and this decade will see a proliferation in use.

Our conceptual, development, and realizable ingenuity, capitalization, and commercializa-tion need more devotion and ardor in eco-logic harmony. *Solar energy is principal to global habitability. Every site enjoys direct and indirect benefits of solar radiation.* To quote from the State of the World 1990: "Direct conversion of solar energy will be the cornerstone of a sustainable world energy system. Passive solar architecture (can now) cut artificial heating and cooling needs to virtually zero in millions of buildings." The author has substituted "can now" in deference "to the year 2030" of the text. *The urgency is now!*

The fact that solar energy is intermittent and not uniformly as copious in all locations requires that its practical and economic use has to be carefully considered. Government subsidies are needed for commercial, industrial, and institutional uses of solar energy in place of polluting and environmentally degrading energies. It is to the common good that ecologic materials, products, and systems be ecologically aligned. Ecologic global concerns are a necessity. An ecologic public mind is growing.

Solar systems are further addressed in the guideline section of this book for Ecologic Residential and Commercial Architecture and Ecologic Interior Design.

EARTH SYSTEMS

The earth itself is a passive and active receiver of the sun's energy. Its interseasonal response to the sun is to gain energy during the summer, retain it into fall, and for the earth to cool by a lower angle of the sun in winter as its rays penetrate the atmosphere so that the earth's coolness carries into spring.

The molten core of the earth contributes heat to geothermal manifestations as hot springs, volcanic vents, geysers, and other displays of geothermal energy. Some of this geo-energy is being used practically and profitably for electric power generation. More extensive use could be made by deep drilling into the earth's strata. Massachusetts Energy Lab under the direction of Jeffrey W. Tester has been researching a hot dry rock (HDR) technology in which deep drilling to great gradient earth depths and sending water down to earth fractures, letting it heat there, and then drawing it back up could product temperatures of 475 to 575°F (246°C to 302°C). An estimated probability is that HDR could supply energy in a magnitude greater than all fossil and fissionable sources. It would be clean energy for power generation and other sources. A proposal to tap into a Hawaiian volcano with drilled vents has met strong opposition from the native people whose religious attachments to this sacred ground find it a provocative defilement.

The earth is a shelter, a moderator of climatic extremes, a resource of minerals, clays, sands, and rocks, the medium for vegetation and other forms of organic life, a providential thermal mass, and the realm of natural energies. From caves to skyscrapers it has been the habitat, work place, and playground of man. But as earth people we have separated ourselves by our architecture and technology further and further from the earth.

We are now strangers on our planet. We dress in unnatural technologic materials and conduct our lives and architecture at peril to our wondrous earth's planetary systems. Further, we plunder the earth with unseemly acupuncture from the wound of which we extract fossil fuels. But unfortunately these repositories of ancient solar energy and earth pressure on ancient vegetation are a poison to the atmosphere and an agony to our earth.

The earth is our sustainer, the chain of ecologic survival. Renewability is the key to our human continuum and our prime resource for architecture. Trees are the "tree of life." The living tree provides oxygen and absorbs carbon dioxide. A dry piece of wood for construction wood remains the most time-honored, adaptable, structural, and workable renewable material of construction and finish work. The question is, does it come from a sustainable growth forest? The question is, how distant is the tree from the final place of use? The question is whether the wood is from an "old growth" forest area or how does clear cutting victimize the forest and its ecology?

Seldom have these questions in selection and specification been addressed. In architectural and design practice the focus has been on the properties and suitability of materials and products to purpose. The resource and its processing, handling, packaging, and journey to point of use should intimately be a concern within multifarious conceptual and technical facets of prevailing practice.

EARTH FORMING

Earth sheltering, earth handling, and earthscaping are more clearly pronounced in the vocabulary of architectural planning and design. Trees for shade and windbreak can bear a consideration in architecture and landscaping. But generally landscaping is regarded apart from the architecture, whereas in ecologic design it is most effectual as an integral part of the architecture and interresponsive with it in land forming and landscaping.

In ecologic design the earth is valuable as a shelter, particularly in conjunction with landscaping. Earth coupling is not in the usual architectural vocabulary but is a very effectual way to benefit the architecture by more stable earth temperatures than those of the atmosphere. Earth temperatures stabilize at varying depths depending upon climate and geologic characteristics.

Because commercial projects very often have large internal heat loads of lighting, people, and equipment, earth coupling has a particular advantage. For the Hotsy Corporation project the author used this principle to a considerable advantage. The lower level is subgrade on three sides with grade level to the east. The main level has a northwest and north landscaped earth berm that both shelters from northwest and north winter winds as well as provides a degree of thermal coupling with the earth.

Both residential and commercial projects can benefit by earth sheltering and earth coupling. The cut and fill from excavation can be well utilized to save utility energy initially and during the useful life of the building. The greater the proportion of space within the building envelope and the less the ratio of its external surface, the greater is its thermal stability.

EARTH TECHNOLOGY

Earth technology research and formulations beyond that of adobe, rammed earth, earth concrete, and clay products are needed in alignment with Nature's ecosystems. Experiments have been conducted by a soils engineer with the author in the practical use of waste product additives and stabilizers with site-specific earth. The intent was to technically analyze the soil of any site with the objective of using it as a major material of construction. By certain insulative additives or by increasing its thermal mass density, the thermal and structural behavior of an exterior or interior wall could be programmed.

The prime advantage of such earth technologic strategies would be in the use of on-site material, conservation of present construction methodologies, and associated transportation of materials. However attractive this concept is in ecologic and possible economic terms, further research, methodology, and compliance with structural building codes is essential.

Earth technology would be most suited to low-rise buildings. The site-specific properties and characteristics of the earth, its specific stabilizing requirement, and availability of the possible use of waste products could determine its practical and economic feasibility.

Another aspect of earth technology is of underground residential, commercial, and storage facilities. Thermal stabilization is a major benefit, as well as possibilities of radioactive fallout protection, external noise isolation, reduction of exposed building envelope, and compensation to natural ecologic continuity over the architecture.

Underground design can benefit by natural ventilation, daylighting and solar thermal strategies, and control of radon and other possibilities of geologic radioactivity.

The displaced earth in excavation for underground architecture should be used *in situ* with the least disturbance to the site ecology.

RADON

On the less constructive side and more provocative of earth concerns are the radioactive decay products radon and thoron that can be harmful to health. Every site has potential levels of their radioactive daughters that can pose a threat to our respiratory and physiologic well-being. It is not uncommon to find a radon level of 100 picocuries per liter (100 piC/l) at a soils depth of 12 to 18

Fort Collins Solar Residence

Situated on a large land parcel of a subdivision, this residence was energy efficient, ecologic, and economic in construction cost. With earth berms from excavation embanked on the north, optimal passive solar, and active drain-back solar collection system for heating domestic hot water, the owners were delighted with the comfort and utility cost savings of this house.

South patios with an area designed for the support of a summertime sun shade and direct connection to the interior from the living room and due south greenhouse augmented architecture and site space use.

The airlocked solar-heated southwest entry was south-glazed with a dark tile thermal mass floor. The living room had a solar/thermal mass banco. The attached greenhouse and south clerestory to the central hall provided multiple solar advantages and daylight. Summer shading was part of the architectural design.

Large trees lying on the site that were dry and structurally sound were used as major members of the construction. Outsulation literally put a airtight thermal encasement around the outer walls and parapets of the house. An earth-tone color was chosen in keeping with the southwest character of the design.

The house had a central air destratification system, was fully cross ventilated, and had wind turbines for direct ventilation from floor-level awning windows.

inches (30.5 to 45.7 cm). Concentrations are usually greater at an 8' to 10' (2.4 to 3.0 m) depth. It is advisable on all projects to get not only the usual soils tests but also radon track-etch tests. The short-term test using the charcoal method is not informative enough. Either method is not absolute but is an indicator of related remedial action.

Designing so that by adequate sealing off of the radon gas or otherwise by other intervention and forming a vent system under concrete or other floor system to the outside air (but not near operable windows), the occupiable space should be preferably under 2 piC/l and not over 4 piC/l. The standard set by the Environmental Protection Agency and ASHRAE is 4 piC/l. Indoor air ventilation and negative ionization can also reduce the indoor level of radon gas.

BIOELECTROMAGNETISM

Another natural attribute of the earth are its electromagnetic fields that can be salutary or harmful to our biologic wellness. Ancient peoples were well aware of the beneficial and harmful points of electromagnetic energies from the earth. Modern evaluations attest to this sensitivity in the precise location of ancient dolmens, Stonehenge, and other sites identified with sacred architecture. All creatures of land, air, and sea inhabit places in earth magnetic locations favorable to their species.

In Germany cancer and other maladies have been associated with geopathic anomalies of the earth fields. It was found that the incidence of malady correlated with the vortexian geopathic electromagnetic energy, principally in the location of a bed within a bedroom. Identified strong negative and positive earth fields, the regularity of the Hartman grid, and the Curry grid diagonal to it have a biologic effect upon our position relative to them.

We are essentially electromagnetic beings. Our personal sensitivities to the earth and its atmosphere affect our state of being. The Schumann resonance between the earth and ionosphere conditions all life, be it plant, animal, or ourselves.

AIR SYSTEMS

Air is the most immediate necessity that we have. Without breathing we cannot last too many minutes. Be that as it may, we treat air badly. We produce a constant attrition upon air quality in our fossil fuel and technologic society. Architecture is no exception. By the materials we select, the means and methods we use, and all of the processes and transfer systems that accompany them, we pollute our local and global atmosphere.

In earlier times in winter there was often a mild to dense pall from industrial smokestacks and homes and buildings that burned wood, coal, coke, or oil to stay warm. But with horse-drawn vehicles of those times, the contamination was more on the pavement than into the air.

AIR POLLUTION

Today with natural gas and electricity serving urban and most rural populations, the electric power generating plant with its air pollution is usually farther from the urban center and most residential neighborhoods. The motor vehicle is most often dominant as the major polluter within the urban environment. Its ubiquitous fumes invade homes and buildings.

Fireplaces comprise a surprising amount of urban air pollution. Ordinances that restrict the burning of wood or other air-polluting fuels are not uncommon. A switch to natural gas with ersatz logs is promoted by utilities. But it is the waste of a finite resource when such relatively "clean" energy can be more effectually used.

For remote areas some stoves approved by the EPA can be a choice. But people do want fireplaces along with all of their mental and emotional attachments to them. Industrial designers need to enter the scene with a fireplace insert that uses nonpolluting fuel, efficiently provides heat, and can be a supplement as needed to a principally solar-heated and energy conservation home. Gelled alcohol is available but is relatively expensive. A 15-ounce can will burn for about four hours and produce approximately 10,000 BTU during that time. A better ecologic and economic viewpoint is to detach the public from its cherished connection with the fireplace.

Escaping air pollution can be a choice in locating away from a city. But not to be overlooked are fireplaces and other possible sources of outdoor air pollution. Outdoor air pollution becomes indoor air pollution in the necessity of ventilating our homes and buildings with oxygen for removal of CO_2 from heating, combustion, and other sources.

Indoor air can be largely more polluted than outdoor air as all of the added toxic gases and particulates from the architectural interior and its contents assail our respiratory system. Smoking is the most pervasive source of harmful indoor air pollution. Smokers should be relegated to separately ventilated rooms that in no way feed back fumes into mechanical systems or other indoor spaces.

More and more businesses and governmental agencies are prohibiting smoking. In architectural planning where smoking is permitted, measures can be taken to greatly increase the ventilation rate, exhaust the smoke to the outside with a negative pressure, and to not place nonsmokers in the path of the tobacco smoke.

The attrition of smoking on the architectural interior is very great. Tobacco smoke is an odoriferous and noxious entity in the indoor environment. It not only harms the smoker and nonsmoker but also coats interior surfaces with a viscous residue and lingering odor. Cigarette fire risk and burns on surfaces and floor coverings should be considered in selection of materials. Maintenance, repair, and replacement add to the ecologic, economic, and human loss from smoking.

Automotive fumes should be kept from entering operable windows, exterior doors, intake air vents, and mechanical systems. Further concerns and considerations are set forth under "Vehicles."

From a human ecologic health standpoint the indoor air should not be contaminated by the toxic outgassing of materials, devices, or equipment nor by other contents of the interior. An answer has been "healthy homes" and buildings. But not enough regard is usually given to Nature's systemic ecologic vitality and sustainability.

"Sick building syndrome" has been a well publicized concern in office and institutional buildings. The answer has been a recommended increase in ventilation that is finding its way into building codes. The syndrome has spawned some indoor environmental sleuths who seek to ferret out the problem. "Sick building syndrome" can be alleviated with controlled negative ionization (10,000 to 12,000 small negative ions per cubic centimeter per second) combined with Schumann positive pulse resonance at 7.83 Hertz (the electrophoresis effect).

Indoor air quality is a complex problem. Not only is the interior architecture involved, but all of the contents also, including furniture, furnishings, equipment including occupancy types and occupant proclivities. Everything within the indoor environs is suspect in its effect upon the well-being and wellness of the occupants.

IONIZATION

Microorganic life of bacteria, yeasts, and molds tend to proliferate in tight buildings with low ventilation rates. Negative ions are depleted by equipment, people, and mechanical systems. Positive ions that remain tend to favor the growth of bacteria leading towards "sick building syndrome." Negative ions stimulate the endocrine system, aid the transport of oxygen into the bloodstream, and suppress environmental bacterial growth.

Negative ionizers, however, in negatively charging air particles tend them to be grounded on nearby surfaces. In this process the air is cleaned but the unsightly accumulation of soilage on ceiling, walls, and other surfaces can be discouraging. To overcome some of such problem, a plate or ceiling panel that duplicates the Schumann positive pulse resonance within effective calculable proximity will receive the particles. "Pure air" alone is not equal to air that has been made vital by negative ionization appropriate to conditions of indoor space. While a median level of 4000 to 5000 negative ions per cubic centimeter may be appropriate for a residence, 10,000 or more can be appropriate to an office workplace.

The author 12 years ago had this type of electrophoresis effect installed in his research facility located in an urban area subject to air pollution. Persons entering especially on high pollution days are struck by the mountain air crispness. With an ion discriminator the author established the negative ionization at 4500 0.001 micron negative ions per cubic centimeter per second. With considerable sensitivity the author established this median. At 5000 the stimulation was too great and at 3500 the effect was too flat. The electrophoresis effect is particularly being used in clean rooms and laboratories. It is proving to be more effective than HEPA (high-efficiency particulate air) filtration when the system is properly engineered.

VENTILATION/COOLING/FILTRATION

Our chemical world sends its toxins and aberrant particulates out through the products of architecture, the interior, and systems. Within the enclosed indoor environs they are inescapable. Carpeting, other floor coverings, wall coverings, finishes, plastics, furniture, clothing, and household products all conspire against our respiratory health. Copy machines and other office equipment outgas and contribute particulates to the indoor air. When nearly finished and with newly provided interior carpeting, furniture, and other furnishings, a period of maximum ventilation should be sustained until detectable odors and removal of the toxic emissions are reasonably assured before occupancy.

Mechanical systems may come first in thinking about our systems for buildings. But from an ecologic perspective they should come last. *Ecologic architecture is the system.* Small buildings and homes of any size naturally ventilated are basically duct systems with varied spacial volumes and openings that let air in and others that let it out.

The comfort level and thermal utility of the home or building depends upon how the ventilation and interior air are conditioned by the heating and cooling of solar, natural, or mechanical systems. The shortcoming of natural systems is that incoming outdoor ventilation air cannot be desirably filtered without a power assist. The most effective particulate filters (such as HEPA) require an extra amount of power. Ordinary furnace filters and central commercial duct distribution system filter are inept relative to air quality. More effectual pleated filters are available, compatible to the limitations of the air-handling blower.

In relatively dry climates in summer with hot days but cool nights, filtered pressurized nocturnal cooling is most effective. The author has been using such a system for 12 years. A quiet squirrel cage blower located in a daytime living area away from bedrooms brings in nighttime cool air through a self-actuating electrostatic filter to remove particulates. Opening vents in bedrooms and a roof stack vent at ceiling level opposite to the incoming air at floor level allows controlled air flow during the night hours. With the advantage of a large interior thermal mass (although the principle works for any type of construction), the interior is effectively cooled. During the hot daytime hours the architecture is buttoned up to retain the cooling. The higher horsepower, noise, and unfiltered disadvantage of an attic fan exhaust are avoided. The system is most effective and can also be designed for adjunct refrigerated cooling under very hot conditions or stay-dry evaporative cooling (no moisture introduced into the indoor spaces due to a heat exchange principle). Refrigerated mechanical systems are not recommended with Freon or other CFCs.

Residential and commercial buildings that heat up from internal sources or from too much solar gain can be cooled with cooler daytime air by the same pressurized "space flushing" system. It can function automatically with outdoor/indoor thermal controls to conserve on refrigerated cooling energy.

EARTH COOLING

Earth temperature cooling has been mentioned under "EARTH SYSTEMS." The author has used this principle. Six-foot (1.8-meter) diameter corrugated steel culvert vertical half sections about 8 feet (2.4 m) high were arranged in a cloverleaf fashion in an excavation around an operable window to cool and temper air to lower-level spaces. A grade-level wood decking with a metal open grille section allows the passage of outdoor air to be cooled by the extensive surface of the metal in direct contact with the earth. Even on very hot days the air is notably cooled. In winter the cold entering air is warmed by the relative warmth of the earth. Cross ventilation through lower level spaces is to a roof stack at the ceiling that functions as a temperature inductive and venturi flow system.

A master bedroom on the main level of the author's research facility has a metal plenum under an earth berm. The earth berm extends to the roof around the exterior concrete walls (insulated on the earth side). Outdoor air enters at the floor line and the earth in summer cools the plenum air as it passes through an insulated self-actuating electrostatic filter (low density for air flow) with an insulated hinged panel for air control. In hot weather it is principally used at night. Exhaust is through a solar west-facing metal chimney with eutectic salt tubes that are heated by the sun's energy and sustain the heat at night, assisting inductive air flow. The vent opening is at the ceiling with an operable panel.

FILTRATION

Room-size portable air-cleaning machines vary greatly in their filtration and air quality characteristics. The best have a pre-filter, an HEPA filter, an activated charcoal or other molecular adsorber, and a last negative ionization stage.

For central systems, better filters appropriate to environmental conditions are needed for the majority of homes and buildings. Nega-

Ecologic Residential Research Facility

This 7000 square foot project included reference and test facilities for research, a home office, principal living quarters, two apartments with separate entries, and an indoor swimming pool area. Completed in 1980, it has served for weather, internal space temperature, and daylighting monitoring.

In practical evaluation all systems (solar heating, inductive cooling, air tempering, daylighting, outgassing and drying of items and materials, earth and thermal mass air cooling and temperature stabilization, concordant humidification) function well and most notably better than originally calculated and predicted. The swimming pool as a central heat sink is 100% solar heated.

All of these systems provide a research base. Within different space environs, various materials and products are tested under different conditions analogous to those of most commercial and residential architecture.

Landscaping, architecture, interiors, and the interresponse to sun, earth, air, and water energies of the site were interfaced in design with biophysical, psychoneural, and behavioral consequence. The holistic ecologic approach included a particular concern with the bio-effects of toxins, particulates, pathogenic microorganisms, bioelectromagnetism, and geologic electromagnetic fields.

Ecologic Design Concepts, Strategies, and Process   55

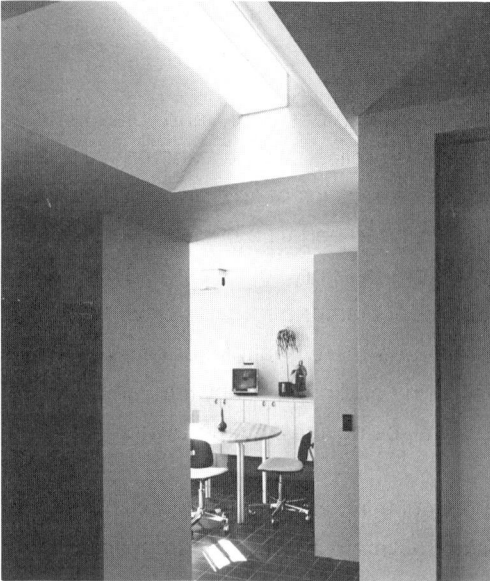

Research has specifically included the effect of:

- ecologic coherence, energy and water conservation, site planning
- solar, wind, and climatic land forming and landscaping
- solar and climate-responsive architectural envelope
- passive, hybrid, and active solar systems
- materials thermal response
- solar inductive ventilation
- performance of solar devices
- earth temperature cooling
- venturi ventilation
- interior bioeffects of electrophoresis (intereffect of negative ionization and Schumann resonance)
- daily monitoring of outdoor air, subsurface, and interior temperatures (readouts from thermocouples)
- indoor readings of alley power line electromagnetic fields
- testing of manufacturer's air cleaning machines
- anti-microorganic coatings in a high humidity environment
- air quality testing of molecular adsorbers, electrostatic, ionizing, charcoal, and HEPA filters
- biologic effect of chemical sensitivity
- belief systems and their ecologic and economic consequences

See Ecologic Residential Research Case Study, pages 135–148.

tive ionizing systems have to be either independent of or at the supply outlets of central duct systems.

WATER SYSTEMS

Water is basic to Nature's planetary systems in sustaining life on Earth. We are composed of about 60 to 70 percent water. The hydrologic cycle makes possible the forests and oceans that oxygenate air and supports agriculture that supplies our food.

Oceans, lakes, rivers, streams, and underground aquifers of water cover a major part of our planet's surface. The patterns of precipitation define the arid to more lush foliaged areas of the earth. Our latitude to solar radiation, the microclimate, and rain and snow that a building site might receive set the conditions for how we can ecologically design.

For the most part, water is piped to us from a municipal supply. But wells are not uncommon. Sites without sewage lines require septic tanks and leach fields. Where the sewage goes is critical to the environment. The water we obtain from a municipality or well is critical to our health.

Chlorination and other chemical treatment restrain the growth of undesired microorganisms in the water supply but have a contrary effect upon our health. The Environmental Protection Agency is concerned about viruses and parasites that are proliferating in treated municipal and well water

supplies. Most water supplies should be adequately filtered or otherwise *treated for safe potability at the point of use.*

WATER PURIFICATION

A magnetic device is available that installed on the incoming main water service will suspend the minerals in the water so that they do not adhere to piping or build up in water tanks. Adsorbing materials such as natural zeolites, charcoal, and certain resins can be used to remove water impurities. Reverse osmosis uses a semipermeable membrane process in which a relatively large amount of water flowing over it results in the removal of unwanted contaminants. But the resultant amount of "pure" water produced is considerably less than the amount introduced across the membrane.

Under development is a new strategy to retain essential health-giving minerals in water while removing contaminants. This process will also remove harmful metals that have an economically useful purpose. It should be available in the very near future. This strategy will have a broad range to applications for homes, businesses, and industry. The reclamation of valuable metals from water will unburden in measure the great ecologic damage from mining.

Distillation of water is accomplished by heating water to a vapor state in which it then condenses on a cooler surface and is collected apart from the impurities that were in it. The disadvantage is the amount of energy needed to sustain the process (unless accomplished by solar distillation). Also, volatile organic substances with boiling points below that of water can recondense into the distilled water at increased concentrations. Furthermore, distilled water lacks beneficial minerals for the body and has a "flat" taste due to lack of dissolved oxygen. It has been claimed that drinking distilled water leaches minerals from the body. Natural waters that retain minerals and vitalizing oxygenation are more pleasurable to the taste and are likely to be more healthful.

Coastal cities are confronted by large ocean areas. The unpalatable ocean water can be distilled by solar energy, as was accomplished in Chile for many years. The economic cry is that inland sources, despite sometimes lengthy pipeline distances, are less costly and problematic. But the oversight is that inland waterways and subterranean aquifers are being grossly depleted by population growth, agriculture, cattle raising, and industry. Interstate competition for terrestrial waters is likely to grow more acute. As ocean water might be distilled (sooner or later), the question would be how to retain its desirable minerals and molecular ionization without the sodium and other undesired constituents.

CONSERVATION

Meanwhile water conservation is either being advised or forced by regulation upon the public. Water-conserving landscaping such as xeriscaping, prescribed water days, and other limitations on water use; water metering; and low water demand toilets, showers, and faucets are moving from recommendation to requirement. Roof water can be collected in a basement cistern and used for toilet flushing (with some primary filtration if needed) or other secondary uses where purity is not a principal factor.

Ecologic design for homes, buildings, and industry in water conservation is by constraints on use, more efficient use, secondary uses, and avoidance of waste. We are a water-intensive society. Average household and per capita use represents an excessive number of gallons per day. Industrial and commercial usage tends not to be discrete. Because reprocessing water for use can be costly and time consuming, the dumping of sewage and toxic waste back into rivers, lakes, and oceans is often the occurrence. Large industrial as well as lesser water polluters are no exception to probabilities of illegal dumping.

It is unfortunate that laws and surveillance become necessary to constrain these ruthless acts against the ecologic sustainability of our waterways and oceans. Aquatic life suffers and the phytoplankton of the sea that supply our planet with oxygen are on the endangered list.

Architects and designers can take a constructive ecologic position in their work. Presenting workable alternatives that are not economically drastic of "water as the medium of life" can be thought of as an entre to clean industrial and commercial processes and good public relations. The rate of public ecologic awareness is rapidly increasing. Rather than act in retrospect, a positive ecologic position is good PR.

DIVERSITY

Water has many remarkable attributes. It is a solvent, a lubricant, a cleanser, a diluter, a wetting agent, and a carrier of substances. It can act as an electrolyte, a thermal mass, a vortexian energy, a gravitational mass, a hydraulic fluid, an extinguisher of fire, as a conductor for heat and cooling, and as a generator of electric power. Absolutely *pure* water does not carry an electrical current. Equally remarkable is how water serves as the medium for aquatic and terrestrial life. It exists in notable energy transformations as a fluid, a solid, or a vapor. The properties of ice vary vastly from those of steam. It can be electrolytically disassociated to oxygen and hydrogen (clean forms of energy). Hydrogen can serve architecture and cleanly power vehicles and other power needs of society. Oxygen efficiently supports combustion.

Solar photovoltaic cells or bioelectric conversion can electrolytically split the atoms of water (H_2O) into hydrogen and oxygen for storage or direct use. Means to a hydrogen technology have been explored in the past. Interest and research are gaining momentum for hydrogen as a replacement for finite and polluting fossil fuels. Inasmuch as water is the primary source of energy, entrenched fossil fuel interests appear as a formidable road block. An electric generating plant under construction in West Germany and another in Saudi Arabia will use solar energy to electrolytically produce hydrogen from water. Prototype hydrogen-powered vehicles are being tested by a consortium of European manufacturers. A converted Cadillac In the USA has been running entirely on hydrogen since 1983. It would make the perfect clean supplemental power source for ecologic architecture. Innovative breakthroughs are in the making. A sustainable solar hydrogen healthy community can be realized. Technologic safety in the use of such powerful gases is a must.

Sun, earth, air, and water are primal to our existence. They should be primal to our power.

Other power generating aspects of water lie within ocean currents, tides, and surface to depth temperature differentials. In research initiated by the Ben Gurion University of Israel, the negative and positive ion interaction between salt and fresh water by means of plastic membranes could sustain the generation of electricity. Such concepts could change coastal and inland cities to sustainable from polluting ways to generate electrical energy.

OBJECTIVES

The built environment needs to be served. But while self-sufficiency by holistic ecologic design can be the objective of new projects, new development and construction usually comprise less of the total urban environment. Municipalities are requiring water meters, limiting water for landscaping for existing homes, and encouraging low flush toilets for all residences. Other water-saving techniques for existing residences are the use of restricted-flow shower heads, displacement in toilets to reduce water in the tank, and replacement of old equipment with high-efficiency hot water heaters and boilers.

Our water resources of the surface and in underground aquifers are being depleted or have been contaminated at an alarming rate. Wells for residential or commercial use should be tested if suspected of toxic substances and for the presence of radon. The remedies are individual to each project.

As discussed under "Ecologic Landscape Design," ground and roof surface water used for irrigation by planning, land forming, and landscaping water retention can considerably reduce the demand on municipal supply. In climates where snow prevails, relatively flat and low-pitched roofs structurally designed for the snow load gain a thermal advantage. The snow acts as a climatic buffer and intervenor against cold and winter winds. It is more conserving of materials and more economic to build relatively flat or low-pitched roofs than steep ones to shed the snow. Greater care has to be exercised, however, to install an adequate, structural, tight, and durable roof with adequate insulation.

Vehicles

The petro-fumes of vehicles assail us on the highways and byways, around buildings, and from the garage. Pollution from motor vehicles has been greatly reduced by emission controls, but the toxic gasses and volatile vapors remain contrary to our health.

The most ecologic vehicle is the bicycle. Minimal materials comprise its structure. It is more efficient than walking, running, or any motor-powered vehicle. Unless more people of our planet switch to being self-propelled or in using pedal or other "clean" power instead of fossil fuel motor power, air pollution will increase. Unless we switch to clean fuels, our atmosphere will continue to suffer.

Hydrogen is the best candidate. New technologies plus older concepts make its commercial possibilities a practical likelihood. Meanwhile electric, natural gas powered, and cleaner burning ethanol, methanol, and reformulated gasoline are appearing as less polluting motor vehicle energy sources.

BIO-EFFECTS

The intrusion of automotive fumes into homes and buildings is more pervasive than commonly realized. The proximity, concentration, duration, and volume of toxic automotive gaseous emissions and particulates into the openings of buildings can have a pernicious effect upon the respiratory well-being of the occupants.

Windows that open, ventilation air intakes, and entry doors are all susceptible to the entry of vehicular fumes. Diesel fumes from trucks and buses are particularly noxious. Loading areas for passengers or commodities especially suffer from concentration of heavy emissions. Architectural proximity to traffic is less than desirable, as well as the accompaniment of noise with the pollution.

Many persons knowingly or unknowingly are mildly or more seriously affected by automotive fumes. Attached garages of commercial, institutional, and residential occupancies pose an indoor pollution problem. Not only are the occupants at levels of risk, but invading fumes with hydrocarbon particulates can increase indoor maintenance.

PETRO-INVASION

Urban planning and the location and siting of architecture and the location, configuration, and attributes of its openings relative to motor vehicles are germane to internal problems from their emissions. The use of outdoor space, pedestrian pathways, and gathering places can be untenable when inundated with clouds of toxic vehicular fumes, and noise from stop and go, upgrade, and roadway traffic.

Places where vehicles stop with running motors should evoke special attention to avoid emission intrusion into indoor space.

Vehicles are both a product and a system. They are a mobile element, a systemic link between and within urban centers. They are in a broad sense a piece of rolling architecture moving people, goods, and services from building to building.

Until "clean" fuels may come into general use, motor vehicles will concentrate their fumes in city canyons and pyramid pollution along traffic-clogged streets and highways to the detriment of ecologic and human health.

Better alternatives are communication by phone, fax, or letter; moving information instead of people; architecture that provides more intercoordinated services; conference calls; the likely proliferation of closed-circuit television; consolidating automotive destinations; and the decentralization of business activities.

Ecologic Economics

Everything that happens in our society goes through an economic sieve. Every project has its budgetary limitations. But the desires and expectations of clients often tend to exceed the actualities of cost. Holistic ecologic design has a value-added factor that translates into ecologic and our own vitality. This extra dimension with frugality in planning and design can often be realized relative to the cost of conventional construction.

The real world is one of Life, our inventory of possessions, property, and our level of knowledge, vitality, health, and adaptability. We are territorialists creating and protecting our sphere of capability to support ourselves financially and gratify our desires. We have not only to satisfy physical but also psychologic desires. We all live upon expectation.

From ancient times our primal support, vitality, and sustainability has come from ecosystemic energies of sun, air, water, and earth. Nature has given form to our earthly habitat and provisioned it with organic life forms that we consume for nourishment and organic and inorganic matter from which we shape our cities, our architecture, our interiors, landscaping, products, and systems. This is the real world cognizant of and connected with Nature.

TECHNOLOGIC CHANGE

But our aggressive, inquisitive, and manipulative mind was not content at this basic level. Through centuries of human history progressions of technology developed irrespective of any direct or unseemly side-effects upon Nature. Functional needs, visions of power, position, and wealth influenced design in form, energy, methods, and materials. Regal and princely purses were patrons of stylistic architecture, lavish interiors, cultured landscaping, products that fit their fancy, and systems of society, politics, and technology.

The pattern was set by the elite mind of aristocracy. Lessor strata of position in the royal realm to the disenfranchised poor sought to emulate the royal privilege. This hangover is with us today. The wealthy and prestigious set the pattern. It is an economic pattern that exploits our global resources and energies within the few and expectations and emulations of the many. The message of unlimited expectation is broadcast by the media.

In this pattern global ecosystems and ecology that give us life have been forgotten. Historic populations were much smaller and Nature's vitality and global habitability were not challenged. Today with exponential world population escalation, Nature's sustainability and global habitation are challenged. We have reached a historic limit.

TECHNO-SOCIETY

We now live in an artificial technologic world of our own making. We spend most of our time within indoor spaces and enclosed vehicles. We have separated ourselves from Nature. Within this isolation of our homes and buildings we separate ourselves from the natural forces that sustain us and rejuvenate our bodies and our mind. We are essentially earth creatures, yet we build high-rise structures and monolithic complexes that ignore this connection.

As technologic architectural design might align with the ecologic forces of Nature, new architectural and renovation projects would fit as ecologic design within this pattern.

Refinements for control over systems, for comfort, and over wastes can remain largely out of phase with solar and natural energy systems or be recast within an ecologic concern, action, and realization. To do less than give honor to Nature and her elegant life-giving and sustaining systems is not to give honor to ourselves as a remarkable expression of Nature.

ECONOMIC SIEVE

Our traditional concept of the "*economic sieve*" limits our perspective. Our financial and economic illusions need to be in con-

cert with the realities of Life and vitalities that empower our mind and body.

The greater our "gross national product" (GNP) within our fossil-fuel economy, the greater is our ecologic deprecation. *Ecologic values and vitalities should be our economic index.* Our immediate and short-term perspective obscures the constant, near-term and long-term effect of misleading traditional economics. Unless all costs from source to use and final disposition and environmental costs are included within total cost compared to prevailing costs, a logical economic will not be realized.

Our present design shortfall in architecture, materials, products, and systems principally depends upon our petro-infrastructure and petro-economy. In general our petro-technologies and economics are counter to an ecologic ethic. But to disregard the individual and long-term benefits of some synthetic petro-derived materials and products can in practical terms be counterproductive. A priority of ecologic value is essential to pass through the "ecologic sieve."

Among other factors of our techno-society, the true burden of energy costs are hidden. The "hidden costs" that we collectively pay in taxes, major subsidies to petro-energy and nuclear (with fractional support for conservation, efficiency, and energy alternatives) are not visible in the energy bills we pay for electric generation by coal and nuclear power and for transportation.

Large increments of hidden cost are in health and medical bills, loss of employment time, from our anti-ecologic and wasteful military, oil spills, and other forms causing extensive environmental damage.

Until the *true costs* of immediate and long-term air pollution, environmental deprecation, ecologic denigration, environmental illness, and the effect of radioactivity and agricultural losses are clearly evaluated and become *real costs* attributable to what we specifically select, specify, or contract, our present illusionary economic system will prevail.

Ecologic economics is the key of necessity if we deem that necessity to be our own well-being. Healthful food, clean water, clean air, undefiled earth, and a vital environment that accord with species diversity and our own vitality in equity of the world's people is an arrival of social justice. Pollution control is critical to our sharing in the reasonable equity of global regenerative abundance and sustainable ecosystemic coherence.

GLOBAL ECONOMICS

A New Age world order and economy are emerging. Traditional economics is in a state of serious erosion. It is being supplanted by an omnivorous, globe-encircling petro-economic of corporate and political power.

Garnering parts, pieces, and components from around the world to make something is anything but efficient or ecologic. The ecologic "pollution trail" is compounded by governmental abdication and corporate aggression.

How to painlessly switch from a capital-intensive and consumer-intensive society is a perplexing ecologic question. Capitalism and other governmental systems have in the main undervalued the *ecologic reality*. Our capital system is a misguided economic counter to ecologic and social justice.

The structures of governmental external support and subsidy and internal institutionalization need a primal inception and accord within a responsible global ecologic economic.

Trade balances are meaningless. The only inherent values lie within sustainable and renewable habitability in all segments of world population. A key to a direly needed economic equity is the restructuring of the executive perspective, education, job training, and the total infrastructure of corporate and governmental meaning into a holistic perspective and functional ecologic values.

Internalized self-sustaining economics for essential needs are a first step for stabilization. From such base ecologic means, methods, and trade systems can be providentially initiated. A global trade environment and economic with ecologic coherence requires modelling in the light of the stability of reliant, internalized economics.

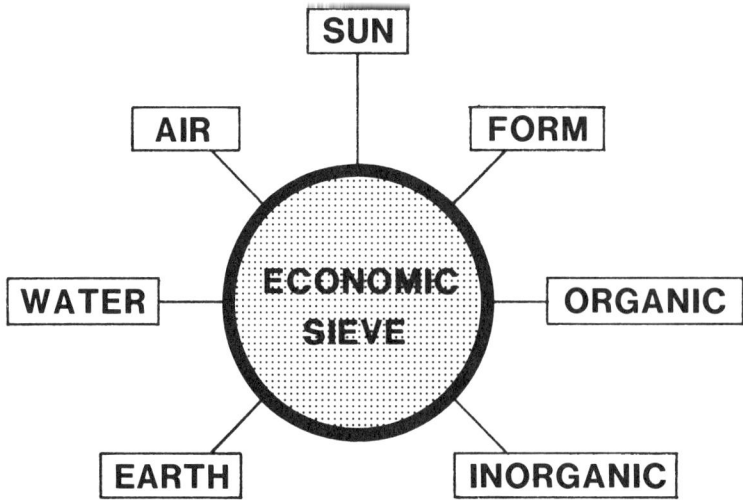

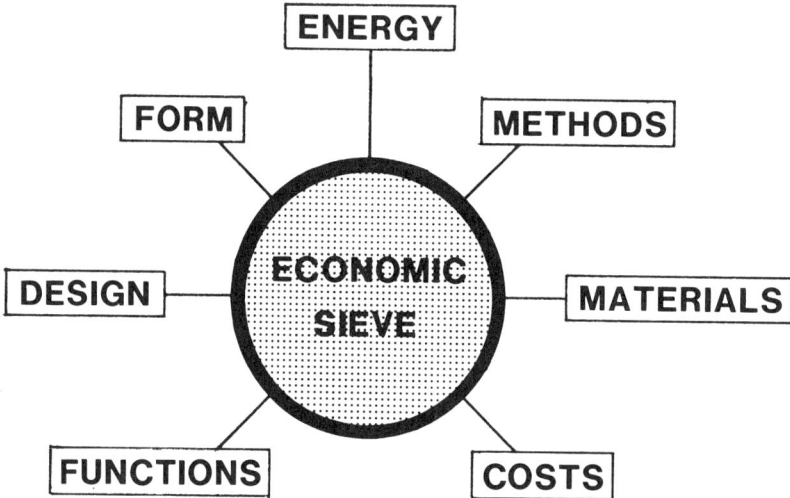

ECOLOGIC DESIGN FACTORS

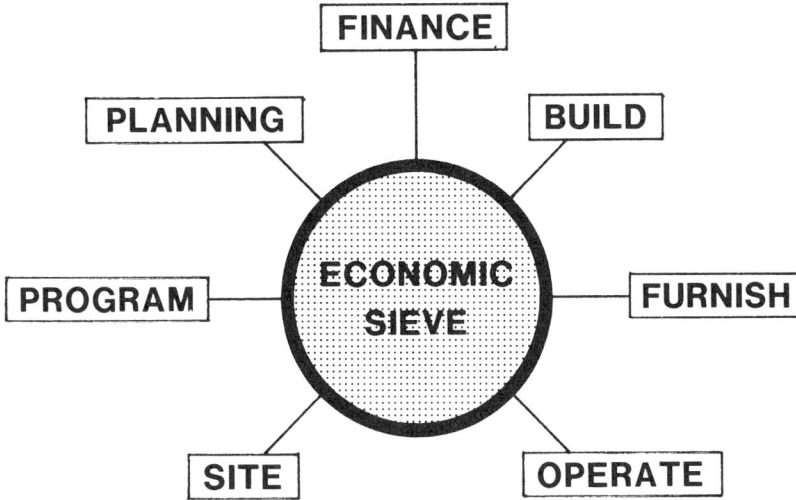

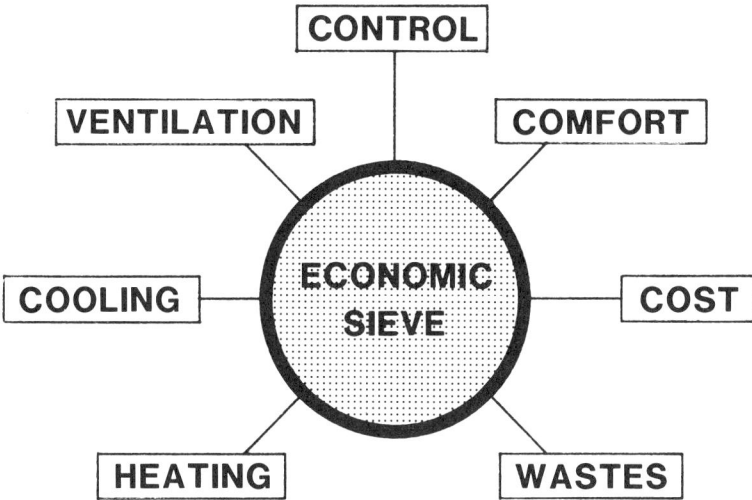

ECOLOGIC DESIGN FACTORS

Energy Policy, Action, and Expenditure

In the light and promise of "clean" energy by the year 2000 or 2010, government ecologic policy, protection, and expenditures with this objective are needed NOW. It is essential that the *move away from* fossil fuel and fissionable energies be urgently regarded and implemented.

Architecture and other elements of the built environment, vehicles, products, and systems can as within the issues of this book be served by energies not antagonistic and deprecating to global ecologic viability, vitality, and sustainability. Planners, architects, and designers can do their part, but governmental ecologic policy, legislation, and funding are needed to address the magnitude of such initiative.

Both the role and funding for solar, renewable, and geothermal earth energies are within our national interest and global responsibility. The global atmosphere is in great distress as a protective shield, a thermal moderator, and as a reservoir of unwitting technologic pollutants. Air quality is primary to breathing. "Clean" air for the interior of homes and buildings depends upon outdoor air quality.

"Tougher" standards over the emissions from vehicles, power plants, industry, and other sources are critical. But addressing the *sources* of air pollution *directly* is more economic and effectual in ecologic terms

and more sensible in terms of human health. *Our human penchant has been in addressing problematic situations after they happen rather than before.* This stance no longer works on a national or global scale. Government resource and energy policies need to be high on the agenda as to global consequence. The policy structure needs to be evaluated in the light of "clean" energy and ecologic viability.

ECOLOGIC ETHIC

Can American inspiration, creativity, and ingenuity be stimulated and motivated towards an ecologic ethic? Inventive practicalities, breakthroughs on ecologic technologic alignment, and how alternatives and existing technologies can be altered to align with global ecosystemic sustainability can be highly rewarding.

Architects, planners, designers, inventors, and creative persons in all walks of life and within business and commercial enterprise can effectually contribute to set forth an ecologic paradigm. For too many decades we have lead the technologic revolution at the expense of the global environment. Now we can take leadership within an ecologic conscience and responsibility. In 1989 at the American Institute of Architects convention, the Board passed a "Critical Planet Rescue" resolution and created an open Committee on the Environment. It has embarked on the initial task of an environmental resource guide. A local chapter of Architects, Designers, and Planners for Social Responsibility elected to pursue the critical issue of environmental design. These policies, directions, and actions are notable towards ecologic design as the prime architectural discipline.

Business will make what people will buy. Business will manufacture or otherwise provide what architects, planners, and designers will specify. When an adequate market is not perceived, business will not jeopardize its organization, its investment, or its ability to make a profit.

To become ecologically minded and productive in coherence with ecosystemic values is no light decision. Adding ecologic materials, products, and systems to existing lines is apt to be the cautious matter of choice. It is obvious that many products, materials, and systems have no redeeming value on a scale of ecologic worth. Policy and expenditure into ecologic channels for such will be a tenuous consideration. The question is, how quickly and to what extent will a demand develop for materials, products, and systems that have greatly reduced, little, or no adverse impact on the environment?

The more quickly a transition to an ecologic ethic is realized by the design professions, the construction industry, and the suppliers, the more quickly is the environment protected. Numerous materials, products, and systems now in production are notably more efficient and conserve energy. But in holistic ecologic architecture that relies first on site-specific energies and individualistic design strategies for optimal self-sufficiency, most items will require a close scrutiny.

Not only the policies and expenditures of government and business, but also the design and specification of each project encompass expenditures of resources and energy. But our own and global monetary systems have little meaning unless they are tied to the ecologic reality.

ECO-INCOHERENCE

Nature's expenditures in regeneration and renewal have persistent and vast proportions. The wondrous development of mature plants and trees from tiny seeds and the proliferation of the species of the earth, water, and air are genetic investments that have no parallel. *The real world is that of Nature's energy coherence and dynamic equation.* The least we can do is to honor this organic investment and cherish the continuum of Life.

Nature's investment of resources and energy that serves, supports, and sustains Life and ourselves is not a statement of policy. It is the working of evolutionary formative energies of which we remain as a fragile part. Our global overproliferation of people seriously threatens ourselves as a most active global species in taking without heed from Nature's bounty. Our human policies and expenditures should agree and attest to rather than overtly test the vitality and sustainability of our global habitat.

But *conspicuous possession* and *status symbols* are a conspicuous part of American life. The freedom to have, to acquire luxuries, and to display position and wealth is ingrained in our culture. Unmeasured is the ecologic exploitation that accompanies this state of mind and the quest for its gratification.

It is a paradox that in residential architecture the size of interior space, the energy-intensive bathrooms, energy-intensive kitchens, energy-wasting elaboration of the interior and exterior, and disregard for solar and climatic orientation vie against frequent claims of the energy-efficient home. While insulation, tightness of construction, glazing, and other "features" save energy, the *total energy quotient* of materials and methods invested in construction is not factored in, as well as the *total environmental impact.*

PERCEPTIONS

As the public is likely to become more literate in ecologic concern in the effects of choice and lifestyle, hopefully a simpler, less stressful America will evolve. The large, cumbersome, maintenance-heavy, multilevel residential behemoths of ersatz prestige are likely to become the white elephants of tomorrow. In perspective, following World War II two-story houses were unwanted and difficult to sell. Now even three-story houses (particularly with a garage under

townhomes) prevail. Walking up and down for individuals in normal health is good exercise. But regardless of the extra maintenance of extra floors (stairs require more effort in cleaning) and land conservation by the stacking of floors, the point is that the American mind does change in perspective over comparatively few years.

The point is that NOW is not THEN. With the media of television, magazines, books, and newspapers casting their barrage of expectation and the "American dream" on one hand and messages of dire consequence to the environment on the other hand, the public is entitled to some confusion. In preference the public takes the road of gratification. In the media reinforcement of gratification, the dire environmental consequence message falls into the shadows. *But the public mind remains reversible with time and circumstance.*

Gratifications in the mind of the architect, planner, and designer are usually preconceived within a framework of education, beliefs, and experience. *"Belief"* is a key word. Our conventional monetary systems, architecture, transactions, and way of life are products of "belief."

If there is no strong and overriding conviction at a public, professional, corporate, or political level for a *prime ecologic ethic*, all else matters little. *Energy policy and expenditure at every level are the marks of attachment to a "belief."*

If we *believe* in ecologic and human vitality and a world of coherence within the spirit of earthly wonderment, the miracle of Life will have been affirmed. *Actions can speak most loudly of our ecologic beliefs.*

Ecologic Urban Perspective

We need ecologic, site-specific, self-sustainable architecture. We need ecologic, integrated, locational, self-sustainable communities. We need an urban context that is coherent with and ecologically interresponsive to the communities and architecture that comprise it.

The productive forces of community within a context of Nature's regenerative and vitalizing powers are principal to sustainability. Envisioned is a garden habitat with land lost to building coverage compensated for by roof gardens and greenhouses. In coherence with Nature, human vitality is stimulated within and among persons. The psychoneural ambience and aspects of place can have a potent effect upon attitudes of mind, endeavor, and satisfaction. But in the scheme of things friction between people cannot be dismissed. The more closely knit a community, the more that regulations over conduct are needed. The rewards of a sustainable community need to overshadow minor to more overt occurrences of conflict.

Community planning and architecture subservient to an ecologic structure of community are the keys to community vitality. Keeping the dynamic processes of communities accorded with the dynamic processes of Nature and within the dynamics of sun and climate requires a constant adaptable discipline. Every day and season are not exactly like another. There are similarities and expectations but no exactitude.

SOCIETAL CHANGE

Although urban spaces and architecture may be ecologically and ergometrically planned does not rule out the advantage of adaptability to change. In keeping with the dynamic propensities of life, people may not change in physical stature and articulation but can change in patterns of activity and other ways of life.

Looking back to early colonial times in this country, the keeping room was a family place of production activity. Candles were made, fabrics were loomed, and other necessities and comforts were attended to. Food preparation and cooking and other routines were part of the keeping room sustainabilities. Shared activities were part of life.

More in principle than a suggestion for duplication, modern homes often have activity spaces, workshop, art, music, writing, or craft rooms, lofts, or other spaces that can presage common space in co-housing or other architectural formulation.

In new projects architectural elements can be within holistic concept. In renovation, additions, and infill housing and nonresidential projects, existing conditions, zoning and building codes, and budget can be particularly limiting to an ecologic viewpoint. Architects and designers have the imagination and ingenuity to make the most of what is. To this add an ecologic discipline.

SOCIOLOGIC REALITY

The acculturated and diverse segments of our urban fabric enrich society and do not have to be abandoned. But revitalization and an ecologic infusion into the urban scape and architecture is needed in most of our cities. Rehabilitation has been successful for many neighborhoods. But often it is a displacement of occupants in an accommodation to an influx of new occupants.

As older parts of the city have "run down," poor and low-income people and often minorities have moved in. In extensive or in substantial cases the rehab and upgrading lies beyond the income of the prevailing occupants and so a more financially capable population segment moves in.

A major social question is how to care for and provide housing for the homeless, low-income, and destitute families and persons. Tying an ecologic conscience with the problem can help lighten the distress by a self-sustainability viewpoint. As subsistence may be optimized on the site with food raising, home industry, inter-sharing of abilities, and common value and use items, hope, well-being, survival, and morale would be encouraged.

Equity in any society is difficult. History abounds more with societal stratification than equality. But as our nation professes to equality and justice for all, Nature and her ecosystems and her ecology of which we are an inseparable part aid in which we all can share. We all share the site-specific energies of the sun to earth, air, and water energies. But only in part are we so benefitted while in measure harmed by earth contamination and air and water pollution. Our prevailing architecture and urban infrastructure for the most part does not fully benefit nor does Nature in the context of how we have designed and built.

Ecologic Urban Planning

Architects may view the urban environment as space between buildings or as a supportive infrastructure for architecture. Urban planners may view town and city planning as a sociologic environment with activities and connections.

Life and cities have become overwhelmingly complex and uncertain as effectual societal and business environs. Highways and byways that were avenues of escape have become clogged and impede the freedom they once offered. The petro-fueled vehicle has become the oppressor rather than the liberator.

Architecture cannot ignore its societal, business, and economic relevancies to the total urban fabric. The urban plan cannot ignore the changing needs in architecture and an urgency for ecologic revitalization.

ECOLOGIC/TECHNOLOGIC

Technology is leading to decentralization. More things can be accomplished at home or nearby. Viewed in ecologic terms, the less distance travelled by motor vehicle, the less pollution. Concentrations of building, pavement, and traffic do not provide the most hospitable environment for people.

As satellite offices, retail sales pitch and participant television, fax machines, technologic communications, information on any desired issue become available within the home or home office environment, the conceptual structure of urban planning and architecture will change.

The question of urban employment is likely to become more critical. Automation, robotics, and computer systems will continue to make inroads on managerial and labor employment. Urban planning and architecture usually follow societal customs. But the time is too late, our misdirected lifestyles and unbridled technology are far afield from ecologic necessity. Society can be influenced by ecologic design. Within the context of the prevailing conscience of an energy-conscious public, the way is paved for the broader need of ecologic design.

ECO-RESPONSIBILITY

Awareness, responsibility, and commitment on the part of urban planners, architects, and designers can exhibit a leadership for a public accord to these values. The precept that *every* choice in urban planning and architecture has a plus, minus, or benign effect upon our local communities and global environment is a choice that affects or will our human well-being and destiny.

Excesses in the use of materials, methods, and energies that deplete our global environment, mutilate its ecosystems, and destroy its ecology leave little room for Nature to remain vital. Frugality in resources and petro-energies and "clean" ecologic alternatives can sustain ecologic margins for ourselves and our progeny.

A succinct point to be addressed is the dichotomy between the efficiency and effectiveness of central urban systems versus ecologic sustainability and site-specific self-sufficiency. The weight of conventional economics obscures the essential *ecologic economic.*

Ecologic Landscaping

Indigenous varieties of trees, bushes, plants, and grasses in most cases are best suited to effectual sustainability within the climate of their locale. Being mindful of their natural ecologic environment is a key to their viability and regenerative propensity. The compatibility of vegetation as to sun and shade, water requirement, type of soil, and the microorganic and insect ecology is critical to the health and vigor of the vegetation.

Water retention and drainage are factors that should not be overlooked. In most dry and relatively dry climates the grading, type of soil, and type of planting for maximum water retention is desirable. How the earth may be covered with wood chips or other materials to reduce surface evaporation can be a plus, as well as retained and channelled water from roofs or paved surfaces. Roof and surface water can be retained in a cistern where by gravity or siphoning can provide the most timely irrigation of landscaping.

Experienced assistance should be sought for every locale, condition, and effect of outdoor space use and upon the architecture. The effect of neighboring vegetation, architecture, grading, and other conditions on the landscaping of any site should be accounted for.

MICROCLIMATIC VITALITY

Every tree, bush, plant, or grass has its effect upon the microclimate of the site and upon the architecture of the site. Planting for aesthetic pleasure only neglects notable microclimatic advantages.

The daily and seasonal solar radiation, vagaries of climate, climatic extremes, and the outdoor and indoor use of space can be substantially conditioned by choice and treatment of landscaping. Creating zones of sun and shade, effectual constraint over unfavorable winds, control over air movement, outdoor spaces appropriate to use, and an integration with indoor spaces can be fortuitous to activities, relaxation, and pleasure.

In general, en masse planting has the advantage of moisture retention, better climate control, and better scale relative to architecture. However, rows or groups of trees or even a single well-placed tree can be a most effective agent of microclimatic control. Low, dense evergreens can block cold winter winds. Large evergreens can attenuate and turbulate north cold winds. In summer months shade is more needed and the placement of deciduous varieties can provide welcome shade to outdoor spaces and shade the architecture and its openings. Vine-covered arbors can offer summer shade also. Mist spray heads judiciously located to water plants and grass or paved or gravel surfaces can by evaporation effectively reduce air temperatures near building openings. They can reduce indoor air temperatures.

In contrast to native grasses that remain in a natural state, cultivated lawns are energy intensive and water demanding. They do provide, however, more oxygenation of the air than trees and offer a surface appropriate to a broad range of uses. Lawns and plants can be maintained by natural organic methods without toxic chemicals. Power lawn mowers and leaf blowers pollute the air and have a raucous output of noise. Their use should be discouraged. As the solar climatic architecture of the site and design of the landscaping are intereffective as to self-sufficiency and sustainability, an ecologic accord is struck.

Human vitality and self-sufficiency are part of this ecologic equation. The flow between Nature and the architecture within our senses and mobility engenders our vitality and experiential pleasure. The design of landscape, architecture, and interior becomes one within a province of ecologic design.

ORGANIC GARDENING

An added attribute is how gardens, fruit-bearing trees and bushes, and the spaces of the site and architecture can accommodate the growing of organic food. Composting becomes an element of this edible endeavor. The more food produced at ground surface, roofs, or attached or detached greenhouses and sunspaces, the less is the impact upon our global environment. Distant agriculture and food production, processing, preservation, storage, transportation, and packaging are energy intensive and encourage the loss of nutrients. The packaging and advertising that attend it from source to use alone account for a formidable contribution to waste and concomitant pollution.

What we do for ourselves within the boundaries of our property that lessens our dependency upon external sources is a vote for Nature's well-being. Not to be lost sight of are the physical benefits to self. But what we either do not or cannot raise at our site, the next choice is for local organic produce and community gardens.

Urban planning can circumscribe areas for community organic food production. At all ages the greater the amount of participation at the community level in gardening, the safer communities become and the greater are the collective and ecologic benefits.

URBAN FOREST

Concepts of the *urban forest* need initiative and development for old and new neighborhoods. Private residential and commercial properties are good candidates for forestation. But to be thoughtfully and legally observed is the solar and climatic influence on adjoining and sometimes nearby properties.

Passive and active solar systems can be compromised not only by neighboring architecture but also by the size and position of its trees. Older neighborhoods which comprise most of the built environment can benefit naturally by community-planned urban forestation. As climatic extremes and summer solar intensities are reduced, less heating and cooling requirements are needed.

New and older subdivisions are most often too barren and open. But the most effectual and ecologic planting of trees should not have a negative solar, wind, or other adverse effects upon a neighbor.

Ecologic Residential Architecture

THE SITE

Every residential site is site-specific as to its location, topography, organisms, vegetation, solar access, and its microclimate. It is site-specific as to the development and condition of neighboring properties and to roadways and utilities that serve it.

The ecologic initiative is how in project planning and design to conserve and sustain the organic life of the site with the least disruption. Or how to devise an indigenous ecologic setting of microorganic life and vegetation.

Every site has its locational distance to provisionary needs and to places of education, work, play, exercise, dining, socialization, and entertainment. This locational distance and the frequency of automotive travel to needs and activities translates into increments of pollution per mile. The greater the self-sufficiency of site and architecture that can be originated and realized by planning and design, the less is the environmental impact.

ORIENTATION

The volumetric needs of the architecture and its footprint are environmentally relative to the size of the site. The trend towards small sites, infill housing, and larger single or multiple dwellings reduces opportunities for passive solar and landscaping. For some residential projects the solar and landscaping benefit is incidental. But the more fully packed a site is with connected living units, the more that total energy loss is reduced.

Under the foregoing conditions, south orientation (preferably within 20° of true south) can hopefully be attainable for sunspaces, roof-top greenhouses, roof gardens, and active solar collectors for space heating and hot water.

Single-family and multifamily developments that accord with architectural, topographic, and landscape options on a site can be oriented to the best interseasonal solar and wind pattern opportunities.

Orientation relative to solar radiation and prevailing and cold winter winds is one of the factors most frequently not regarded in site planning and architecture. All openings within the architecture bear a thermal and experiential relationship to the sky, the sun, external views, the earth, and seasonal change.

The orientation of architecture and outdoor space use relative to avoid street and highway noise, automotive fumes, and other externalities is often not well resolved. Local fumes and noise from industry or other external sources such as airline flight patterns may not be well considered.

FORM

The possibilities of architecture are limited by ecologic form. From an ecologic standpoint, the *least* energy and resources, construction equipment, and energy-intensive materials, means, or methods our plans, design, and specifications call for, the least we will impact the environment. But the more we can incorporate purpose, adaptability to long-term probabilities of use, durability, "clean" energy use, and freedom from maintenance and repair in our construction and systems, the better off is our local and global environment.

Ecologic architecture acquires its form in response to site-specific solar, earth, air, and water energies and to planar and volumetric needs, with the location, size, and type of glazed openings as the important receivers of daylight and thermal energies. The architectural envelope can through added insulation or superinsulation and tight construction be an intervention between the energies of solar radiation and the outdoor and indoor climate.

Ecologic architecture should by necessity be obedient to the ecologic well-being of the occupants and site-specific solar, air (wind), earth, and water energies. The fundamental choice and specification of materials, products, systems, and their interrelevancies and redundancies conditions and gives form to the project.

Within an ecologic architectural paradigm are the experiential, functional, ecologic, daylight, and thermal systems and the economics of global sustainability. Every system within architecture and its structure has a salutary or contrary effect upon its holistic ecologic accord and upon ourselves.

Our body's ecologic organic system, our mobility, and our propensities are subject to the holistic life-giving, protective, and supportive factors of our environs. Our visual, auditory, tactile, and olfactory sensitivities are affected by our encounter with people and our environs. We are benefitted by eustress (good stress) or unfavorably or more seriously overstressed. The architecture we plan and design not only has this experiential aspect but also other biologic stressors that are favorable or unfavorable of our environs.

Steady-state systems are antithetic to the dynamic exercise of our senses, experiential mind, and physiologic vitality. Variations within thresholds of reasonable tolerance can be more providential. The architecture itself as a fixed state construction has to contend with the dynamics of people and the dynamics of the sun and climate. Within its "fixity" adaptive ecologic attributes can be given to architecture by design.

Residences in particular have more possibilities for ecologic congruence than most commercial projects, given time-of-day differentiations in space use, less internal heat loads of lights and people, lighter more

Cook Street Residence

This 1972 residence was designed by the author/architect as his energy conservation, natural systems house and included a rentable apartment with separate entry. The principal main single-floor residence was designed to handicapped guidelines and had an attached garage opening to the alley.

Occupancy of the two-story apartment was for security when the author and his wife were on frequent out of state trips. It was designed for and later totally used as a one-family occupancy.

The main single-floor plan had skyshafts of the author's design that with solar rays and daylight illuminated a dressing room, master bath, a corner of the living room, and avoided usual skylight energy loss.

The dining area with a heavily planted moat around it provided CO_2 absorption and oxygenation. This high ceiling solar area had a seven-foot diameter transparent bronze double dome skylight. Full glazing under an exterior reflective solar light ledge and an upper overhang received direct sun and reflected advantageously to the interior ceiling, with winter thermal gain and controlled summer shading. The northside master bedroom and kitchen had exterior projecting vertical architectural fins to shade the low angle of the setting summer sun. To obtain privacy from the passing bus route, aspen trees were used to act as screening in line with south windows. The bare trees in winter permitted direct solar gain.

All interior spaces were cross ventilated. The master bedroom had a horizontal ventilation slit air intake and a west-facing solar gain plenum that projected above the roof and had an exhaust stack to augment the inductive ventilation. A similar arrangement was provided at the roof ceiling of the dining area with intake inductive air flows from all interior spaces. The absence of operable windows in deference to the security of screened louvered air intakes and infiltration reduction added to energy conservation.

The HVAC system was housed above the kitchen in a fire-protected space with direct exterior access for maintenance and outside combustion air. The system was designed with high destratification heating returns and low air conditioning returns (to stratify the cool air near the floor in hot weather for comfort and to reduce the warmer interior ceiling air to hot temperature delta-T outside air thermal exchange). The author has used this energy-conserving principle for commercial and residential projects. Cool air delivered by the HVAC to a comfort zone of occupancy need not wastefully cool the entire volume of space it serves.

Thermal break as well as exterior cavity wall, roof, and perimeter insulation under the slab on grade effectively intervened the drastic diurnal temperature swings. Snow retained on flat roofs provided a thermal benefit of reducing interior heat losses to cold outdoor air.

Flush panel doors, no trim, all white highly reflective interiors, and clean-line contemporary furniture required minimal cleaning in a luminous daylighted environs. A sliding panel from a studio room in closet allowed visual projection onto a living room wall. Carpeting was a commercial grade very tight cut pile with a polypropylene and jute backing.

adaptable wood construction, and more adaptability to optimization of solar and natural energy systems. This is particularly true in the matter of solar *subsystems* most appropriately devised *for each space of categorical use.*

In residential architecture major desires contrary to ecologic design lie within either the criteria of a client or within speculative marketing design criteria. Multiple numbers of bathrooms (an energy intensive and maintenance-demanding space) are not only desired but demanded. Kitchens tend to be overdesigned (another energy-intensive space), increased and inefficient square footage is often present, and an exuberant display of dormers.

OPENINGS

Many windows are apt to prevail in current housing irrespective of their solar and climatic orientation. Unshaded two-story west windows can create a solar hothouse through much of the year. In cold weather climates, solar radiation is particularly welcome in wintertime. A general ecologic dictum:

• most of the glazing should be south;

• glazing to the east should have some protection or attenuation in type of glazing;

• west glazing should be limited in area, be largely reflective, or have an external means of solar intervention; and

• north glazing should be minimal, nonexistent, selective against internal heat loss, or otherwise have a means of exterior thermal protection.

Seasonal solar angles and thermal gain should be calculated and determined for all glazing. Skylights are particularly vulnerable to interior solar overheating during spring, summer, and fall. Skylights also lose energy being generally located along a roof line or existing as a roof. They lose energy to the clear sky temperature which can be as much as 25° to 40°F (-4° to 4°C) cooler than the ambient temperature, depending upon project location. They are also vulnerable to dirt accumulation and possible leakage requiring maintenance.

Clerestory windows have distinct advantages over skylights or glazed portions of a roof. With careful calculations for south-facing clerestories, they can be designed to be self-shading, and interior solar penetration can be ascertained as to the effect upon interior space use, daylighting, and furnishings. North-facing clerestories will have considerable interior heat loss during cold weather, but with appropriate insulative and low emissivity glazing the advantage of uniform interior daylighting (without direct solar radiation gain) can be desired for a particular purpose. This can apply also to northside glazing for an art studio, drafting, and other home tasks for which uniform daylighting is desirable. East and west clerestories share the same problems as window glazing at these exposures. As all glazing is *tailored* to interior purpose for effective daylighting and thermal gain, different appropriate types of glazing and installation will save energy. Heat Mirror, argon-filled low emissivity, tinted and highly reflective, and high transmissivity with little energy loss glazing can provide technologic options for *selective glazing* to meet conditions desired rather than *general glazing* with one type of glass.

Thermal mass must be mentioned relative to its role in the reception and thermal retention of solar energy. To be effective the mass must be sized and placed in regard to the thermal relationship to solar gain and indoor space use. Thermal mass principally can be concrete (colored or with applied dark tile), masonry, water in dark containers, and eutectic salts for direct gain passive or hybrid solar systems. Solar-heated air transfer can be stored in gravel bins or effectual thermal mass inter-spaces within the architecture.

Glazed openings have more purpose than for daylight and solar gain. They provide a view to the outdoors and of earth and sky, of human and other creature activities. They can provide ventilation. But better cross ventilation is usually possible by screened louvered or other weather-protected openings that are low to the floor for intake ventilation air and other stack action and

venturi means to effectually vent the upper strata of warmest air, allowing cooler intake air to displace it. The separation of such ventilation air intakes from conventional window ventilation allows for the advantage of fixed glazing and the ability to best accommodate for daylighting, solar gain and control, for view of the outdoors, and most favorable interior furniture and furnishing arrangements. Fixed glazing in standard patio door sizes is most economical. Set into the architecture without frames, it can more effectively prevent thermal loss than is possible with thermal break frames and without air infiltration.

If windows are elected, an awning type at the floor line is both effective for ventilation and to exclude precipitation. Operable windows in the center of the exterior wall of a room are a poor choice. From a daylighting and ventilation standpoint they are generally less accommodating to interior room arrangements. Windows so placed can cause visual glare inviting scrim or solid draperies to reduce the visual discomfort.

Daylight and direct sunlight, depending upon what reflective surfaces are outside and inside, are less intrusive on vision when windows are closely located to light-colored interior sidewalls. Regressed windows acting like dark shadow boxes accord well with a non-glare vision of the outdoors. The retina of the eye is quieted as a light-receiving surface and the fovea then is less disturbed in a clear view of what is happening outdoors. As we eliminate draperies we

Bellaire St. Residence

Designed for a sculptress, the central solar gallery, south patio, north studio, and front living room comprised flow-through spaces for people gathering. With privacy from the street and neighbors, it internalized private showings.

Daylight from the north for the studio and from the south for wintertime solar gain and light to the central gallery provided an ever-changing interior luminosity. With its natural materials and form, the architecture was in balance with the materials and form of the landscaping. Case study page 161.

eliminate their expense and their accumulation of dust and odors and concomitant maintenance. Vertical blinds provide better light control and have less maintenance problems. Horizontal blinds accumulate more dust but can be effective for in-depth reflection against the ceiling and for privacy. Not to be overlooked are thermal blinds that can be installed for vertical, angular, or horizontal applications.

Doors can be more effective ventilators of indoor space than windows. Louvered grilled doors can provide greater security, offer a substantial opening to desirable prevailing winds, can be fitted with an insulative thermal blanket or panel, and an inside thermal door can act as final security and control over the desired amount of entering air.

In planning, all openings should be located to avoid the entrance of automotive or other fumes and particulates. The word *ecology* has not been mentioned in this review of openings. But the more in residential planning and design that solar and other natural energies can heat, air temper, ventilate, and cool without mechanical use, the more ecologic is the design. The more that daylighting and sunlighting can avoid the need of artificial illumination, the less is the demand on electric utility power. As the architecture is the system by natural site-specific means, it is ecologic.

INTERVENTION

Architecture is an intervention upon Nature. It protects us from the intensities of solar exposure, climate, other humans, and roving animals. The home is a place of security. Doors are locked and windows bolted to keep intruders out. Security has its ecologic side. As we keep our possessions, ourselves, and our loved ones secure, we are not at loss. We are ecological beings. Our vitality, well-being, and possessions sustain our being.

In-depth security planning can assure more protection than a burglar alarm alone. Residential bedrooms tend to be a target where valuables tend to be. It is where we are likely to be at night. Daytime and nocturnal security should both be considered. Operable windows are particularly vulnerable to entry, although an experienced intruder may seek out patio and other exterior doors.

An in-depth system in which an alarm is sounded inside (preferably also to a central alarm station) and in which the intruder has to further break in one or more times to get to you or your possessions can buy time until help may arrive. It can be a strong discouragement to the intruder. Designing a residence or other building with security in mind is better than trying to fit an alarm system in later.

Solar and climatic intervention is a traditional tenet of architecture. In our energy-conscious technologic age, super and "extra" insulation and tight construction have been major tributes to intervention. They have with insulating glass reduced the utility energy demand of dwellings and other buildings. But without regard to solar and climatic orientation they do not enjoy these thermal and experiential advantages. "Outsulation" without CFCs in steam-expanded styrofoam board manufacture can with a monoacrylic stucco-like finish more fully intervene to the climate with thermal break insulating performance than exterior in-wall insulation. But this does not infer the omission of in-wall insulation.

Not so clearly recognized have been climatic buffers that intervene against the cold. Northside earth sheltering, cold wind attenuation with evergreen trees and shrubs, intervention by the architectural elements of garages (avoid garage doors to north), storage areas, closets, bedrooms, and rooms not frequently used, interior stairways, and exterior walls are planning elements that can enhance interior comfort and conserve energy. *Unheated* entries as airlocked vestibules should be thought of as a *must* for all homes and buildings in a cold-weather climate. They will reside at a temperature between that of indoors and outdoors and avoid the needless extravagant waste of heating. Entries are best located south, east, or west but not north, respectively.

Sun rooms, solar atria and galleries, enclosed sunspaces, and attached greenhouses to the south act as climatic buffers as well providing daylighting and thermal benefits. East exposures, porches, and enclosures can be designed to enjoy the morning sun. West exposures are more problematic, but intervention enclosures can considerably protect interior spaces from both climatic coldness and solar overheating. These intervention spaces offer an ideal opportunity to provide in-depth security against intruders. The author has such intervention space in his residential research facility. With a burglar alarm taping and wiring to an outer patio door, doors from the space to the interior are glazed with high-security polycarbonate plastic glazing. Intrusion through the glass side-sliding patio doors (vulnerable to entry) would set off an interior and central station alarm. The difficult to breach inner polycarbonate glazed doors present a more formidable barrier. Heavy doors with peep holes separate and protect the bedroom area from the general living area. Retreat from the bedrooms can be made to a bath dressing area also with heavy doors and locks with direct connection to a central station police alarm. It is of note that the main bedroom has a panel to sensors that indicates the point of entry of any intruder.

Exterior walls, fences, and shrubbery can help to attenuate climatic extremes, provide privacy, and protect outdoor patios. But also they can provide cover for an intruder. How walls and other exterior planning and design are accomplished should not overlook negative as well as positive advantages. Landscaping is the most ecologic and effectual means of site-specific micro-climate conditioning and control. As an external intervention to the vagaries and extremes of climate and solar control it can be a most economic technique. See the chapter on "Ecologic Landscape Design."

EXPECTATION

With ergometric planning space can be conserved. In the criteria of today's custom residences, expectation usually results in more space and more elaborations. The budget is strained by expectations and desire.

Needs are distorted as *desires* are perceived as *needs*. The thought of a client is often that they will only build it once and so they can have little thought for restraint in any category of construction. Ecologic considerations are apt to be subjugated by egocentric personal visions and the quest to fulfill them. Self-gratification is a priority on the American agenda.

A bathroom for every bedroom, fireplaces, elaborate concepts, energy-intensive distant sources, and excessive waste by design, specification, and construction of materials, means, and methods are anti-ecologic. Design reflects the expectations of owners but also the perspective, scope, experience, preconceptions, responsibility, and decisions of the architect or designer. Architecture in practice covers an extensive number of disciplines. Ecologic disciplines added to the great number of usual concerns require

a reordering into holistic relevancies and redundancies much beyond that of prevailing professional practice. An ecologic commitment changes the scope and form of the criteria and the conceptual inspirations and includes a perspective that accords with the dynamics of ecologic systems (that inescapably include ourselves) and an in-depth ecologic informational and knowledge base from which to order the planning and design. The *ecologic reality* equates with wellness and survival. Our anti-ecologic technologic design, inspiration, and ingenuity are misapplied in ecologic terms. A scrutiny and reordering of all expectations and design creativity is essential if we value a habitable planet. Our present habitation is undermining global habitability.

CONSTRUCTION

Construction is not only disruptive of the ecology of a site but also of the neighborhood and also of its local and global effects. The ecologic result of all of architecture is a degree of impact upon the local and global environment.

"Ecologic" should be germinal to the first inception of an idea. In the design phase a constant tendency for a dilution and even elimination of some ecologic values often occurs in deference to more compelling design options. But *ecologic discipline is ecologic discipline* that needs a primacy from idea to completed construction.

Construction materials and methods availability can preclude those more ecologic in being less available within the construction time frame. For a non-wasteful consistency with dimensional lumber sizes and other standard dimensional items, drawings planned on a 4-foot (1.2-meter) or other conserving modular grid have added advantages to eliminate a considerable number of job dimensions, make job layout easier, and the coordination of trades easier during construction in agreement to the modules. Over-the-phone and other communication reference to specific concerns can be more definitive.

Waste not is a simple axiom but takes careful forethought and incorporation into the planning, design, and construction process. Frugality is not a common precept of our wasteful society. But to be frugal with all materials in all means and methods of construction, to align concepts and design to the realities of construction, minimize the use of heavy earth-handling equipment, inter-trade job conflicts, and least impact the site and neighborhood is within an ecologic direction.

Advantages in initial economic savings to the client are multiple in the design and completion of a project with frugality and lack of waste. Energy conservation measures that may initially cost more may be included that have life-cycle energy savings benefits. As the public consciousness to an *ecologic concern* escalates (beyond present energy-conserving features), resale value should be better than homes of less environmental concern. Hopefully the *ecologic home* that embodies design for *ecologic and human wellness and sustainability* will become a status symbol.

Healthy homes and energy-efficient homes are to be commended. But holistic ecologic design for individual and multiple healthy ecologic homes and in particular sustainable ecologic communities is the key to an ecologic way of life.

Architecture does not end with its foundation and outer walls. But the complete design infrastructure of urban planning, interior, landscape, product, and systems design are part of the ecological architectural perspective. The more that an ecological sustaining relevancy and integrative coherence are the order of our decade, the better will be our fortune of destiny by the year 2000.

Ecologic Commercial Architecture

THE SITE

Every commercial site has its site-specific characteristics and influence of the surrounding environment and development. Private and public institutional and non-residential projects can be categorically included within commercial ecologic generalizations. But every project for any type of use has its profile of specific needs and uniqueness of its organizational structure.

The ratio of architectural coverage to the area of the site can preclude any significant new ecologic site development and landscaping or sustain what may exist. Most zoning laws require some open space or setbacks to provide light and air to buildings. Some zoning laws are now requiring landscaping for commercial projects and screening of parking areas.

Parking is a major requirement for need and codes. It is often the major determinant of site and limitation of architectural development. The ubiquitous motor vehicle is anti-ecologic in its energy-intensive materials and manufacture, its omnipresent pollution, and the infrastructure of roads, service facilities, and parking spaces.

ORIENTATION

The location of commercial and institutional buildings has seldom been equated with sun and climate. Determining factors most often have been the aspect of street or road frontage entrance and a definable "face of the building." Loading and unloading facility has its influence. In retail stores street frontage is very defined, and in a shopping center where the mall becomes the street.

For the most part little regard is given to the definitive path of the sun and to aspects of seasonal climate. Most commercial and institutional buildings are a statement of independence except from the sky. Atria, courts, skylights, clerestories, and office building configurations that give view and light from the sky to the occupants are not uncommon.

But much can be done to use more daylighting that conserves electric illumination and air conditioning in the majority of structures. The architectural "skin" of the building and roofs can be designed as a thermal element using solar radiation as a source to in measure provide heating, cooling, air tempering, and ventilation. The full benefits of building design derived from interseasonal solar radiation, optimal daylighting, and correspondence to the climate are seldom being realized. "Glass skin" buildings are a case in point, very often with a mirrored facing that can cast intrusive reflection upon their neighbors. But buildings can be designed to benefit by capturing winter solar radiation and aid needed cooling by the envelope design and selection of glazed and other surfaces.

FORM

Within our technologic fossil-fuel economy, energy-demanding buildings and structures exist where many people gather to watch an event, attend a conference, or otherwise congregate. The energy intensities of travel must be added to the causation of air pollution. States and cities vie for business and tourists, but architecture that supports these activities and transportation has an erosive environmental effect. In a sense polluting motor vehicles and airplanes are elements of the architecture that take us from building to building.

Clean transportation fuel is as important as clean energy for architecture. Polluting fuels are a blight that we do not need. Until we switch to *clean energy sources*, our environs and planetary ecologic systems remain at considerable peril.

Today's societal, industrial, and economic revolution has no decisive and absolute structure. The heterogenous form and incongruity of architecture answers to these form givers. Decentralization is most likely to occur. Instead of moving bodies, we are more apt to be moving information, extending the connections and processes of work, and likely visual instant communication and interaction. The scenario is already unfolding with fax machines, computers, and sophisticated copy machines. More homes have a home office or work space, a network in business communication and process.

Satellite ecologic sustainable mixed use communities are likely to be a coherent design form of architecture. Interfunctional community relationships, tasks, and activities can enhance the security of person from young to old and collective self-sufficiency through solar, other natural energies, and food production. Garden-type ecologic educational, business, cultural, and spiritual sustainable communities could reduce most of the present stresses. An amalgam of education, work, cultural, spiritual, caring, shared effort, experiential learning, play, physical and spiritual exercise, and recreation could be enjoyed within a natural vitalizing environment.

Commercial and institutional architecture usually is burdened with the internal heat loads of lighting and people. Cooling is usually the most dominant energy need. Ecologic cooling can be either partially or totally accomplished in numerous ways. Most give form to architecture.

- *Earth coupling* is where a significant portion of the building is in contact with the earth. Underground architecture is a prime example.

- *Earth air cooling* (and air tempering) occurs where plenums or underground tubes cool incoming air or heat exchangers act as an earth cooling source for indoor space.

- *Solar inductive ventilation* -- where a cooler stratum of air is heated and exhausted by the sun and incoming cooler air displaces it.

- *Stack action ventilation* -- cooling and ventilation by temperature differentials within vertical forms or stacks of the building.

- *Venturi ventilation* -- roof stacks designed with a constriction to increase air exhaust by negative pressure developed by the wind.

- *Solar lithium bromide absorption cooling* -- high-temperature solar collectors can be used for absorption cooling.

- *Ice storage cooling* -- ice made by winter temperatures by waste heat or off-peak energy can be used or stored for summer cooling.

- *Nocturnal cooling* -- mechanically induced flow or pressurized air (preferably filtered) can cool by cooler nighttime temperatures. Better than roof exhaust fans and requires less horsepower.

- *Clear sky temperature cooling* -- clear sky temperatures 25°F (-4°C) to 40°F (4°C) cooler than ambient temperatures can be used for cooling.

- *Reduction of internal heat loads* -- reducing lighting equipment and other internal loads.

- *Heat pumps* are most desirable with the best coefficient of performance (COP). Air-to-air: outdoor air is the thermal exchange medium. Water-to-air: A cooling tower, pond, or other body of water of adequate size can be the thermal exchange medium. Earth-to-air: the earth can act as a heat sink for heat pump cooling.

Earth coupling, earth shelter, earth berms with trees and other vegetation, and the building itself acting as a natural cooling and ventilating system with solar radiation and air temperatures can have an ecologic accord in total building design with building form.

The envelope of the building, how direct sun openings are shaded, how daylighting is optimized, and how interior space is best served for comfort and function lie within the ecologic paradigm. Other form givers to commercial architecture are zoning and building code regulations and parking requirements. The client is notably in the position of acceptance or rejection. Initial cost looms big in a client's mind. Functional and economic feasibility presages acceptance. Budgetary considerations and functional practicalities often have their impact on what can be considered and what may be built.

Ecologic considerations for the most part have had a low or secondary priority against what the budget may otherwise buy. Very often the economic feasibility depends upon lease space. It is a prime yardstick of project worth.

But many ecologic options tend to reduce cost, to simplify the form, use less costly materials, and avoid all elaboration and waste in the design, specification, and building process. Frugality in budget generally aligns with frugality in form. Minimal surface to building volume ratio, the least demand on utility energies, and avoidance of overdesign of the building and its appurtenances relate to form and a reduction in construction costs. The selection of one structural system over another is critical to cost and to building form, depending upon how the envelope is treated and its effect upon the utilization of interior space.

Many low-rise buildings are either residential or semi-residential in character, and as such reference is made to the chapter on Ecologic Residential Design.

OPENINGS

While small commercial and institutional buildings may have residential type or other operable windows and possibly patio doors that open to a terrace or balcony decks, most large and high-rise structures are more apt to have fixed glass. The advantage in such case is that the uncertainty of how many windows may be open and adversely affect a mechanical heating and cooling system is eliminated.

On the other hand, in some classes of occupancy such as hotels, motels, and apartment buildings the mechanical system is not likely to provide the desired amount of ventilation to specific space occupancies. This is particularly true of transient occupancy buildings like hotels and motels in which the incoming occupant may find lingering odors distressful.

At grade level or balconies, access doors from individual occupant units can provide both ventilation and a physiologic and psychologic relief from indoor space. Schools and other educational institutions could benefit by the ability of classes under favorable weather in climate-protected areas to use outdoor space.

Large or more limited glazed roof areas prevailed in shopping arcades, office buildings, hotel lobbies and restaurants, and other occupancy types of years past. A pleasant and often most enticing indoor court environment was created. Daylight served the functions. Similar architectural resolutions are common to numerous architectural projects of today. The positive side is the protection of indoor space and the experiential stimulation under a literal canopy of daylight. The negative side is that such architectural devisements are energy intensive, relatively high in first cost, and high in maintenance. They also are subject to considerable cold weather and clear sky temperature heat loss and possible leakage. In summer shading may be required depending upon the use of the space, and they present a high air-conditioning load.

Before the days of electric illumination, daylight was architecturally sought and introduced into buildings as an oculus, an eye to the sky, peripheral windows around a dome or other raised ceiling, or by day-lighted glazed lanterns above the roof. Clerestories can be especially effectively and appropriate to serve indoor purpose by specific design that equates with the seasonal position of the sun or for north light for uniform interior daylight.

Daylight that enters or can be directed laterally across indoor task areas improves the acuity for reading, writing, and drawing. Strong downlight can reflect from a paper surface and, with the reflection from dark lines or typeface, can make it less comfortably visible than lateral illumination. But concentrated shafts of sunlight or artificial light can make objects more sharply visible. Daylighting or electric lighting as reflected from ceiling surfaces in a diffuse manner can, however, provide a comfortable reading, writing, and drawing environment.

Psychoneural responses to variation in sunlight and daylight exercise our visual and physiologic system. We are rhythmic beings to which our sensory responses need stimulation within reasonable psychologic and physiologic tolerances. But the stimula-

ting stroboscopic effect of fluorescent lighting can cause fatigue and stress.

The spectral characteristics of light have an effect upon our perception of space, the color of objects, and the degree of our visual and psychologic composure. Natural light is more calming than fixed-state electric lighting. The electromagnetic fields from quartz halogen, fluorescent, and other types of lamps and transformers can in our proximity to them have a harmful electromagnetic physiologic effect. *Most new and older buildings are overilluminated with artificial light.* Most offices, schools, and other commercial applications have too great a footcandle level of light and light fixture surface brightness. This extravagant use of light is overstimulating and does not favor best visual acuity. Excessive artificial lighting can result in hyperactivity and degrees of symptomatic distress. Task lighting with reduction in lighting level and correspondent air conditioning will reduce utility costs. Vision is not harmed by lower lighting intensities.

A prevailing wasteful commercial situation is an unnecessary blast of overhead electric illumination when adequate interior illumination is provided by daylight entering through windows and other openings. The proclivity of humans not to turn lights out when space is not occupied is another gross energy waste. Control and design are predeterminative of economy in energy conservation. Enough switching to separately control banks of lighting or a number of lamps in a fixture is ecologic and eco-nomic when appropriately used to task and need.

Every project at its location and latitude and for best suitability to occupant tasks and purposes requires examination as to the most appropriate daylighting resolution in the light of *all* visual, psychoneural, and ecologic considerations. It should be noted that certain light intensity and artificial spec-tral index (Kelvin rating) can be therapeutic for some depressed, visually impaired, older, or otherwise specific dysfunctional persons.

INTERVENTION

Within their usual size and bulk and proxi-mity within an urban environment, buildings act as a solar and climatic intervention to the street and to each other. High-rise clusters have a certain fascination in their visual limitation of sky. These city skyscrap-ers dwarf street-level activity and act as an immobile backdrop.

Mirror-like buildings reflect the sun's radia-tion upon their neighbors, often contributing to their air-conditioning load. Fast-moving elevators can be a greater activity than slow-moving street traffic. In the city canyons of architecture, site choice and ecologic options are usually narrow.

In contrast are buildings in a country-club-like setting, with often copious greenery separating them from other architectural expressions. Such sites can offer a par-ticular freedom for solar and climate-respon-sive orientation. Daylighting and passive, hybrid, or active solar for space heating, air tempering, or as an assist to inductive ventilation can be appropriate ecologic design modalities.

Smaller-scale commercial buildings gener-ally have less constraints to ecologic coher-ence than those of larger scale and often monolithic proportions. Depending upon site, solar orientation, solar access, the microclimate of the site and its proximity to traffic, noise, and fumes affecting natural ventilation, solar utilization for air tempering, heating, and as an assist to ventilation can be possible. Architectural form and insula-tion can be tailored to the directional expo-sure to cold winter winds and winter warm-ing sun. Superinsulation of north and other-wise tailored to conditions of other exterior walls and or the roof can act as a substan-tial climatic buffer.

Clerestory daylighting to the interior north-side can compensate and balance interior illumination with direct southside interior daylighting. Dependence upon electrical illumination can be minimal during daytime with adequate daylight and solar radiation. Reflective roof decks can enhance the solar gain upon air-type active solar collectors that heat gravel in a basement storage insulated bin for space heating. Clerestory daylight can be augmented in winter from a reflective relatively flat roof. An overhead angular reflective canopy can provide late spring, summer, and early fall shade over the clerestory. But in summer the roof deck can not only act as a reflective solar intervention but also to secondarily contribute some reflection to the angular surface of the canopy above the clerestory, bringing in a soft amount of light to the interior.

In the particular case of the perspective and sections of companion Cherry Creek Office buildings designed by the author in 1976, the foregoing description applies. The roof had reflective white marble chips and the overhead clerestory reflective canopy had mica flakes embedded in a smooth white stucco matrix. Other interventions specifically were 10" (25.4 cm) of rockwool insulation with thermal break sheathing and 16" (40.6 cm) of blown-in rockwool between the flat roof trusses.

In experience of approximately 5000 square feet (464.5 square meters) each building saved about $3000 per year in utility costs. The strategies of intervention including earth coupling and the effectual use of daylight, solar air tempering, solar space heating, and solar thermal storage (in the gravel bin), southside entries and natural ventilation added a minor contribution to initial construction costs. An air-to-air heat pump mechanical heating and cooling system was phased with the solar and natural inductive air flow system. But the total cost due to planned non-wasteful use of materials and labor, close attention to sub-trade coordination without construction conflict, simplicity in form, standard (patio door glass sizes) non-framed glazing, the total tradeoff cost

was that of conventional construction. Or equating the cost above the actual tradeoff frugalities, the payback was 3.8 years. The cash flow not paid to the utility company was an ongoing bonus.

In recent years the two buildings were joined under new ownership (planned as a possibility within the original design). The author designed a south-facing clerestory as a connecting link. Under such conversion into one building the climatic impact was reduced and utility energy demand further decreased. The notable point is that scale relates to the proportion of climatic intervention. As new buildings may be planned for and existing ones be designed with energy-efficient and climate-responsive links, energy conservation is improved. Pre-planning in original design for the possible joining of the two buildings had its practical and economic advantage.

Architecture is a major intervener upon Nature. As the world population increases, more homes and buildings are needed. And the automotive connections to architecture likewise increase with paving and other necessities for the vehicles. Human population and the energy and resources of our planet are under provocative stress.

Our ingenuity and expectations have gotten us where we are. Can these same attributes solve our wayward dilemma? Ecologic design can attenuate and reduce ecologic stress. But people of the world who do not have an ecologic conscience and way of life

Cherry Creek North Solar Office Buildings

These active solar superinsulated buildings together saved over $6000 per year in utility costs. The conservation measures and the air-type solar collectors storing heat in an insulated gravel bin had a cost payback increment of 3.8 years.

The north building contained the author's architectural office and his environmental research and educational facility. The south building was integrated in design and later joined (as potentially designed) into one building structure. It initially provided offices for a corporate designer.

The superinsulation of the building is more than R-60 for the roof, R-45 for the north exterior wall, and R-30 for other exterior walls. Heating and cooling supplemental to the solar and inductive heating was with heat pumps.

Ecologic Design Concepts, Strategies, and Process 97

retard or nullify the evolution to ecologic design. They remain the interveners to a habitable world.

EXPECTATION

Expectation is the feeding ground to commercial enterprise. The incessant bombardment through every conceivable medium of beguiling and potent messages plays on the sensory appetite of the public. Everything that encourages attention and possession is programmed to the mind of the consumer.

Exploitation of finite global energies and either nonrenewable or dwindling resources is seldom equated with *expectation*. In architecture and all other products of imagination and design, this symbiotic relationship is seldom addressed or publicized. Energy efficiency, energy conservation, and "smart" buildings have become bywords, but the *full possibilities* that lie within an ecologic paradigm are not in usual practice. Nor can they be without an extensive ecologic informational base that needs to exist.

Expectations need a new equation that prioritizes *all* ecologic factors in architecture and in vehicles, products, systems, and services that pertain to architecture. Expectations provide business continuity and employment, but the switch to an ecologic opportunity is essential.

Environmentally "safe" products have been entering the marketplace. Usually they are more evident in catalogs that in stores. But along with implications (rather than always the actuality) of being environmentally safe, the consumer is responding.

An ecologic awareness and ecologic sensitivity is being fostered in the corporate mind at many levels. Time is in favor of business consciousness being skewed to *ecologic design*. Architecture as a major product and major investment is ripe for the expectation of ecologic design.

Whereas architects and designers may be on the forefront of techniques and methodologies in the creation of commercial and institutional site development, architecture, and interiors, holistic ecologic design offers a widened sphere of attention and acceptance.

CONSTRUCTION

Ecologic design and specification can pose a dilemma for contractors used to traditional and time-honored ways of building commercial and institutional buildings. Plans and details need to be especially clear in ecologic intent. Specifications should admonish the contractor to order early materials, products, and equipment that are "ecologic." Inasmuch as subcontractors in particular and general contractors in general do not like to lay out money ahead for these items, reimbursement clauses are needed and penalties called out for delay in getting what is specified. This is often a problem within the usual process of construction in which products not so common or available may be specified.

The general contractor and subcontractors need to be made well aware of the ecologic responsibility and to accord with in all procedures, processes, means, and methods and to adhere to such precepts. Close administration of the contract documents is advised by the architect and communication should remain open on all issues during the progress of construction. Substitutions from items specified can pose a particular problem as they may be requested by either the client or the contractor. New to construction ecologic procedures, means, and methods can require a very definitive description to be fully understood by the contracting trades.

In the conceptual preliminary planning and design process the comparative costs of construction within ecologic design and specification are best evaluated when schematic drawings, an outline specification, and sufficient construction structural, electrical, and mechanical information are determined. The greater the planning and design attention to the most effectual and efficient use of materials and methods and intercoordination of all trades involved benefits cost, reduces time for construction, and enhances the ecologic well-being. Initial as well as life-cycle costs should be assessed at various steps along with development of the construction documents for the client's evaluation and acceptance.

Ecologic Interior/Architectural Integration

SPACE AND FORM

The ecologic interior is most fortuitously conceived and planned as the space and form giver to the architecture. People live, breathe, and conduct their way of life in the interior of homes and buildings. People spend about 80 to 90 percent of their time *within* the architectural interior.

To optimize ecologic orientation and openings to daylight and solar radiation, external views, and psychoneural connection with the sky and earth, and to create interior space and form most appropriately to day and season is appropriate and energizing to the occupants.

As an ecologic form giver and delineator of architecture, interior design should encompass our physiologic, psychoneural, and behavioral receptivity and responses. Every nuance of the interior affects us. Every environment we attend leaves its imprint upon us. We are changed and modulated by our experiential impressions within the architecture and the attributes and characteristics of its interior. A fusion among interior spatial elements, their visual, tactile, acoustical, and aromatic characteristics, and the architecture is best realized in an interactive harmony.

DISCIPLINES

Thinking of the architecture as a creative expression without its integration and interrelevancy with every element of the interior is like an attentive package without any contents. Light, space, form, and surface are the ingredients of our mind, of architecture, and of the interior. Holistic architectural interiors and landscaping ecologic design must be a simultaneous and interrelevant conceptualization, coherent process, and project realization. Projects designed and built for a predetermined purpose contrast to speculative housing and commercial spaces that will be leased to others. But in principle the ecologic perspective can still apply.

Interior design can be appropriate and integrated with the architecture as an ecologic form and system, or interior design can be contrary or superficial to the functional and ergometric planning and a coherent interrelevancy with the architectural design. The ecologic design of necessity addresses our experiential and ecologic biophysical and psychologic needs and vitality.

The disciplines of the ecologic interior and architecture are demanding upon each other. The architecture and interior are responsible to Nature's earth, open sky, and atmosphere and to the ecologic health and well-being of the occupants.

Where the interior and architectural needs and form resolve and the exterior dynamics of sun and climate meet becomes the responsive architectural exterior form. Ecologic openings to the exterior should be those most suited to human purpose and wellness. The forms of the exterior should be most compensatory to the forces of Nature.

Interior architecture and interior ecologic design have a special responsibility due to the exposure of occupants to the materials, finish, and maintenance requirements of indoor space. The effects of electromagnetism and of radioactivity should not be omitted. Composite and synergistic effects upon health and vitality should not be overlooked.

In a way of thinking, the interior becomes the control mechanism within the architecture. The light-reflective properties, shading of windows, visual aspects of color, texture and form, acoustical properties of materials, tactile influence of floor surfaces, and the opening between spaces control the indoor environs. The indoor environs then conditions us. But also the outgassing and particulates emitted by materials as surfaces can have an unnoticed or noticeable effect on our health.

INTERACTIONS

Feelings of both security and liberation depend upon the attributes of the architecture and interior. Much of our reaction is by vision. We feel more composed and secure in a restaurant, waiting room, or work situation when persons or objects do not move across the alarm zone of our eye or do not approach in visual confrontation in entering a private office.

The composure and ease in approaching someone is most agreeable when the area of the vision is between the alarm zone (far to the corner of the eye) and direct visual confrontation. The same response holds in persons passing each other in corridors or otherwise in close proximity.

Persons in an office or other situation feel more at ease and secure when they can observe what is going on but in which their personal territory is clearly defined. The Hotsy Corporation office building designed by the author clearly exemplifies both this design resolution as well as "see through" from space to space for visual and psychologic escape. (Case study pages 125-130).

Ergometric planning creates the efficiency of closely organized space and assurance that goes with it. Ergometric practicality establishes attitudes towards organized activity and performance.

Space can be quiescent, centrifugal, or centripetal in our planning and design. To be quiescent it can be private, quiet, and offer composure. To be centrifugal it can tend to lead people away from each other. It can act as a separator in the workplace or among people at a gathering. To be centripetal space tends to bring people together. It becomes a space of socialization, inter-participation, or gathering in common interest or that becomes an audience. As an audience it can be in attendance at a lecture, visual projection, concert, ballet, demonstration, exhibit, or any other type of event or presentation.

Every interior space succeeds or does not measure up by its combined architectural and interior appropriateness. It is primarily a planning and design adventure in human ecology. Our ecological sensitivities and state of psychoneural and physiologic integrity can be augmented or diminished by the environs we create. How we accomplish the *best* within respect for and in harmony with Nature's ecologic energies and sustainability is critical within ecologic design.

INTEGRATION

In ecologic architecture and interior design the key word is "integration." Ecologic concern and frugality in the use of our planet's resources and energy is paramount to an ecologic ethic and responsibility. To evaluate possibilities of ecologic integration of the architecture and the interior, Construction Specification Institute (CSI) categories are used as a reference.

Every conflict or problem that arises through lack of integration equates with some loss of energy and ecologic consequence. The numbers are CSI designations of category. Certain categories expressly relate to

architecture and the interior. But ecologic significance and impact have to be specifically evaluated as to consequence.

1. General Conditions
General conditions circumscribe responsibilities, standards, process, performance, and legalistic considerations. The line of connection and definition between architecture and its interior can vary with each project, but ecologic expectations in design and specification should be added as a clause.

2. Site Work
How the site is land formed, views are developed or existing ones enhanced, along with landscaping affect not only architecture but also the point of view and correspondence between the exterior and interior. Interior design also is a terminology but outdoor patios, garden enclaves, and literally room-like outdoor spaces can have a close and desirable affinity with the interior. Making the best use of outdoor space with extended interseasonal comfort can save in some cases an economic and compensatory reduction of interior space.

3. Interior Concrete
Concrete is more apt to relate to the surface for outdoor patios but can also serve for indoor sunspaces and greenhouses. In the past some smooth hand-trowelled interior concrete floors have been beautifully stained and waxed for entire homes or portions thereof. A durable nontoxic coating over a fiberglass mat with a wide color choice is

available. Concrete thermal mass furniture can be most appropriate for indoor sun-spaces.

4. Interior Masonry

What has been stated in a general way under concrete can apply to masonry. Thermal mass walls can particularly be both an effective thermal mass to receive solar radiation and a stabilizer of indoor temperatures.

5. Interior Metals

Metals can apply to architecture and the interior as shaped forms, railings, and for fountains and sculpture. Circular and other metal stairways and ladders can be space-saving elements of architecture and the interior. Metals are energy intensive, and they should be adroitly used. Plating and anodization reduce maintenance over that of applied finishes but also add to the increment of energy. Wood can often be used to take the place of metal.

6. Interior Carpentry

Finish carpentry is pertinent to the architecture and the interior. The minimization or better the absence of interior trim, the less are the energy and materials used to make and the life-cycle maintenance in cleaning. Flush doors, frameless fixed windows, and windows without mullions also lessen detailed cleaning.

Clean-line contemporary design fits better with an ecologic concern than superfluities of tradition. Ergometric kitchen cabinetry saves space, materials, and functions more effectively than conventional cabinets. Aromatic and exotic woods from the tropics should be avoided and can be counter to individual sensitivities. Common construction lumber and treated wood for exposed areas such as decks, porches, and exterior members and surfaces can adversely affect the respiratory system of some people. Obtaining lumber from sustainable yield forests as close as possible to the construction site conserves transportation energy. Old growth forests should be avoided as sources.

For hardwood floors or other interior uses, white oak appears to have little observed effect upon persons sensitive to outgassing from the terpenes and other constituents of wood. Built-ins and wall paneling should be considered as to their possible respiratory effect. Interior grade plywoods and particle boards can outgas formaldehyde. Nonallergenic, nontoxic finishes for wood surfaces are advisable. Most people are not affected by plastic laminate covered cabinetry and other surfaces. Completely covered surfaces (visible or not) can seal in outgassing of plywoods and other wood materials. Coatings are also available to seal surfaces to prevent outgassing.

7. Interior Thermal Protection

Exterior intervention of direct solar radiation through windows, skylights, or other glazed openings is more effective than when applied internally. However, thermal window blinds, movable insulation, and insulated shutters are more effective than draperies or regular blinds. Draperies tend to be cumbersome, thermally inefficient, and require considerable stacking space and maintenance. Regular vertical blinds are a better choice for definitive solar control, privacy, small stacking space, and maintenance. Horizontal reflective blinds can project solar light to the ceiling, reflecting natural light more deeply into interior space. Overheating of the interior can also be lessened by the reflectivity of the intervention materials. The shading effect can lessen the solar intensity upon the furniture and furnishings and other contents of a room. West solar exposures can be particularly intense and troublesome. Exterior rolling shutters operated from the interior are most effective for thermal control and security, including control of west solar gain. Solar rolling shades are most appropriate as an external shading device to intercept the heat before it enters the interior. Rolling shades can be installed internally to attenuate direct solar intensity while others can function as a thermal intervention.

8. Interior Doors, Windows, Glass

Operable windows, louvered or grilled screen doors that prevent entry, and other screened openings that take in outside air appreciably affect interior room arrangements by the size, location, and the characteristics of glazing, size, placement, and type. In natural ventilation furniture and equipment can have a significant effect upon air flow through a home or building. The ventilation and comfort for the occupants can so depend. Particularly for commercial and institutional indoor spaces, the effect of furniture and other interior items on mechanical or natural air flow behavior can be predicted in to-scale fluid chamber studies.

Direct solar radiation can be disturbing to occupants and also have a deteriorating effect upon furniture and furnishings. Glazing that provides UV protection can avoid fading. In totally sealed buildings with fixed glass, mechanical air conditioning can cause discomfort where supply and returns are located near people. Interior planning should avoid such conditions.

There is a salutary relationship between home and building occupants and their ability to see outdoors. Windowless spaces within architecture are not conducive to visual and psychoneural relief. Where windows and other glazed openings may be located is critical to interior planning. Within naturally ventilated homes and buildings the location of operable windows, outdoor air intake vents, and interior door and other openings can be critical to directional views, optimal ventilation, and penetration of daylight. Glazed interior and exterior doors can add a contribution of light and view.

9. Interior Finishes, Paint, Carpet, Flooring, Ceilings

These are major sources of indoor air pollution. Carpeting is usually the most pervasive source. Its odor and chemical outgassing can linger on for weeks or months. Carpet harbors dirt, dust mites, and bacteria. Added bactericides leave open to question their effect upon people. Paint and other applied finishes to the architectural interior, furniture, case work, and equipment can outgas harmful toxins. Paints reputed to be nonallergenic are made from plant resins. They are expensive but provide a margin of greater nonallergenic probability. Plain water-based latex finishes tend to be less troublesome to most people, but they also tend to flake off small particulates during their lifetime. Oil-based paints can harden out but heavily outgas during and following their application. Natural stone may require less energy intensity in preparation and has been used since ancient times. But it can have radioactive properties which can be checked with a scintillometer. Natural slate is likely to require less upkeep than stone.

When possible finishes for doors, cabinetry, and other wood items should be applied in a well-ventilated place away from the project until there is little evidence of outgassing and odor.

Other surfaces of varying plastics for floor coverings and walls can be heavy on odor and toxic emissions. Tile in a natural mortar setting bed with masonry grout is least apt to be counter to health. Dark unglazed or matte glazed tile over concrete is an effective receptor of thermal gain from direct solar radiation. But imported tile or for other materials like marble, considerable energy can be used in their preparation, processing, and transportation. Linoleum that is cork

based is reputed to be less likely to cause allergic reactions than vinyl and other synthetic plastic floor coverings. Wood flooring is touted for "healthy homes," but the finish, maintenance, and noise factor can be counter to biologic well-being.

Considering that the vast majority of items in this general category will have direct and indirect ecologic consequences in inquiry, information, and evaluation, choice is not easily made. The consequences upon human health are seldom clearly defined. Prudence is better than lack of caution. A liquid coating material is available to seal in the toxic chemistry of carpeting and other floor coverings. It is reputed to be FDA and EPA approved as being nontoxic and nonallergenic.

10. Interior Specialties
Of particular note should be external sun screens, awnings, canopies, and other external sun intervention methods that can shade glazing and exterior walls. The result can be a cooler interior and also as with canopies and awnings act as an exterior shaded area for rain and sun protection.

Under specialties are also air venting louvers that can be used with screening to provide an intake air port for cross ventilation. Such divorced from the glazed areas for view, daylight, and thermal gain provide an interior advantage for natural ventilation and avoidance of the insecurity of operable windows. The panoply and diversity of specialty items requires an "ecologic mind" to sort out and qualify an appropriate choice or alternative.

11. Interior Equipment

Equipment covers a broad range of items that are specific to each type of business or other commercial category. Equipment is more general for residential projects. Equipment should most efficiently fit with the process by which a project functions.

There is no ultimate guide within an ecologic perspective for the selection of commercial equipment. In residential planning and specification, kitchen and other appliances can have energy efficiency ratings. These should be used for evaluation. But further, the question of what can be better and less ecologically impactual from source of materials, processing, distance of transport, durability, freedom from maintenance, and life-cycle operational energy demand should not be absent from the evaluation.

Does the equipment optimize efficiency within the context of use? is a basic question. But an in-depth ecologic concern calls upon investigative scrutiny and assurance before choice and specification.

12. Interior Furnishings

Furnishings call to mind furniture and other accoutrements of the interior as to appropriateness, practicality, aesthetics, and cost. But not accounted for in usual selection and specification are the ecologic factors of resource, energy intensity in extraction, manufacture, and delivery nor the final

disposition or recyclability upon termination of use.

Chairs and other seating pieces may be selected for comfort and practicality but with a neglect of how the upholstery or its finishes may affect the respiratory system of the user or more so of users in a room crowded with chairs is a health concern. Plastics, aniline dyed leather, fabrics, and wood finishes can outgas odors and toxins.

Look for high quality construction, serviceability, nontoxic fillings and fabrics, ease in maintenance, and reclaimability or recyclability at termination of use.

Commercial grade furniture and other furnishings can be more serviceable than residential pieces for residential use. Multipurpose, multi-use furniture, adaptable systems, and reusable rather than disposable items for residential and commercial planning and specification should be a priority consideration. Office "landscaping," modular units, room dividers, screens, and other movable systems can be very adaptable to needed change and more effectual layouts. Durability, convertability, and cost savings can be time-extended advantages.

13. Interior Special Construction

Passive and active solar systems are listed within this category. Solar applications have had a greater use in residential than in commercial architecture. But for either they are a most neglected planning and design strategy. Considering that the sun is the earth's prime source of energy, it should be the prime source of energy for architecture.

The sun's direct site-specific radiation should be the first energy priority of the site and the architecture. It takes design ingenuity and a thorough understanding how the sun's energy can be optimized for *every project*, to capture and best use "free" and "clean" solar radiation. Interior planning and design play a major role in how effectively the sun's energy can be utilized. How sunspaces, attached greenhouses, and the architectural envelope may be most functional and useful is germane to each project.

As various forms of thermal mass might be employed, furniture and furnishings including floor or wall elements that might intervene can seriously affect expected thermal performance. An imperative is not to use materials in direct solar exposure or super-heated conditions that are likely to fade, warp, or otherwise be damaged by UV radiation or by heat. Glazing is available that stops the ultraviolet penetration. However, a certain amount of UV radiation is beneficial for us and has a beneficial effect upon indoor plantings.

At certain times the sun's direct radiation can be most welcome. But for many of our tasks, activities, and times of rest may not be desired. Time of day and season and the level of our own sensitivities to light and heat and in what we may or may not be

doing are all pertinent to the conditions of a solar space and the solar experience.

Thermal mass furniture or furnishings such as heavy earthen pots with planting can well fit into the scheme of a solar space. Or the furniture or other objects can be suspended above or have minimal legs or other support to avoid shading a thermal mass. Highly polished specular surfaces when appropriately planned can either compensate for some shadowing or can direct solar rays towards a thermal mass.

On the other side of the coin, with a hybrid solar system it can be desirable to heat the air of the solar space as quickly as possible and to convey it away to a place of more effective use or storage. Various forms of intercepting dark metal blinds or other interceptors that accomplish this purpose should be selected to optimize this conversion of solar radiation to heated air.

Under this hybrid strategy, depending upon the design of the solar space and type of furniture and furnishings and their arrangement, floors and walls can be treated without regard to a blocking of the sun's rays as no thermal mass is required.

The author has used very narrow spaces, sometimes only several feet wide, with inner and outer full south glazing in residential projects. The solar-heated air by a duct and blower system is forced through a vertical double wall masonry plenum containing gravel remote from the sunspace. This thermal mass has been in most cases centrally located to provide both radiant and convected heat to surrounding rooms. Returns are at the bottom of the sunspace. In one case a north masonry wall was used. The glazed sunspace with intercepting blinds functions like an active air-type solar collector with less cost, better use of interior space, and minimal maintenance than might be the case with a sunspace thermal mass system.

"See-through" sunspaces designed by the author provide a visual connection with the sky and earth. As designed to latitude they receive secondary solar gains through the inner glass and the depth of the sunspaces can provide a solar shading cut-off in summer. The sunspaces were designed with stack action ventilation, as an air-tempering space with glass side-sliding patio doors at opposite ends of the outer and inner glazing as part of the strategy. The double glazed sunspaces act as climatic and security buffers and avoid the degree of radiant loss from a thermal mass such as a Trombe wall that can also block a full-glazed visual and physiologic correspondence with Nature and other outdoor happenings.

Trombe walls can have a purpose in receiving direct solar gain and by thermal lag and convection provided to inner space. But Trombe design and application is most suited to conditions appropriate to planned internalization of space use. The author has such an example at his residence library solar test deck. In addition to testing solar products and materials, the space is used for drying and outgassing anything from clothes to food to magazines and other items that have toxic constituents. The space of necessity to its testing purpose has sloping glass to the south but is subject to dirt, weather etching, and vulnerability to leaks. But it is functional for its purpose. As the most useful type of space for residential use it is not as practical as other thermal mass alternatives and tends to considerably overheat, loses energy to the clear sky temperature, and does not have a particular economic advantage. Vertical glazing to the south primarily avoids the foregoing problems.

It should be noted that the dark solid concrete Trombe wall sets back about seven feet from the outer glazed area and is flanked on either side by wide glazed doors to the interior library for access, light, air, and control over the entry of solar-heated air. No book shelves or other thermal impediments are placed against the inside of the Trombe wall. Ventilation of the sunspace is by large horizontal lower and upper louvers and a trailing edge roof shape that aids ventilation by negative pressure. Prestressed hollow core concrete slabs form the library ceiling and solar air can flow through the slabs providing a solar radiant ceiling for the library.

Commercial roof-glazed atria and galleries are quite common. As central lobby or access spaces for interior daylighting and delight in seeing the sky, they can be dramatic. But they are expensive, lose much more energy than an insulated roof, trap solar heat in summer (increasing air conditioning loads), can suffer in summer, late spring, and early fall from direct solar intensity, and require considerable maintenance.

Interior use of the space varies with every project, but for its euphoric advantage, less glamorous clerestories carefully calculated to year-round solar angles and designed to seasonally optimize solar control and minimal energy loss to the clear sky, indoor space can with much less energy, greater comfort, economy, and practically be realized.

Solar did not acquire a position of status until the latter part of the 1970s. As such it is a tail-end category of CSI "special construction." This relegation obscures its primal importance and in general the great headway that was made in passive, hybrid, and active solar architecture for nearly a decade. Since then it has been clouded by relative indifference in consideration of the great amount of new residential and commercial architecture that has been designed and constructed. Solar is more demanding of knowledge, ingenuity, and effectual design than conventional construction. But the sun's energy is primal to all life, and the habitability of our planet is essential to replace our misplaced love affair with fossil fuels and nuclear energies. "Time waits for no man." The sun and Nature's ecologic

systems and our well-being and human survival depend on it.

Technologic structures and systems under the heading of "special construction" require examination in the light of ecologic sustainability. Most are obviously at odds with their use of resource and anti-ecologic energy manufacture, distribution, use, or final disposition.

14. Interior Conveying Systems

Many low-rise, all high-rise buildings, and relatively few private residences have elevators. As earth creatures the question is whether we should be propelling ourselves toward the sky. High-rise buildings have a probability of being vulnerable to decentralization. They have the advantage of a relatively small footprint for their multiple floors and an occupancy concentration relative to site. Comparative low-rise structures will occupy more land area and are likely to have a greater per occupant energy demand ratio. Elevators remain an energy- and maintenance-intensive element of any building.

15. Interior Mechanical, Plumbing

The early 1930s ushered in the advent of refrigerated air conditioning. Before that time people depended largely on fans at home and in the workplace. As with all technologic systems that provide convenience, comfort, and ease in operation, mechanical air conditioning was rapidly accepted in the marketplace, workplace, eating places, theaters, and other places where people gathered. Residential applications came somewhat later.

After ammonia in the earliest systems, the nontoxic refrigerant medium Freon was developed. The more recent discovery that Freon in the family of CFCs is destroying the earth's ozone layer has sounded a disturbing note within the widespread use of this otherwise desirable product. How soon an ecologic alternative might get in common use is open to question.

In any case, whatever is now being accomplished with more energy-efficiency mechanical heating, cooling, and hot water heating systems, the least demand that can be put upon the utility power grid, the less is the concomitant pollution at the power plant.

Air-to-air, air-to-water, and air-to-earth heat pumps with a broad range COP (coefficient of performance) conserve energy. On an all-electric system, heat pumps have a marked advantage over resistance heating. But when a solar home or small commercial building is designed to be highly efficient in thermal performance, electric hydronic baseboard units (located near but not directly under exterior windows because of energy loss) thermostatically controlled within each interior space has the advantage of heating only the space being occupied. Spaces not in use can be maintained with either none or very minimal heat.

Radiant electric hydronic baseboard or radiators also do not deplete negative ionization like open resistance heating coils. Radiant electric ceiling heating is not recommended due to the electromagnetic field that it produces. The field from an electric hydronic baseboard unit is relatively negligible at the distance most people will be from it.

In most commercial and industrial buildings duct systems are chosen in their ability to distribute heat, cooling, and air for ventilation. The drawback is that the ducts can harbor harmful microorganisms and dust as well as ground off beneficial negative ions. Most mechanical systems have inadequate filters. From a health standpoint if electrostatically charged filters are used, activated charcoal filters should be located after the electrostatic filter to remove any ozone generated by them.

New, more efficient filter types (not requiring electrical energy) are available that are electrostatically self-actuating and others that are able to capture smaller sized particulates. HEPA filters due to their density are efficient but require more horsepower and do not remove airborne gases. Portable air purification units are available.

With the considerable number of varying types of filtration units, a selection should consider the area and air volume of the space, suitability of the unit to purpose, and the negative ion vitalization of air as well as its purification. A multi-stage filtration system in such units can not only remove small particulates with a HEPA filter, but an activated charcoal or other efficient adsorber can remove undesired gases and negative ionizing in the final stage can vitalize the purified air.

Although they have no filtration capability, Casa Blanca fans and vortex fans can aid the destratification of warm air near the ceiling in winter and act as an agent in summer for cooling our bodies by air movement.

Destratification can also be accomplished by a high air return in a forced-air duct system so that in winter the ceiling warm air stratum can be distributed to the floor area. In summer a low return air to the air handling unit can keep the cool air in a stratum near the floor occupied by people while not disturbing the upper heated air of the room. Thus on a yearly basis a savings in energy results by this strategy.

Plumbing fixtures will conserve materials and labor by a common vent stack, waste line, and water connections. Water lines should not be soldered with lead. Available toilets can optimize water conservation as can that of low water demand but effective shower heads. Insulated hot water lines, tanks and hydronic systems heating lines avoid heat loss. Insulation outgassing is to be avoided in occupied space. The location of hot water tanks (preferably solar) heated close to point of hot water use is practical and energy conserving. Gas-heated hot water tanks and hydronic space heating systems with direct combustion air intake and direct

venting avoid cold wintertime combustion air from entering their mechanical space area with likely attendant heat loss of home or building or depletion of oxygen from occupied space.

Heating equipment fired by natural gas is available with over a 90-percent efficiency. Equipment should be selected with high efficiency ratings and most appropriate to thermal need. Zoning is most important in space heating, ventilating, and cooling. How internal loads may vary as in an auditorium with and without people while other parts of a building may have sustained loads is a condition. But external effects of sun and climate can also alter the zoning demand on heating and cooling. Variable volume systems can address inequities in internal heat loads.

The design of a building that accords with sun and climate and uses sun, earth, and air site-specific energies as principal to design whether low-rise, high-rise, or residential is within an ecologic paradigm.

16. Interior Electrical Systems
There has been mounting evidence for more than a decade that 60-cycle alternating current power lines, line transformers, electrical systems, appliances, and equipment in homes and buildings can cause cancer, neural, and other physiological disorders.

Of the electromagnetic fields generated, electrical fields that are largely intervened by homes and building contrast with magnetic fields that penetrate through concrete, wood, or other types of construction. The plumbing system to which electrical systems are grounded acts as a carrier of the magnetic field energy.

The question is, what is safe or unsafe for our "body electric?" The vortexian DNA molecule programs our body's electrical constitution, mitotic cell division, and inter-correspondence in the electrical activity of brain and body. Where "free radical" occurrence is greatest at the mitotic sites of our body is where we are most vulnerable to physiologic aberrations. The bottom line is, what is our proximity and time exposure to bio-damaging frequencies and amplitudes of electrical and magnetic fields?

We each have our own sensitivities and vulnerabilities. Age has something to do with it. Certain (a growing number) individuals are seriously sensitive and biophysically affected by exposure to electrical but more strongly to the effect of magnetic fields. Such fields abound within architecture and in our outdoor exposure to power lines, transformers, and fields on those poles that carry electrical distribution. It is best that power lines be buried and interlaced to nullify the magnetic fields.

Too often high voltage power lines cross close to school, home, business, and industrial properties. While the risk is not completely known, prudence dictates the removal or other strategies to sufficiently diminish the field to a reasonably safe level.

Within homes and buildings the electrical power entrance, electrical panels, transformers, motors, and all devices, appliances, ballasted lighting fixtures, and equipment and the interior wiring should be viewed as hostile to the well-being of our body. *Proximity and exposure time are critical to sources of potentially harmful electromagnetism*.

Computers are high on the list as the monitor screen puts out X-rays, VLF (very low frequency) and ELF (extra low frequency) radiation, and positive ions that can be intervened with a special screen on the monitor. But the magnetic field from the flyback transformer is not easily shielded and computers in our marketplace do not have this protection. Children it is reasonable to assume and well as has been documented pregnant women should not be in such computer fields for any length of time and perhaps not at all.

The workplace with electrical equipment, devices, and electrical motors and transformers can be possibly hazardous. The fields from electromagnetic diagnostic equipment deserve attention. Electromagnetic fields can be an occupational hazard in industry. Utility electrical field workers have been shown to be subject to a higher incidence of related physiologic problems.

Despite these drawbacks, central electrical power distribution is here to stay for many years to serve the built environment and its infrastructure. Inasmuch as power generation with its pollution is emitted from a location somewhat remote or at least not affecting most urban neighborhoods, the air of the city is kept reasonably clean with the "clean" deliverance of electrical energy. This is in contrast to the early part of this century when coal- and oil-burning furnaces of homes and buildings were the order of the day. However, urban wood-burning fireplaces remain as an anathema to respiratory sensitive individuals.

The needless waste of electrical energy to prevalent overillumination, lights on when space isn't occupied, or when daylighting of interior areas is adequate should be a number-one priority for avoidance or correction.

Other common electromagnetic field producers are electric clocks, televisions, radios, quartz halogen, fluorescent, and other lamps, light fixtures, copy machines, electric blankets, water bed heaters, heating pads, and other devices with which we may be in contact or proximity. Electromagnetic fields diminish by the square of the distance from the source.

The kitchen is particularly energy intensive with appliances that put out specific levels of electromagnetic energy. Refrigerators, electric ranges, and electric ovens and especially microwave ovens put out intense fields (irrespective of a "tight" microwave door). For an electromagnetic sensitive individual it is not a place to be. From epidemiological and statistical electromagnetic studies over 3 milligauss magnetic fields are deemed to be of hazard and 1 milligauss to be harmful and possibly dangerous depending upon exposure time. In Europe not above 0.3 milligauss is considered prudent.

But within close or very close proximity the fields produced by the aforementioned sources can well exceed 3 milligauss and many will be above 10 milligauss. *Prudent proximity* is the measured distance in which you should prudently stay away from each source of electromagnetism. Field meters are available to make this determination. Every electro-sensitive person should have one.

The general *urban* background electromagnetic field level may be about 1 milligauss more or less. Very sensitive persons may not prudently care to reside in this electro environment. Outside and inside electrical panels and transformers should not be near bedrooms. Wiring a home or business with grounded metal conduit will ground off electrical fields but not magnetic. Bedrooms can be wired in conduit at least to ground the electrical field.

Too often lighting is not designed to fit the task. This particularly applies to reading, writing, and drawing in which over illumination is more frequent than under illumination. As downlight intensity increases the reflection from the dark or colored image and of the surface on which it appears, the retina is over-stimulated, putting the fovea under stress for the best acuity of vision. Then again, point sources of illumination can work better for acuity in observing small, intricate, and three-dimensional objects. Indirect ceiling reflected light can be most suitable for computer tasks. Low surface brightness is usually most desirable in most lighting fixture installations.

A basic problem is that with overlighted classrooms, offices, and most other places of gathering, people have become "light junkies." For the acuity of vision relative to task, lower levels can be a benefit in avoiding fatigue and in saving electrical energy. But after an acculturation for very often long periods of time, individuals can feel the necessity for over-stimulating light intensities. People need to be reprogrammed to effectual levels for the task at hand. Without doing so, electrical power waste continues along with inefficient lamps and light fixtures.

But there is an extensive movement in commercial architecture for more efficient lamps and light fixtures in new buildings and replacement in older buildings. Quartz halogen and more efficient fluorescent lamps and light fixtures for interior space and high-pressure sodium and metal halide lamps for outdoor use are available. Despite the long life and efficiency of these lamps, the question not broached is, what is the materials and process energy intensity in manufacture? Every effort as well as for lighting to reduce the electrical energy demand load of buildings is a plus for the environment. Appliances, heating and cooling equipment,

hot water heaters, and other devices are available as energy-efficient items. But regardless of improved efficiency and less utility energy demand, photovoltaic solar cells, wind power, or other forms of *in situ* electric power generation have the advantage of clean energy and avoidance of the power loss from central generating plant to point of use. Photovoltaic costs are becoming ever more economic.

Photovoltaics in particular phase in well with hybrid and active solar. When the sun shines and provides thermal gain is the time when the sun's energy can produce electricity to run blower motors or operate pumps to distribute and use solar energy or to put it in thermal mass storage for later use. Photovoltaics can be effective in solar and natural energy systems control.

A more *ideal* situation would be for a solar photovoltaic system that electromagnetically is in phase and resonance with our human body. All electrically powered items of the household or workplace would also have to be so designed. But if we do not look at ideal conditions for our indoor environs, we are selling ourselves short in ultimate well-being. Photovoltaic cell construction and other accoutrements have a certain energy intensity in their manufacture. But their longevity, replacement of polluting energy sources, and potential to be in phase with rather than counter to life can be a compelling objective.

**holistic ecologic architecture/
case studies**

In bridging from contemporary commercial art and product design in the late 1920s to holistic contemporary integrated architectural design in the 1930s until today, the author evolved through the 1940s in ecologic concern to ecologic architecture.

Unparalleled advantages of holistic design preside within bioresponsive form and function and effectual economics. With a "waste not" frugal, practical, and functional perspective on life instilled by the cataclysmic Depression of 1929, the author has plied his practice in architecture and associated fields of design.

Science to technology to design has been the modus of the author's precepts and work. Physics, biophysics, and ecology are primary to configurations, form, and holistic integration in concept, planning, and design. An ecologic economic and human interresponse are the denominators of design.

Architecture is the most "fixed" element of the holistic design equation. The dynamics and interrelevancies of microorganisms to the site-specific ecosystems of the site and those of human activities and interactions contrast with the "fixity" of the architecture. How to make *all attributes* of the site, the architecture, and the interior a setting most agreeable to biologic and ecologic congruence is the quest. The building envelope becomes the interface between the dynamic internal happenings and dispositions of people and the external daily and seasonal ecologic forces of sun and air movement. The earth within coupling, sheltering, and air tempering methodologies can notably balance the thermal equation with the forces of sun, outdoor air temperature, and wind velocity.

Prior to 1976 about 80 percent of the author's work was commercial. But with a concentration exclusively on an optimization of solar and other alternative energies, residential projects became more into focus. They offered a broader base of design and technical opportunities in keeping with the author's conceptual and research initiatives. Hence the case studies herein presented are mainly residential. But the concepts and techniques are in measure applicable to various types of commercial and institutional projects.

Commercial projects, with greater internal thermal loads, more often require cooling than heating during times of occupancy. Such can apply even during wintertime in which a well-insulated building with large internal loads principally of lighting, equipment, and people can require cooling. Nevertheless, air tempering for indoor ventilation can be a major requirement for commercial and to a lesser but equally important extent for residential architecture. Air tempering is an effectual element of the author's work for indoor ventilation by solar and earth thermal design strategies and to compensate for tight building construction.

Whereas the author has designed all his residential projects as a holistic integrated sun, climate, and earth energy system, commercial projects as to type and requirements of occupancy most often with a size-restricted site as to building volume ratio, multiple floor levels, limitations as to solar access and daylighting, mechanical systems necessity, internal thermal loads, and technical considerations most often have had more restricted ecologic design options. But commercial and institutional buildings offer other opportunities for conserving energy by building configuration, control over interior volume to exterior surface ratio, ergometric planning, efficient reduced intensity lighting, energy-conserving controls and systems, thermal comfort with economizer cycle systems, air purification, and systemic solar air tempering and earth landscape climate moderation as may apply. Interior space to occupant density of residential or commercial projects is a relative *ecologic space use index.* The less the per capita space and energy use, the less the utility demand.

All of the author's commercial and institutional projects were designed with an "eye" to adaptive change as to immediate and future space use, space needs, and possibilities of change in occupancy. Architectural, structural, natural, mechanical, and electrical systems as well as site adaptability were initially designed not only with integrative frugality but also to minimize the work and cost to meet probabilities and even some improbabilities of change.

Time has been the witness to this most important ecologic design concern. The author's initial design for space adaptability, ease of conversion within space redesign and redevelopment, minimal need to change basic systems have been through the years give witness to the ecologic, practical, and economic benefits of this parameter.

Architecture is the most fixed element of the holistic design equation. To make it most adaptable to change can conserve materials, labor, and costs within the life-cycle considerations of initial design. Every project has to be a "site-specific custom design" if it is an "ecologic design." Even "cookie cutter" housing subdivisions could ecologically and economically have individuality in design by using a marriage of manufactured core modules and stick-built or panelized construction. The case study "St. Paul Street Residences" (pgs. 142-147) encompasses a core module concept as well as other coordinate manufacturing/site options.

Architecture is an art exercised through technologic strategies. Creating coherent order and design within its multitudinous complexities is no small matter. Every element bears some relevancy to the whole.

The degree of *ecologic relevancy* is germane to its parts as well as to the architectural totality. Not to be dismissed is how people within architecture will exist within it, manage its interior elements, and be programmed by the configurations, form, and attributes of the architecture.

The author recognizes that it is fully debatable in any specific case study in measure of its parts or whole being fairly called *ecologic architecture.* In our petro-energy, petro-economy in the *purest* sense, it is literally impossible to ecologically design and construct any architecture that fully meets personal or collective societal desires and expectations. Even to build a small backyard shed draws its material source from petro-cut, milled, and transported lumber. Even the hardware for its door is of petro-energy-intensive metals, processing, packaging, and delivery.

All materials, means, and methods from inception to final construction, from completion to terminal use, and as ultimate use or reuse in the light of *ecologic design* require close scrutiny and evaluation.

To what degree every decision impairs Nature's regenerative, sustainable, and ecologic vitality is a constant issue. The author has taken a view of how architectural and infrastructure needs can be met employing the *most responsible, ecologic, site-specific holistic design options and strategies.* The case studies present effectual projects that were designed and constructed to avoid the extensive ecologic incompatibility in most of architecture.

CHERRY CREEK NORTH SOLAR OFFICE BUILDINGS

PROJECT

Companion site-specific, ecologic solar and natural energy architect/separate building owner integrated 1976 project. Design intent to develop a corner location with two analogous optimal energy-conserving, climate-responsive buildings. Initial coordinated planning expedited the joining of the buildings by the architect into one structure in 1983 for new occupancies.

The initial project consisted of joined properties, each 50 feet by 125 feet and zoned for office use, with separate buildings of 4500 square feet. The south corner Monigle office building on two levels was planned for corporate design services. The north Crowther building on two levels was planned as a environmental demonstration and educational facility and architectural office. In 1983 a final connection and enclosure between the buildings resulted in a single energy-efficient building (with separate new respective occupancies for medical and accounting uses).

ENVIRONS

In the redevelopment area of an older residential and business neighborhood. The adjoining sites were located on a corner with full solar access. This site at the edge of the business district benefitted by the more relaxed character of the adjacent and redeveloping residential neighborhood.

CONSTRAINTS

Primary concerns were that the south building not significantly block the winter sun from the north building and that the two buildings would harmonize in planning, design, and energy efficiency. Future maximum adaptability of interior space and solar, thermal, and electrical systems was a focal concern within the criteria.

ECOLOGIC CONCERNS

The architecture was designed to respond to the sun, to wind, the movement of air, and to the earth. The predominant use of renewable non-energy-intensive materials, the architecture as a thermal system, spatial daylighting, task lighting, ergometric planning, inductive ventilation, microclimatic control landscaping, solar thermal storage, and minimization of energy demand were all elements of ecologic design.

Excavation and land forming were a concern as to the minimization of earth handling equipment, time, pollution, and the least disturbance in connection with the residential neighborhood.

EXPERIENTIAL

The buildings have a composite relationship with functional diversity. With a dark warm grey texture they are a background to landscaped land forms with a solar and wind-protective screen of aspen trees along the west and south frontage. South lower-level courts provide outdoor space and interior daylighting.

Main building entries are to the south with a split level interior stairway daylighted to the south by a light scoop. Northside clerestories with horizontal banks of windows to the south are designed to concentrate wintertime direct solar radiation to the upper level and through a large light well to the lower level. Clerestory daylighting through the summer season is subdued reflected solar light from the reflective roof decks and reflective overhead angular canopies oriented due south.

With windows principally to the south and the clerestory direct and indirect solar interior illumination, supplemental interior electric illumination was minimal. The changing ambience of daylighting was a vital visual benefit and contrast to usual fixed-level interior artificial illumination.

The initial interior plan in 1976 for the north Crowther building was with a solar, natural energy, and conservation display area in the main front upper level. It was an open-to-the-public exhibit addressed to our environmental necessity. The front lower level was a meeting and audiovisual projection room seating about 60 persons. It was for the meeting of environmental groups and professional and governmental agency environmental seminars and workshops. These areas remained intact for about three years. The environmental educational portion of these facilities originally was not intended to produce a financial return. But in a subsequent desire to bring a return it was leased to an interior design firm.

The upper and lower level rear was the author's architectural office. A circular table in the conference room allowed for equal discussion and participation. The drafting room on the lower level was daylighted with a bank of windows to the east and from a greenhouse to the southwest.

All of the main upper-level spatial divisions were designed as "see through" spaces. While sense of space and "openness" prevailed, privacy as appropriate was provided. All interior surfaces were a reflective white with neutral tight pile carpeting (for ease of cleaning) except for bright color fabric accents of contemporary oak furniture.

Natural flow-through cross ventilation in all parts of the buildings when outdoor temperatures were equitable for indoor comfort was augmented by a west-facing venturi venting system located above the roof of the south building. The north building had double wind turbines mounted above a roof penthouse. This sunspace penthouse was designed with a black lateral duct that received and tempered outside air with direct solar thermal gain.

The combined solar and natural systems for solar heating, inductive cooling and ventilation, and the daylighting systems provided a pleasurable and moderately stimulating psychoneural and physiologic environment. A changing ambience (instead of steady state) of lighting and temperature is more conducive to work efficiency as long as it occurs within a gentle range of change and does not exceed tolerant levels.

THE SITE

Corner location had full solar access. The sites prior to building were relatively flat with no significant vegetation. But land forming the west street frontage into protective berms with an extensive planting of aspen trees provided shade for the west elevations of the buildings in summer. Berms with a coverage of low evergreen shrubs and fewer aspens were used for the south side as a climatic buffer and buffer of noise and activity from the street.

The parking area was located to the east, open to the south sun in winter, and partly shaded by a continuation of the aspen trees in a berm that also screened the area from street view.

ARCHITECTURE, FORM, AND SYSTEMS

The architecture was planned and designed into simple rectangular volume split levels most adaptable to the original and projected possible future uses. With the lower level earth coupled and the solar and climatic ratio of an east/west dimension and shorter north/south, the exterior envelope was of minimal surface and most favorable in energy conservation terms.

The all wood construction with 10-inch framing to the north and 6-inch framing to other elevations was superinsulated with rock wool batts. The common ceiling roof joists of 16-inch depth had a full depth of blown-in rock wool insulation. An exterior insulation sheathing over 5/8-inch fire-protection gypsum board resulted in R-42 for the north exterior wall, R-26 for other elevations, and R-64 for the roof. An insulative thermal continuity and thermal break with the outsulation, and an applied stucco coating, provided a "tight" building envelope.

The built-up roofs were covered with white marble chips to act as a reflector for active air-type solar collectors located at a latitude plus 5° angle to the sun below a band of northside clerestory windows, for clerestory window daylighting, and as a summertime reflector of solar radiation back to the sky. The roofs were relatively flat as favored by the author so that snow would act as both a climatic intervention and as a solar reflector to the solar collectors and clerestory windows.

An overhead angular canopy projecting forward above the clerestory windows increased winter solar gains upon the flat-plate collectors and through the clerestory windows in addition to direct solar radiation. The canopy had a reflective surface of mica chips embedded in a white stucco matrix. The stucco of the building exterior was a dark warm grey.

For each of these companion buildings the architecture was designed as a holistic energy system. If a commercial multistory building within zoning code limits might be built across the street to the south of this project, solar and daylighting as major roof elements of the architectural system would not be blocked from solar access. The clerestory and active solar roof forms and Crowther solar penthouse (for testing solar devices and using plants as a filter and oxygenator of outdoor air used for air tempering) were located northside to assure optimal solar access at the time of construction and in the future.

The flat-plate active solar collectors of 175 square feet for the south building and 300 square feet for the north building with an insulated thermal storage bin of approximately four tons of 1-1/2" washed river gravel provided heating.

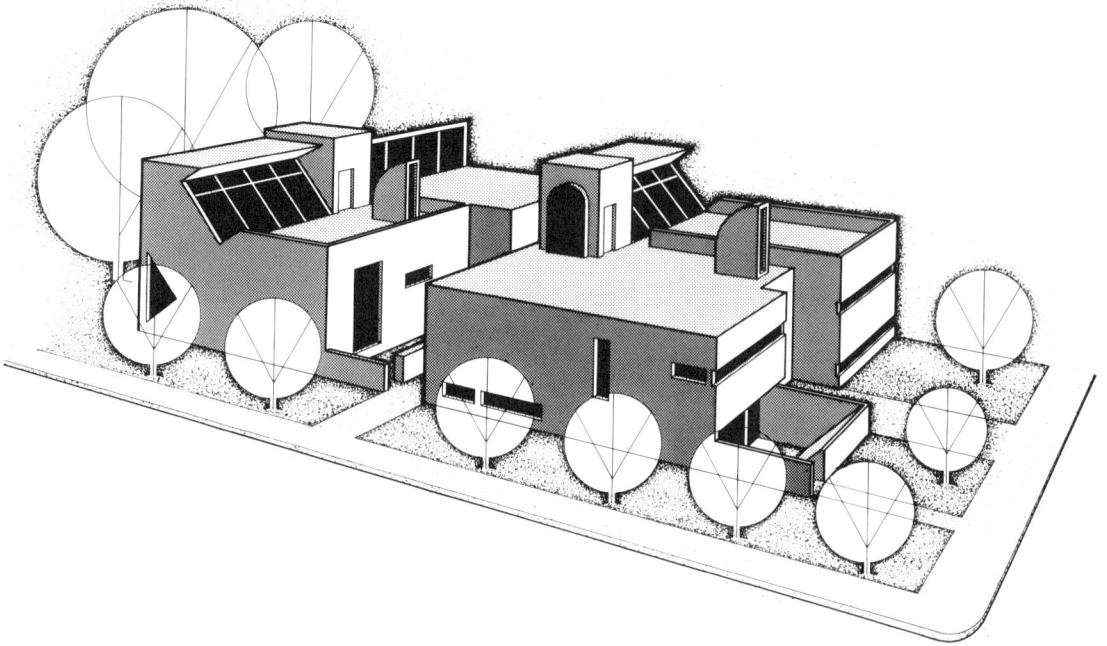

CHERRY CREEK NORTH SOLAR OFFICE BUILDINGS

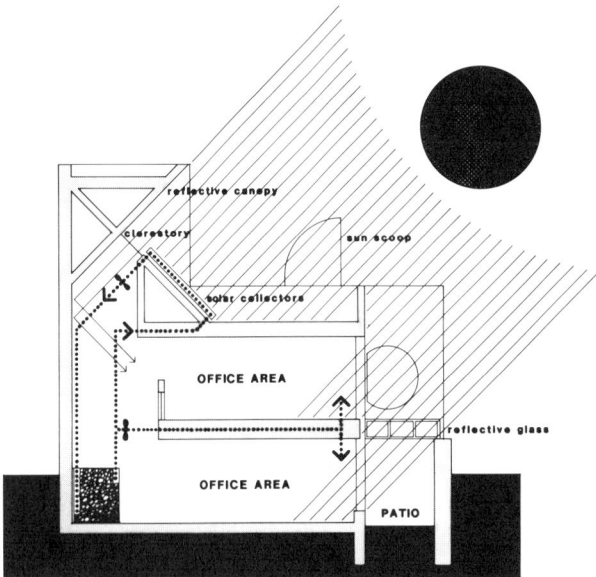

reflective canopy

clerestory

sun scoop

solar collectors

OFFICE AREA

reflective glass

OFFICE AREA

PATIO

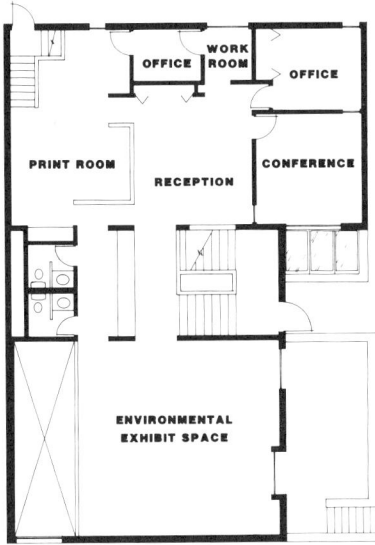

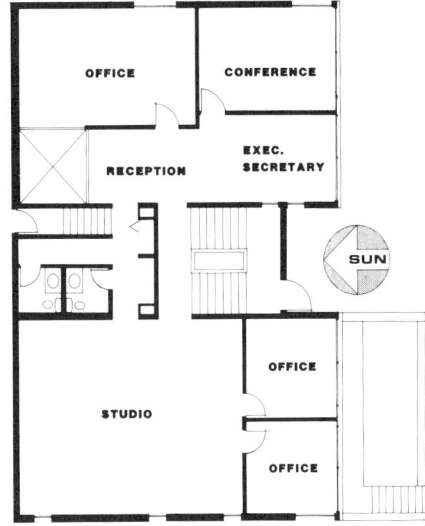

upper level

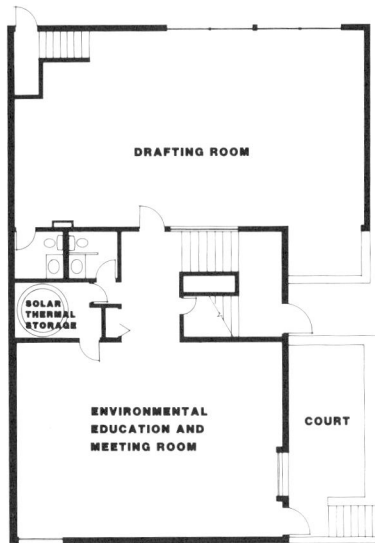

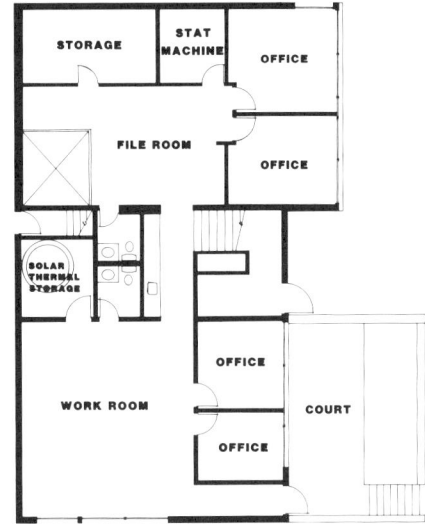

lower level

Holistic Ecologic Architecture/Case Studies   123

The duct system was designed to destratify the warmest air from the peak of the clerestory in the heating mode. For periods of the coldest weather, roof-top air-to-air heat pumps provided the additional heat required. During periods of hot weather when natural inductive cooling and ventilation were not adequate for comfort, the reverse cycle cooling of the heat pumps was called upon.

Despite these sophistications to conserve energy, exterior reflective canopies, superinsulation, double glazing (that was tailored to be tinted to the east, highly reflective to the west, and clear to the south), the total cost of the buildings was comparable to conventional architecture and its systems. The trade-off within frugal concerns of planning and design compensated for the additional cost of the energy conservation measures.

It should be noted that each building saved more than $3000 each year in utility costs. For the combined 9000 square feet of both buildings amounted to a total savings of $6000 per year. Contemporary simplicity in architectural form and absence of exterior and interior trim initially saved money and reduced life-cycle maintenance.

Several years ago the author designed an enclosure (originally planned as a possibility) between the buildings for a cosmetic surgeon when the author relocated his architectural practice to his residential energy research facility. The additional space has a south-facing clerestory band of windows with an overhang for summer shading. The connecting link resulted in a single building of 9800 square feet in which although not monitored could only improve the architecture as an energy form. With the foresight of original planning, the conversion from two to one single building was accomplished with significant economy.

The daily and seasonal change in interior ambient solar radiation and daylight illumination together with the proportions, form, and location of glazed openings provided an engaging psychoneural stimulation.

CONCLUSION

By effective holistic ecologic design, architecture can use renewable, non-energy-intensive materials; optimize the use of solar energy, earth coupling, inductive air flows, and daylighting; and use material, equipment, and labor most effectively to advantage life-cycle utility savings.

By adaptable planning and design, various types of occupancy can be accommodated by minimal alterations. From a realistic perspective these buildings paid back initial costs in 3.8 years the enumerated solar, thermal, daylighting, and energy-conserving techniques. But these strategies as stated did not initially escalate total building construction costs above that of a conventional project of the same space need criteria and occupancy conditions.

HOTSY CORPORATION OFFICE BUILDING

PROJECT

This 30,000 square feet office headquarters and product educational building exhibits significant elements of ecologic architecture. The holistic ecologic perspective included site-specific energies of sun, earth, air, and water as primary to planning and design. This 1980 two-level project as holistically designed by the author included land forming, landscaping, architecture, interior design, organization planning, and architectonic sculptural wall plaques.

The forms of the architecture and internal enclosures of the building were designed as an interface between internal functions (with ergometric and bio-responsive relevancy) and diurnal and seasonal solar and climatic forces. Topography and site access as well as the foregoing factors dictated a two-level building that principally separated office from educational functions.

ENVIRONS

The vacant property was located in an office park site in which landscaping was a dominant requirement. The large site of over two acres was at the intersection of two roads. Adjoining sites of comparable size were well landscaped with contemporary office buildings of recent construction. The location was notably free of urban air pollution.

CONSTRAINTS

The site offered more of an ecologic opportunity than a constraint. The most constraining question was how to realize maximum energy conservation, ecologic, and bio-responsive advantages within a limited budget.

HOLISTIC DESIGN

Architecture, criteria, site development, landscaping, systems, the interior, and artwork were within the holistic design scope of the author. The author also used a Stage 1 and Stage 2 design and cost evaluation feasibility process to control costs. The final project cost adhered closed to feasibility cost projections. Similar projects constructed in the office park that did not have the conservation, solar, natural systems, ecologic, and psycho-physiologic advantages actually cost more per square foot.

There is no greater initial and life-cycle cost and benefit advantage than when the *total* project is conceived, planned, and designed within a holistic paradigm.

SITE

The building was located and oriented on the site as most suited the topography and the side road access. Cut (excavated) earth from the foundation and parking lot to the east was used as fill for the extensive earth berms along the north and west sides of the building. Other berms and grading to aid the retention of roof and surface water were also provided. Topsoil was retained and native grasses of less maintenance and watering requirements were seeded. Pinon pines (to intercept ground currents of cold north winds), Austrian pines (to turbulate north and northwest mainstream winds), and evergreen shrubs were planted to attenuate winter impacts upon the architecture. Deciduous trees, including the sun-screening effect of numerous aspens, were installed southwest, south, and southeast to shade and cool in summer.

The parking was planned to screen the area from the principal road along the south line of the site. The two-level east elevation provided access to an underground demonstration area (daylighted with 7-foot diameter skydomes).

FUNCTIONS AND EXPERIENTIAL ECOLOGIC FACTORS

Experiential factors relate to our perceptions and our vitality. They are critical to our human ecologic sustainability. Bioneural responses and psycho-physiologic reactions are of basic importance within every environment. Lighting, sound, temperature, odors and tactile elements, form, color, and texture have their instantaneous and composite effect upon us. Within these dimensions the perceptions and spheres of collective and personal territory have a salutary or retarding effect upon our energies, our production, and our health. These were ecologic concerns of the author in the planning and design of this project.

Bio-lateral daylighting principally to the south but also to other building elevations together with the light court, stairway clerestory, skyvaults, skydome of the lobby, and skydomes of the lower demonstration area comprised a natural system of general interior illumination. An outdoor court within the plan of the building brought daylight and air to the lower level and daylight to the upper level.

Territorial perceptions and responses tend to be overlooked within the aspects of personal interactions within the environment. In this project the author sought to plan and design territorial space to lower the threshold of interaction between people. Private office spaces were arranged so that direct confrontation was avoided and the off-to-the-far-side visual alarm zone of the eye was not intercepted. Thus for the private offices the most conducive territorial approach was realized. Private offices had recessed light fixtures switched to give either half or full light. It was gratifying to note that the occupants of each office tended to leave the lighting on the lower setting for a more relaxing environment. The higher light level of about 50 footcandles was used for special occasions.

In the principal sales area, floor-to-ceiling clear glass space dividers were used to provide a territorial place for each salesman. Openness and light were preserved from south daylight along a glazed corridor and south light from the outdoor court. The see-through and lateral daylighting aspects made individuals aware of what was totally occurring while retaining a demarcation of their own territorial space.

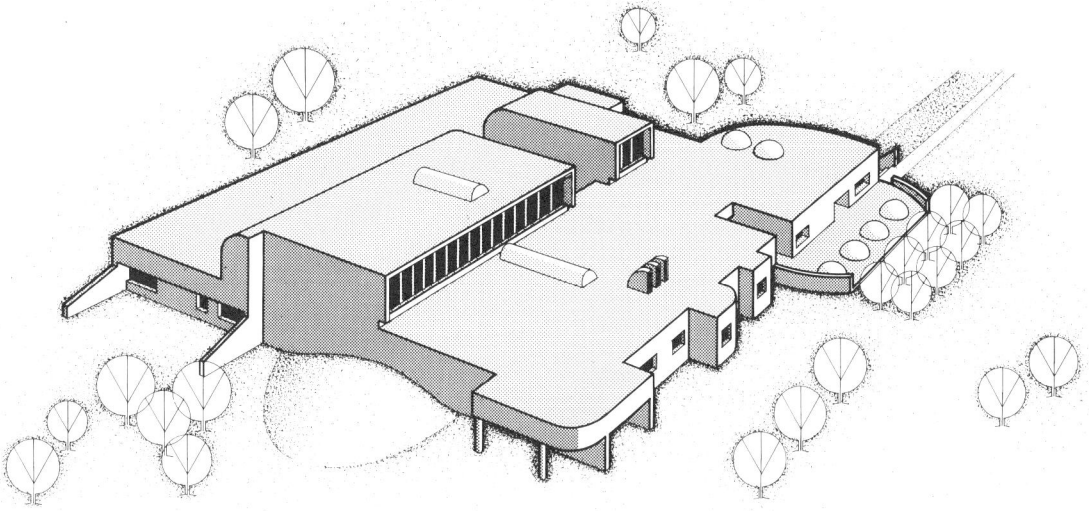

HOTSY CORPORATION OFFICE BUILDING

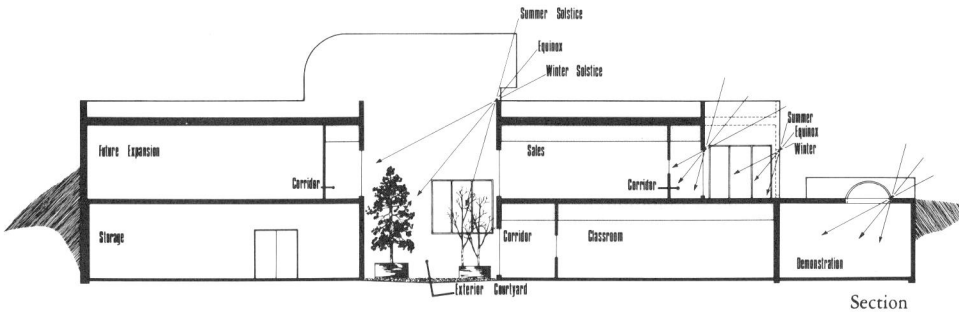

Summer Solstice
Equinox
Winter Solstice

Future Expansion

Corridor

Storage

Exterior Courtyard

Sales

Corridor

Summer
Equinox
Winter

Corridor

Classroom

Demonstration

Section

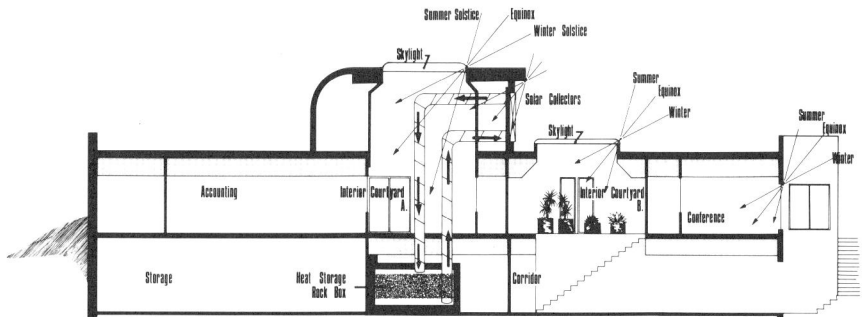

Summer Solstice
Equinox
Winter Solstice

Skylight

Solar Collectors

Skylight

Summer
Equinox
Winter

Summer
Equinox
Winter

Accounting

Interior Courtyard A.

Interior Courtyard B.

Conference

Storage

Heat Storage Rock Box

Corridor

Section

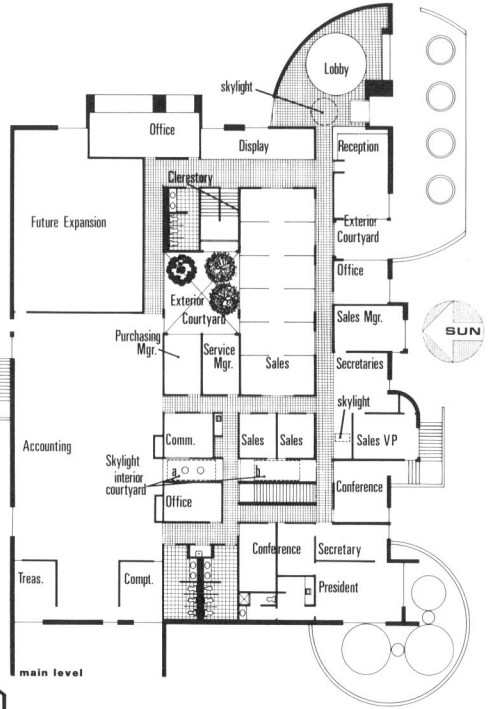

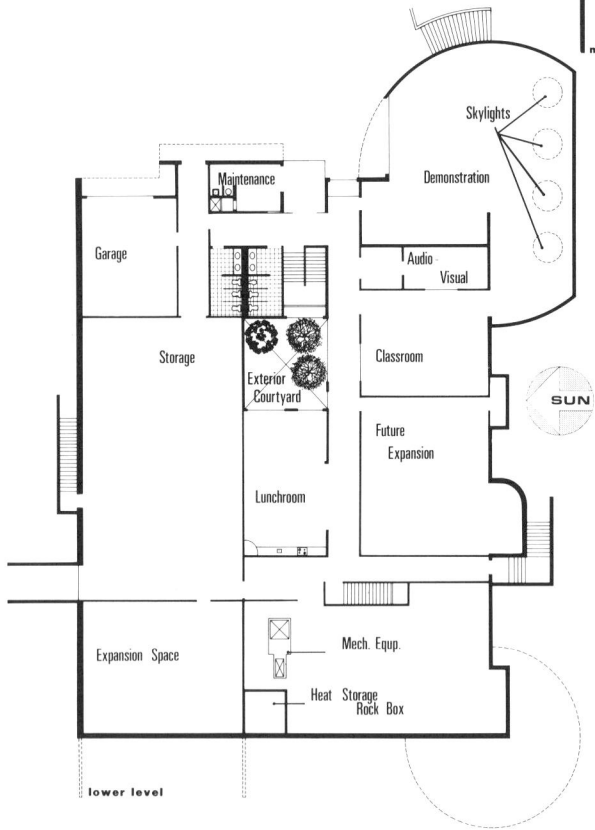

There was also a general selective system for visiting persons from the front desk of the east lobby to the president's secretarial interception at the far end of the building. The president's office had a circular outdoor patio to the southwest mountain view and was deeply shaded by the architecture. Most other private offices offset from the facade captured a distant mountain view as well as numerous interior "see-through" areas. As a passing note, the president in an energy conservation building designed by the author in 1973 had a central position office to optimize control as the center of operations. In this 1980 building the firm's authorities were delegated commensurate with the rapid growth and extendable marketing potential of the firm. The circulation patterns of the interior were planned for the integration of administration, properties management, sales, accounting, promotion, and computer functions. The lower level was designed as an autonomous element for product demonstration and education. A backlighted audiovisual screen was provided for product presentation, use, and maintenance training. A daylighted full-scale truck and vehicle demonstration area had direct access from the outdoor parking area.

The lower level had a lunch room open to the light court that was also used by the personnel of the main upper level for administration and office functions. Daylighted stairways and corridors were located to allow for a nondisturbing tour of all functions of the building. This experiential aspect also served for other visitors and left a notable impression of the prevailing efficient effect and human-oriented organization.

ARCHITECTURE, FORM, AND SYSTEMS

The form of the architecture was derived from the totality of the interior organizational territoriality of functions; internal circulation patterns; solar, daylighting, natural energies within integrated systems; characteristics of the site; and an accord within the planned development with a response to seasonal climatic conditions. Planning and design were optimized to minimize the external envelope of the building while maximizing the internal volume for space use.

To provide a large thermal mass the building was designed with horizontal prestressed concrete core slabs for floor and roof systems and post-tensioned concrete over the lower-level truck demo area and for the main lobby above. In addition, more than 40 percent of the architecture was earth coupled for interseasonal indoor thermal stability. Rigid insulation over the roof mass and "outsulation" (using a monoacrylic stucco-type finish) provided a thermal/climatic shield to the interior thermal mass. The southwest and east portions of the lower level completely below grade were earth-connected below an insulation depth of about 8 feet of the concrete foundation.

Land forming and treatment of the site were complimentary and effectual in microclimatic terms with the architecture. The building form was longitudinal along an east-west axis which minimized the undesired impact of the west sun. Both the building and the parking lot are oriented to the south. The expanded south elevation and the smaller west and east elevations helped minimize indoor winter heating and summer cooling requirements. A dark tone exterior natural color scheme blended in rather than contrasted with the landscaping and the topographic hillock along which the building was located.

The circular form of the lobby on the exposed east end of the building was designed to let cold north winds flow around it and as a welcoming visual form. The rounded form at the west end of the building was complimentary to its east counterpart.

A vertical bank of solar collectors for heating and air tempering was designed with a reflective roof deck to the cool and cold weather season but with an appropriate overhang above to be more shaded during the summer. Skydomes and skylights are discreetly used, being energy losers more than the main stairway clerestory. Other external glazing followed interior function as to proportion, placement, and view.

The exterior was largely an expression of interior functions. The author develops *designs from the interior to the exterior in an interface with sun, earth, and climate.* The functional and ergometric aspect of all interior spaces dictated the size, location, and interior arrangement of all work areas. Daylighting, passive solar, active solar, earth coupling, indoor air quality, thermal comfort, views from most interior spaces to the outdoors, and design with future flexibility for change were all taken into consideration.

In the years since the building was constructed, significant space needs and organizational changes were easily accomplished as "growth" space was initially designed into the project.

The interior was designed to be complacent and comfortable, with "see-through" spaces to provide a sense of quiet and purposeful activity. All windows receiving direct solar exposure had vertical bronze-tone "see-through" blinds. The dark bronze transparent vertical solar blinds absorbed wintertime solar gain. Return air above the blinds and the heat from the light fixtures in the return air space above the ceiling, combined with heat from an insulated gravel bin heated by vertical air-type roof solar collectors, provided heat to a zoned variable-volume air duct distribution system for zoned comfort. Inasmuch as only electrical service was available, the dependence upon solar lighting and other internal heat gains was important to reduce utility demand.

Since smoking was permitted by the company in the conference room, dark bronze pendant light fixtures that encircled the conference table were grounded so that cigarette smoke negatively charged by an outer circle of negative ionizers would ground off inconspicuously on the fixtures. This avoided annoyance to others and cigarette smoke contaminating the return air ducts. The residue is easy to clean off of the fixtures. The outdoor air intakes for indoor ventilation are far removed from the parking area or street traffic fumes to further minimize indoor air pollution.

The general ambience of the interior organizational elements was of light-reflective wall and ceilings, with neutral floor materials of wood and carpet. More than 20 large abstract wall plaques designed by the author, task lighting and daylighting, and contemporary clean-line high-tech furniture (durable and easy to maintain) were provided. Flush surfaces without moldings or extraneous detail also conserved on maintenance. To a visitor the impression is of efficient, clearly defined organization, visible activity within a quiet environs, and a pleasant, well-lighted ambience.

MT. POWELL RETREAT

PROJECT AND ENVIRONS

The ecologic mountain setting of this 1981 active solar project can be described as magnificent. It comprised individual guest rooms with bath, habitable loft space, central living/dining/kitchen area, a solar hot pool and sauna area, and a caretaker's apartment. A broad patio to the south with a southwest view of Mt. Powell and rear decks overhanging the Blue River provided an accord with Nature.

The location of the ranch is between Silverthorne and Kremmling, Colorado. The principal main level with a lower level area of the architecture enclosed approximately 4200 square feet.

CONSTRAINTS

The main constraint was a view of and noise from the major highway that passed in front of the site. Some large old barns to the east of the site were unattractive. Major views to the southwest mountain view presented a late afternoon sun problem.

THE SITE

The site had full solar access and a protective stand of evergreen trees to the north above the arroyo of the Blue River. An unobstructed view of Mt. Powell to the southwest was a principal focus in planning and design. Except for the drop towards the river the site was relatively flat, but excavation for the lower level and foundations was used to form earth berms and provide landscaping to attain privacy, road noise reduction, define the south patio area, and act as a foreground to the distant views. All native plantings were used for self-sustainability under natural climatic conditions. The site extended to the Blue River, noted for trout fishing. The existing natural and added native vegetation made landscaping a minimal endeavor and required little irrigation.

EXPERIENTIAL FACTORS

Colorado is noted for its scenic beauty and outdoor life. The trip to the site is a scenic experience. Staying at the site heightens a rapport with Nature. A contact of view and sound with the river is achieved by rooms on two levels opening to the river channel. The changing interseasonal character of the outdoor landscape is one of intimate accord.

THE ARCHITECTURE AND SYSTEMS

The main area of the architecture was planned parallel to the south property line with an obtuse-angled wing. The east wing was oriented to a direct view of Mt. Powell to the southwest. This principal lounge area had access from the main south-facing passive solar (non-mechanically heated) airlocked

MT. POWELL RETREAT

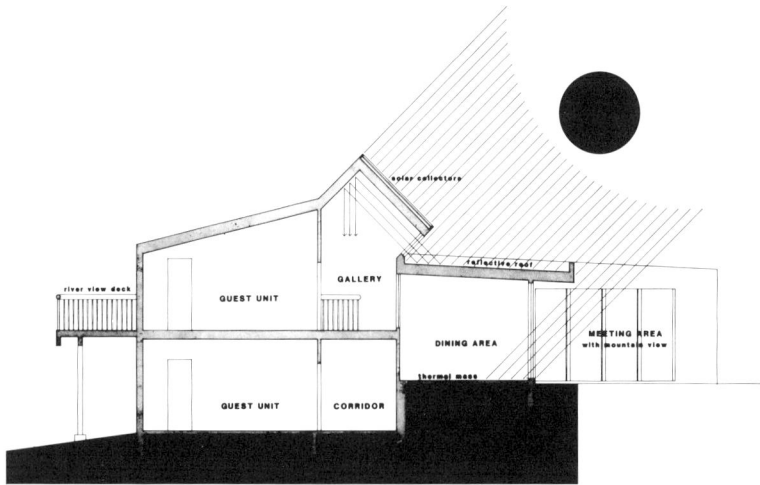

solar collectors

reflecting pool

river view deck

GUEST UNIT

GALLERY

DINING AREA

MEETING AREA
with mountain view

thermal mass

GUEST UNIT

CORRIDOR

Section

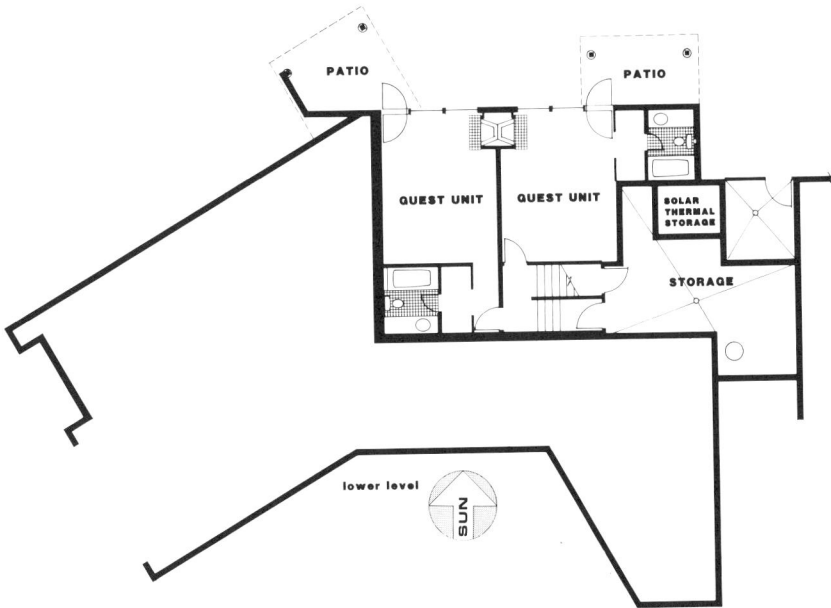

entry. The dining and open kitchen interior space was sequential to the main lounge area.

Although the author has been less than enthusiastic about fireplaces, it was a focal element of the owner's criteria. A metal firebox with circulating convection air exchange outdoor combustion air and glass door fireplace were installed.

Primary space heating and heating of a hot spa pool was by means of approximately 600 square feet of fluid-type flat-plate solar collectors with a concrete solar storage tank of 2000 gallons. A combination of hydronic fan-coil units to individual rooms and slab radiant low temperature heating in principal floor areas provided major space heating, in addition to direct passive solar gains received into dark tile over concrete floors for the principal areas to the south. An electrically heated boiler was used as a backup for the solar heat. Electricity was the only utility energy available. The active solar collectors mounted to due south solar exposure were the main means of space heating.

Passive solar double clear glazing to the south extended from the floor to door height. To capture the panoramic mountain view the largest area of glass in width and height was oriented to the southwest. To compensate for the disadvantage of direct late-in-the-day solar radiation, tall sliding insulating panels were installed to cover the glass. The roof overhang that extended along the south and southwest also acted as a shading element. The use of the outdoor patio in summer was also protected late in the day by the obtuse angle of the west wing. The only glass to the west was a small amount at the caretaker's apartment.

Lower-level rooms cut into the north embankment to the river provided earth coupling. Northside glazing to the guest rooms consisted of triple glazing plus external rolling shutters operated from inside. An angular ribbon window above the bank of solar collectors provided an extensive view including Mt. Powell to the upper loft space open to the principal area below. Overhangs were calculated to provide summer shade over the south glazed areas. The upper clerestory band of windows was self-shading through the summer by a tilt out angle of 45°.

The airlocked entry was south facing and unheated. Rear wooden decks extended out to the river arroyo for warm weather enjoyment and a view of the river. A harmonious relationship was established between the architecture and its setting.

ECOLOGIC RESIDENTIAL RESEARCH FACILITY

PROJECT

Site-specific, holistic, ecologic architecture. Architect/owner 1980 project. Design intent: evaluative research of solar, ecologic, and biologic accords; a climatic oasis and healthful and effectual habitation in the geographic center of Denver. Land forming and landscaping are interresponsive and integrated with the architecture. The total project comprises 7000 square feet (3500 sq.ft. each level). The upper level has the principal residence and home office. The lower level has a solar-heated indoor swimming pool flanked by a front apartment and rear guest quarters.

The project was adaptively designed for conversion at any time to four separate living units as permitted by the zoning code. Adequate parking was also provided for such possible conversion.

ENVIRONS

Vacant site pending development on a corner lot (100 ft. by 125 ft.) zoned for four residential units in an older but redeveloping neighborhood. The area is surrounded by older prestige neighborhoods in proximity to a new top-level retail shopping mall redevelopment.

CONSTRAINTS

The location is in an area of major air pollution. But local regulations during the past few years have somewhat improved the air quality. However, residence in most urban environments from an air quality standpoint is questionable.

Until a few years ago a power line along the south property line and another in the alley that now remains produced electromagnetic fields. For the alley line that remains, electromagnetic field meter measurements taken within rooms closest to the power line indicate levels equivalent to general urban background magnetic fluctuations of about 0.5 to 1.25 milligauss. Extendable exposure time to fields over 3 milligauss is not regarded as prudent. Some researchers believe that exposure should be below 1 milligauss.

Security of person, possessions, and property is another major factor of concern in the urban inner city.

ECOLOGIC CONCERNS

Preserving the numerous trees, the natural grass, and ecologic organic viability of the site were primary considerations.

Major design and construction concerns were how to least impact the site and neighborhood, avoid energy-intensive materials, means, and methods in construction, create a healthful habitat, adhere to a frugal budget, and optimize the site-specific use of sun, earth, air, and water energies, with self-sufficiency as the objective and minimization of utility energy demand.

Excavation and land forming were a concern as to the minimization of earth-handling equipment, time, and pollution.

EXPERIENTIAL

The architecture by its design excludes disturbing external sounds of the city. An accord with the ever-changing nuances of daylight and the park-like interface between the street and interior to exterior points of view is a constant enjoyment throughout the days and seasons of the year. A somewhat restricted mountain view is visible to the west.

The interior design and complacent forms of the architecture, integrated open planning, borrowed light and vision from space to space, careful allocation of wall and ceiling surface reflectivity, natural flow-through ventilation, naturally controlled mean radiant temperature and humidity (40 to 50% relative humidity), and an integrated simplicity of furniture and furnishings provide a symbiotic pleasure and relaxing ambience.

Volumetric relationships of light, space, and form are concordant with interior space use, migrational pathways, and a general exercise of our sensory responses. Experiential concern and values were consummate in planning and design.

THE SITE

Corner location has full solar access. A stand of blackthorn locust trees remains along the south boundary. Earth embankments with these trees and low evergreen foliage were formed to act year-round as a climatic, street noise, and privacy barrier. These landscaped earth berms also channel the cold winter air that moves down from hills along the front, sides, and rear of the property away from the architecture. The earth berms also were a place to use the earth from an excavated courtyard along the south side and for the lower-level area. The sidewalk was moved to the curb so that this frontal landscaped area could attenuate the climatic extremes of summer and winter and act as a climatic moderator through all seasons.

Today a literal urban forest exists with summer shading for a lower courtyard excavated to open a lower level of the architecture to the south for solar gain when the locust trees lose their leaves in the early fall. Natural uncut grass of the site still prevails between the trees. A wooden post and vinyl-covered wire system retains the earth embankments at the courtyard. White marble chips of the courtyard add solar reflectivity to lower-level interior spaces. A 700-gallon cistern at the rear of the property receives roof water down a large internal down spout with solar reflectors at the roof to melt snow and ice. Water from the cistern flows by gravity to irrigate the trees and planting.

The landscaping was designed to further lessen climatic extremes. Austrian pines were placed to intervene and turbulate north and northwest cold winter winds. Pinon pines were located to prevent cold winds from sweeping through the lower courtyard. Broad-leaf deciduous catalpa trees were located to the east and west for summer shading of the architecture. A couple of apple trees to the west provide fruit.

The architecture was located to the north on the site, with a rear earth berm to the roof to accommodate the south solar courtyard and the south passive solar surfaces and openings of the architectural envelope. The roofs are flat to retain the thermal benefit of snow, except for a central roof structure that acts as a place for solar collectors and for clerestory windows of the central solar gallery.

The northside roof was designed to be earth covered for native planting or to serve as a garden area. But the decision was to not take on the extra watering, care, and maintenance. It can always be used for such purpose.

THE ARCHITECTURE, FORM, AND SYSTEMS

The architecture is essentially earth coupled, earth sheltered, solar, and climate responsive. The design and form were entirely dictated by ecosystemic and ecologic site-specific characteristics. Solar energy has been optimized for interseasonal thermal heating, air tempering, ventilating, cooling, solar drying, sanitization, outgassing of materials and items, and for optimization of daylighting. Passive, hybrid, and active solar systems are treated as effectual and economic subsystems, and all systems interseasonally interrelate to interior comfort and to fulfill purpose. The form of the architecture also derives from our human ecologic reality in the orientation, space planning, and disposition of interior and exterior space. The climate-responsive interior planning optimizes daylighting and equates with the daily and seasonal positions of the sun.

With the extreme mountain climate temperature swings of 40° to 50°F in a matter of hours, the large thermal mass of concrete construction, earth, and swimming pool water was logical to stabilize indoor temperatures. North and west earth embankments to the roof have a concrete cover to keep the earth dry and insulative and to divert cold winter winds.

A large solar-heated (to melt ice and snow) roof scupper delivers water to an earth gravity distribution channel that irrigates the front landscaping. The main entry door is recessed to the east for weather protection. Garage doors with a dark paint finish act as a solar collector together with an angled reflector towards the sun that also melts a path through the snow in front of the garage.

The garage acts as a climatic buffer, and as with the general construction, it has concrete thermal walls and an insulated prestressed concrete roof and is earth coupled. The garage has a step riser to the house entry hall and cross ventilation to a roof wind turbine to avoid intrusion of petro-fumes into the interior. The garage has an energy-conserving skyshaft designed by the author for illumination. The 18-foot wide garage door and interior space of the garage were designed to accommodate one larger and two smaller cars. The driveway is fully exposed to the morning sun.

The main level equates with the street-level entry as a handicap provision if ever needed. The exterior and interior doors are wider than usual for such possibility, in addition to allowing a freer passage of light and air. Door knobs and light switches are placed at handicap level.

ECOLOGIC RESEARCH FACILITY

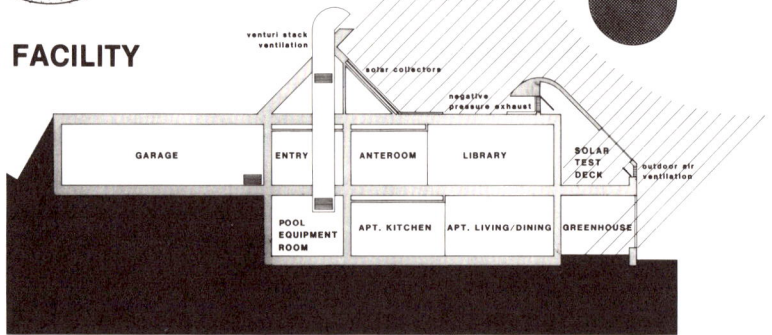

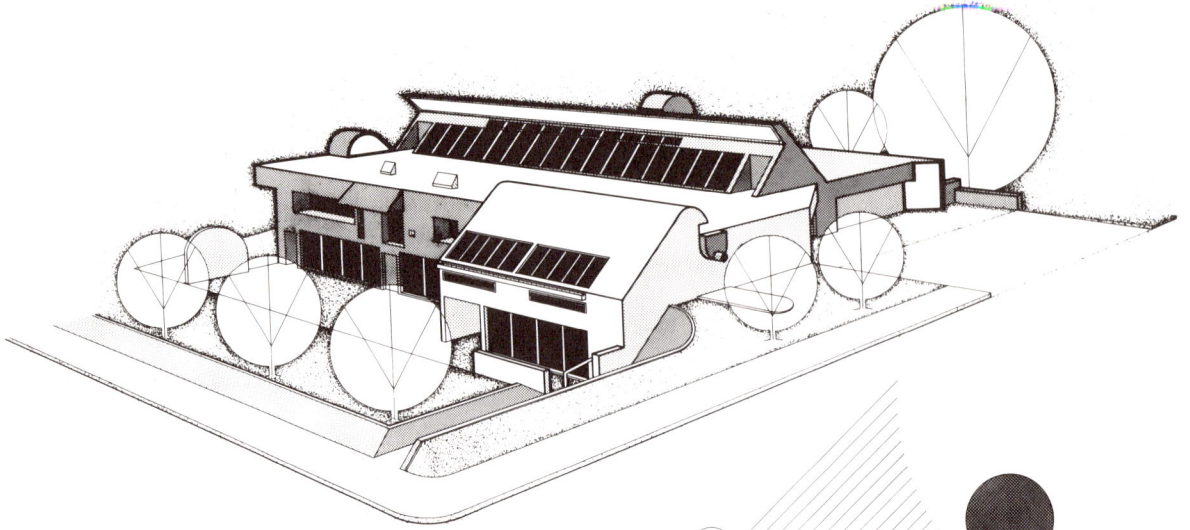

GARAGE	ENTRY	ANTEROOM	LIBRARY		SOLAR TEST DECK	

venturi stack ventilation

solar collectors

negative pressure exhaust

outdoor air ventilation

POOL EQUIPMENT ROOM | APT. KITCHEN | APT. LIVING/DINING | GREENHOUSE

Section

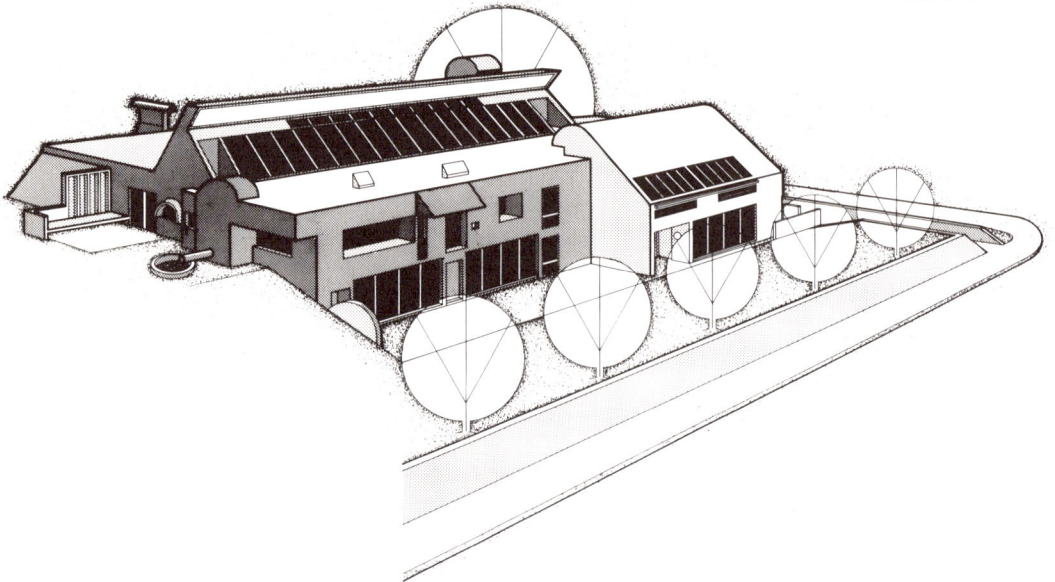

Section drawing labels

skyshaft · skyshaft · reflective canopy · clerestory · solar collectors · reflective roof

MASTER BATH · UTILITY · SOLAR GALLERY · DINING ROOM · BREAKFAST NOOK

STORAGE · SAUNA · HALL

SOLAR THERMAL WATER STORAGE

SWIMMING POOL

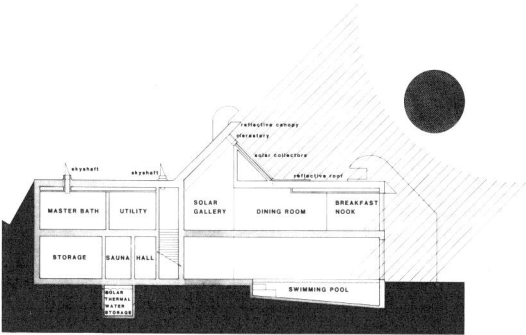

Swimming Pool　Section

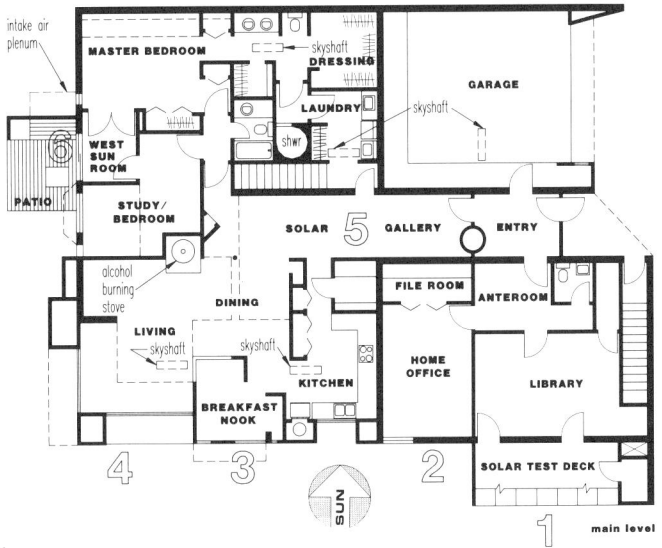

Main level plan labels

intake air plenum

MASTER BEDROOM · DRESSING · skyshaft · LAUNDRY · skyshaft · GARAGE · shwr

6 · WEST SUN ROOM · PATIO · STUDY/BEDROOM · alcohol burning stove

SOLAR · 5 · GALLERY · ENTRY

FILE ROOM · ANTEROOM

LIVING · skyshaft · skyshaft · DINING · KITCHEN · HOME OFFICE · LIBRARY

BREAKFAST NOOK

4 · 3 · SUN · 2 · SOLAR TEST DECK · 1 · main level

SOLAR THERMAL ZONES

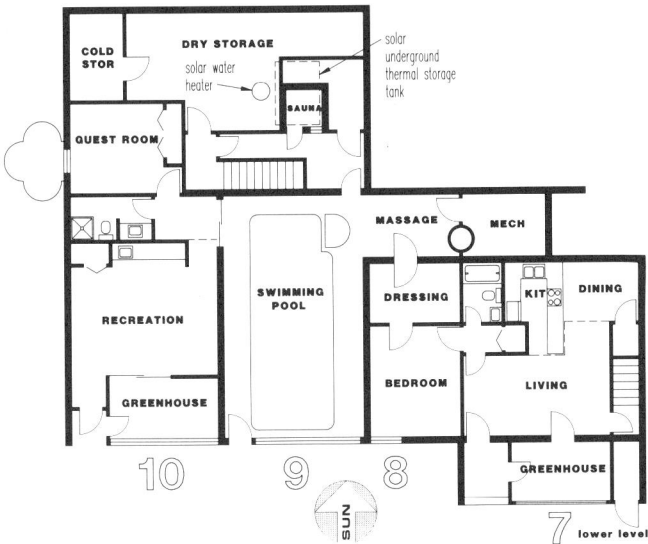

Lower level plan labels

COLD STOR · DRY STORAGE · solar water heater · SAUNA · solar underground thermal storage tank

GUEST ROOM

RECREATION · SWIMMING POOL · MASSAGE · MECH · DRESSING · KIT · DINING

GREENHOUSE · BEDROOM · LIVING

GREENHOUSE

10 · 9 · 8 · SUN · 7 · lower level

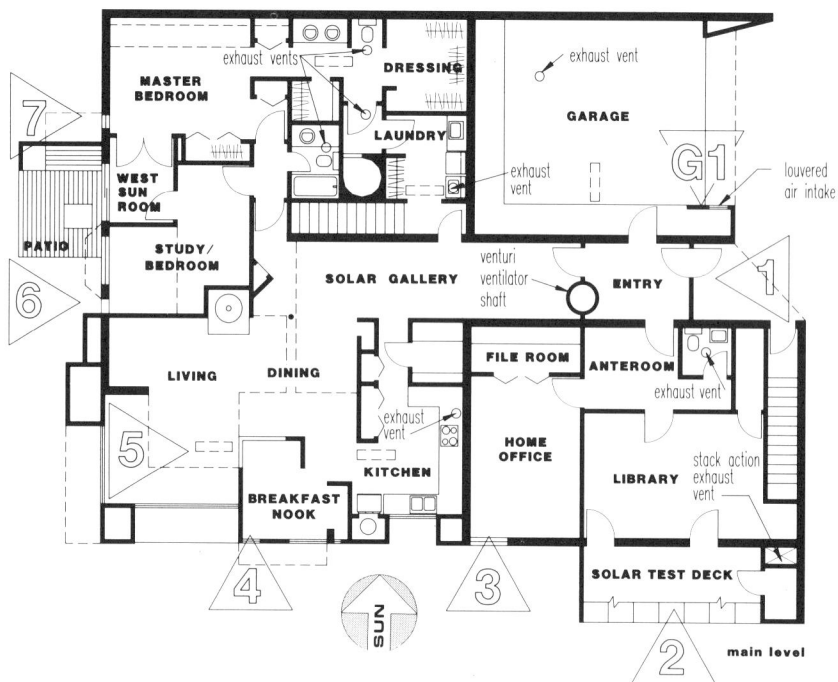

VENTILATION ZONES

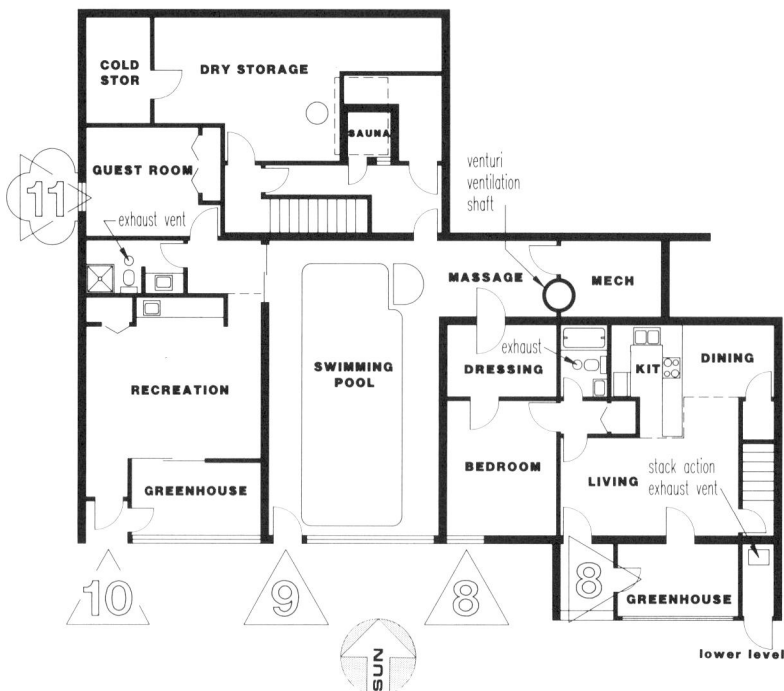

An unheated airlocked main level entryway is of minimal volume and provides access to the garage, the library, solar test deck, home office, and the main-level residence. A security ventilation outer door with winter thermal blanket and inner thermal door has a screening (solar screen) that can permit a night view of the person at the door with the light on outside and dark inside. An energy-conserving mailbox is devised from a short-pile carpeted cylinder that opens for mail and tightly closes against a carpeted surface.

Adjacent to the library is an angularly glazed indoor solar test deck for year-round testing of solar devices, materials, and equipment; drying of clothes and items; and the outgassing of sundry items before bringing them into an occupied space. It should be noted that the author does not advocate small attached greenhouses or sunspaces with roofs of sloping glass due to seasonal overheating, clear-sky temperature energy loss, surface dust and dirt accumulation, possibilities of precipitation leakage, and maintenance required. But for solar testing there is no other alternative. This space is ventilated by large horizontal screened louvers below the glazed area and also at the highest point at the roof line, and with a trailing edge configuration of the architecture, prevailing winds create negative pressure at the roof line that aids the rate of ventilation.

This frontal part of the project including the test deck, library, and home office is about 1100 square feet and was designed if desired to be converted into an apartment. The concrete wall between the solar test deck with a dark finish coating like a Trombe wall provides solar heating to the library by thermal lag. Horizontal hollow core precast ceiling panels can act as a hypercaust solar heat system that provides radiant ceiling heat. Large glazed doors on either side of the wall admit task-effective daylight and secondary wintertime thermal gains to the library. Conversion to an apartment would have a pre-planned separate entry door and a small amount of modification including that of a bathroom shower and kitchen installed to the roughed-in plumbing.

From the low-ceiling entry hall the high-ceiling solar gallery is entered. An exterior horizontal cantilever reflector angled at the highest point of the structure projects a high level of reflected plus direct solar radiation into a main-level central solar gallery through a band of clerestory windows. Convected solar heat from south passive solar systems of the living room and breakfast nook, as well as internal heat gains from kitchen appliances through a ceiling plenum, bring heat to the central gallery. The resultant concentration of heat at the ceiling is summarily conveyed by a thermo-statically controlled (82°F) blower and ductwork to lower-level eutectic salt thermal storage and concrete mass under the north side. A dark concrete thermal mass wall in the gallery receives direct and indirect winter solar gain. In summer reflected solar light only, results in a soft, subdued level of daylight in the gallery. The reflective roof, cantilever exterior reflector above the solar collectors, and clerestory windows add to the concentration of interior solar radiation and concentrate impact on the solar collectors.

An exterior bank of fluid-type flat-plate solar collectors located at a 45-degree angle below the gallery clerestories heats the indoor swimming pool and preheats the hot spa pool, the sauna, and domestic hot water. The swimming pool is located in the lower level and acts as a central heating system by directly heating thermal mass walls on either side of the pool. Thus an adjoining apartment either side of the pool and a precast concrete ceiling system above the pool heats in measure a main floor residence as well as with direct passive solar gains from the south that heat the dark-tiled concrete pool deck and the interior air of the pool area. An insulated concrete 1000-gallon solar tank under the sauna of the lower level preheats it and in turn heats the shower floor of the upper level.

In winter the concentration of direct solar radiation that is reflected from the reflective roof and the overhead exterior reflector provides an intensification of light (200 to over 1000 footcandles) and thermal gain to the gallery. But in summer the exterior reflector acts as a sun shade over the band of clerestory windows while not shading the flat-plate solar collectors. In consequence reflected solar light from the roof deck reflects against the overhead reflector and a soft illumination from 20 to 70 footcandles pervades the gallery at a 36" height from the floor. A central white translucent plastic form in the gallery is a sculpture pedestal and luminaire for night use.

The general interior of the principal residence living space is an "open" plan with dining and west living room (with mountain view) connected to the gallery. The ergometrically planned kitchen and breakfast nook are to the south. The breakfast nook floor is dark tile over a prestressed concrete floor system for the reception of passive solar gain. Table and chairs have minimal legs to minimize shadowing the sun's rays. Cabinets are suspended above the floor. The exterior overhang acts as a shading device. Vertical blinds provide sun control and privacy.

The living room Heat Mirror low-emissivity glazing is reflective against the west sun. The west projection of the roof and exterior side wall provide additional summer solar shading. A large horizontal south window is recessed, providing summer shade to the interior of the living room. During winter the low angle of the sun heats a bank of eutectic salt containers, which subsequently provide heat to the interior along with a dark tile over concrete thermal mass ledge. During summer pressurized cool nighttime air (with self-induced electrostatic filtration) is used for cooling the main-level areas. In winter by a return air system the lower-level guest space greenhouse can provide solar heat to main floor areas or act as a system to temper cold outdoor intake air for ventilation.

To the west from a bedroom study a small wood deck patio is shaded by a catalpa tree in summer and is protected from north and northwest winter winds by Austrian pines, evergreen bushes, and a wooden earth retaining wall. A screened sheet metal rustproof-coated metal plenum under the west and northside earth-sheltering embankment to the roof tempers outdoor air (that is filtered by a self-inductive electrostatic filter) for master bedroom ventilation. A west-facing solar chimney opposite to the plenum intake air retains heat in eutectic salt tubes which as the night air cools and is further cooled by the earth through the plenum ventilates and cools the room.

The west "eyebrow" window on the study/bedroom with clear polycarbonate glazing (for security) and inner heat-absorbing plastic with relief given to solar-heated air also shades from the sun. A screened, louvered grille with insulated panel provides controlled cross ventilation for the study/bedroom. Double-glazed exterior sliding patio doors of the west sun room are reflective. The west sun room provides a climatic and security intervention and massage and sitting space for the master bedroom or optionally, the study/bedroom. Inner double polycarbonate glazed doors provide access from each space. A metal grillework in the patio deck allows ventilation air to be air-tempered by half vertical sections (6-foot diameter) of galvanized steel culvert installed below grade in a clover leaf pattern to the rear of the lower-level apartment. Sunlight and daylight also are provided to the lower level by the grilled opening.

The lower south courtyard aligns approximately with the lower-level floor line. The lower-level greenhouse accepts direct passive solar gain and uses eutectic salt tubes as the thermal mass. The greenhouse with cellular double plastic vertical glazing is the most economic solution. Inner glass sliding doors provide access and also accept secondary solar penetration to the interior. The surface of the greenhouse is covered with white marble chips to increase interior solar reflectivity and benefit greenhouse plants.

A screened louvered section with a full-sized insulated door to the exterior provides air to the greenhouse and also for the forced-air ductwork ventilation and nocturnal cooling system of the upper level principal residence area. The upper breakfast nook area has an exterior wall projection over an acrylic glazed window for summer shading and winter passive direct solar gain into the dark tile and concrete floor. Fixed cellular double plastic windows allow for direct passive solar gains in the swimming pool and surrounding dark tile and concrete pool deck.

The swimming pool is 12 feet wide and 30 feet long with 11,000 gallons of water, 100% solar heated for the past 12 years. The pool water temperature usually varies from about 85°F to 90°F even during mid-winter. With 200 pounds of salt (NaCl) added to the water the atoms of chlorine and sodium are disassociated electrolytically such that the chlorine suppresses algal and bacterial growth. In the interest of conserving energy the pool is covered most often with a transparent plastic cover that allows solar penetration, and the pool area is infrequently ventilated. The experimental use of molecular adsorbing materials did in observable measure inhibit mildew growth on surfaces of the area. More recently a nontoxic mildew control cleaning and coating of the walls has notably prevented the formation of mold, without any ventilation of this area and with humidity most often over 90%.

The pool is cleaned by turbo jets in the bottom of the pool. Other than one replacement of water for an acid cleaning, in nine years no cleaning of the pool has been necessary. The pool is concrete with a white plaster surface.

To optimize cross ventilation upper-level rooms have screened intake air grilles, as does the swimming pool area. A large duct to the roof ventilates by venturi principle the lower-level pool area as ventilation is desired and also the upper-level principal residence. Bathrooms are ventilated with roof wind turbines in which the amount of ventilation is manually controlled.

A centrally located stairway descends to the swimming pool area and to a storage room with an earth temperature cold storage room for food, film, and sundry items. The stairway is designed to accommodate a personal lift if ever needed. The lower-level courtyard has a tennis backboard and forecourt for practice.

The front lower-level apartment is directly accessible to the swimming pool, as well as the guest space to the rear. With a concrete thermal lag wall heated by the pool, the rear guest space of 750 sq.ft. with a greenhouse (using eutectic salt tubes for thermal storage) and largely earth coupled with incoming air tempered by the earth contact corrugated culvert sections has never been below 68°F without any other source of heat. During the hottest days of summer incoming air with culvert earth contact remains pleasantly cool.

The front apartment has its own south patio and a sunspace with a high transmissivity film for glazing that perceives the sun's radiation as double glazing but acts conversely as triple glazing. This front apartment of 1100 square feet has a hydronic electric baseboard heater but is largely heated by thermal lag of the concrete wall of the pool area.

The south courtyard is shaded in summer and has direct solar exposure in winter. White marble chips provide reflection to the lower-level spaces, to the guest space greenhouse, and to an outdoor organic garden. It is an interseasonally protected space for many activities.

The thermal performance of this residential research facility is more than 50 percent better than the original thermal calculations. Interior temperatures of the main living areas have not been below 68°F irrespective of winter temperatures often below 0°F and sometimes as cold as -10° to -20°F. Most interior spaces have no electric utility heat (namely the main entry, solar gallery, kitchen, breakfast nook, dining room, utility room, master bedroom, west sun room, lower-level front apartment bedroom, swimming pool area, and rear guest apartment). When it was -22°F outside, the unheated west sun room was 56°F and the unheated master bedroom was 66°F. Total supplemental electric hydronic baseboard heat on the line for the total 7000 square foot facility is 5.4 kW through most of the winter, with 6.4 kW under extreme cold.

SECURITY

Security of person, possessions, and property was a concern met by initial planning. The main-level airlocked entry has stout insulated doors to the exterior and each interior space. The security grilled door to the exterior and other inner deadbolt doors provide a formidable barrier to intrusion. A slot window to the entry hall and energy-conserving mail slot is at a distance from the inner door latch. An intercom system from principal points of the upper and lower levels to the main entry doors gives primary protection.

The central gallery solar thermal concrete wall acts as a barrier along with solid-core inner doors with peepholes and a lighting control separates bedroom and night areas from those of the living areas and lower pool area. With the stairway within this protection area and a lighted panel in the master bedroom that indicates where any intrusion occurs, the alert is given.

In general the fixed glazing of the exterior with contact security wiring and to outer doors and fixed louvered intake air grilles are a primary deterrent. The polycarbonate glazing of some outer windows and inner doors of the west sunspace to the master bedroom presents unexpected barriers to entry. The retreat capability to the master bath dressing area with stout doors and emergency button directly to the burglar alarm company buys time for the police to arrive.

The skyshafts designed by the author for the living room, kitchen, master bedroom, utility room, and garage are confined to a 7" width through the concrete roof structure thereby preventing physical access.

SOLAR THERMAL ZONES

1. Solar Test Deck. For testing solar devices, outgassing and drying materials, solar heating, air tempering, ventilation, and thermal lag through concrete wall. Daylighting and secondary solar gain through glass doors to interior library. Sloped glazing for year-round direct solar radiation.

2. Home Office. Direct solar gain to due south thin outsulation of heavy thermal mass concrete wall and through double glazed window. Window located to optimize in-depth interior daylighting by reflection of adjacent wall and general interior.

3. Breakfast Nook. Direct solar gain to dark tile covered concrete slab. Exterior architectural overhang for summer shading. Clear plastic glazing to admit beneficial UV radiation. Furniture with thin chrome legs to reflect radiation back to the tile floor.

4. Living Room. To receive direct winter sun a eutectic salt bin is placed to protect carpet and furniture from fading or sun damage. The recessed double clear glass window is calculated for correct sun angle winter radiation and summer shading. The dark exterior box-like form that surrounds the glass creates a warmer micro-environment and preserves the thin air film on the glass, thus reducing internal cold weather thermal losses. It also acts as an anti-glare surround that enhances vision of the outdoors from indoors.

West-facing Heat Mirror glazing reduces interior thermal re-radiant losses and acts to reflect back solar intensity during warm and hot weather. An architectural roof overhang and north architectural projection considerably reduce unfavorable solar impact during warm and hot periods of the year when the west sun angle is very low. These wide horizontal windows provide good acuity lateral daylighting to interior space.

5. Solar Gallery. A reflective roof deck and overhead angled canopy concentrate reflective solar as well as direct solar radiation through a two-foot wide horizontal band of clerestory windows. A dark concrete thermal mass wall receives the energy. Subsystems 3 and 4 and a kitchen ceiling plenum that accepts convective waste heat from kitchen appliances contribute to the centralization of the solar gallery thermal energy.

The upper strata of solar-heated air is subsequently ducted with a blower to a lower-level northside basement eutectic salt thermal mass to heat the floor of the dressing and bath spaces above. The sloping ceiling of the gallery and other surfaces are highly reflective. In winter the light intensity at midday is 500 footcandles, while in summer it is less than 50 footcandles by virtue of the architectural configuration.

On a sunny midday in winter the gallery temperature can exceed 80°F, while in summer it is likely not to exceed 85°F. The mean radiant temperature of the main floor residence area remains above 68°F when outside temperatures can drop as low as -20°F. Supplemental electric hydronic baseboard heat for the 7000 square feet of the two-level facility does not exceed 6 kW during winter despite a home office, principal residence area, a leased apartment, guest apartment, and solar-heated swimming pool.

A thermal blanket and insulative side-sliding panels are used to cover the windows of the living room when temperatures fall below 0°F. The clerestory and other windows have no movable thermal coverings.

6. West Sun Room. This space receives only partial solar radiation in a winter afternoon. But it serves as an affective climatic buffer, a security intervenor, a place for various functions, and as an additive area to the master bedroom or the west bedroom study. Outer burglar alarm glazing and inner polycarbonate clear plastic greatly reduce the risk of intrusion. This sunspace provides daylight and view to the bedrooms that adjoin it.

The limited solar thermal gain has some advantage. At 7 a.m. of a January morning this space was 56°F and the adjoining master bedroom 66°F with no electric or other heating including solar, when the outside temperature was -20°F.

7. Apartment Solar Greenhouse. This lower-level greenhouse has a high transmissivity film between the double glazing. Direct gain solar radiation is received by the dark concrete greenhouse floor and concrete interior wall.

8. Apartment Bedroom. The bedroom receives direct solar gain through a fixed and lower sash awning window.

9. Solar Swimming Pool. The 100% solar-heated pool of the lower level is a central thermal mass heat sink. 360 square feet of fluid-type active solar collectors with added thermal gain from an overhead angled reflective canopy and reflective roof deck heat water of an 1100-gallon concrete thermal storage tank by a heat exchanger. The tank with heat exchangers heat the swimming pool and domestic hot water. In over 12 years the pool temperature has been sustained entirely with solar energy above 80°F and in a usual range of 84° to 90°F.

The deep end of the pool is at the south. South double celled clear plastic glazing and the dark tile concrete deck benefit by direct passive solar gain. The pool and its concrete deck and enclosing walls and prestressed concrete ceiling provide thermal lag heating for the lower-level apartment, guest apartment, and residence space above. A sauna is preheated by its location over the solar storage tank, and the shower above on the main level by its location over the sauna.

10. Passive Solar Greenhouse. This space contains direct gain 81°F phase-change passive salt tubes that improve thermal effectiveness by about 12°F. Reflective white marble chips of the exterior courtyard and in the greenhouse with reflective walls and ceiling add to interior daylighting of the vertically glazed greenhouse. The glazed inner side-sliding doors permit secondary solar gain to interior space.

11. Guest Apartment Bedroom. An opening in the wood patio deck above a lower-level areaway permits daylighting and a degree of direct solar radiation to enter this space. See item 11 of Ventilation Zones.

VENTILATION ZONES

1. Main Entry. This is an unheated airlocked space. The front entry exterior door is a security design with louvered screening. It is deadlocked for safety

and effective for partial or whole main level cross ventilation. This outer security door has a velcro affixed thermal blanket in winter and an inner insulated door that controls ventilation and provides added security. A large mail slot is designed to close in an insulative and airtight manner.

G1. Garage. A screened louvered air ventilator has an insulated operable panel that controls outdoor intake air that cross ventilates the garage to a roof wind turbine. The planned ventilation pattern directs automotive fumes away from the garage door to the main entry. A step curbing in the garage intercepts heavier emissions from entering the entry hall.

2. Solar Test Deck. This sunspace has multi-functional uses: testing solar materials and devices, ventilation, air tempering, and drying and outgassing of materials and items. Large screened horizontal louvers at the base of the sunspace and others above the roof plane have insulated operable panels that control air flow. The sectional configuration of the sunspaces with a trailing edge along the roof augments ventilation by negative wind pressure. A reflective mesh fabric suspended behind the glazing reflects back summer solar radiation and provides inductive convection to reduce sunspace heat. This sunspace cross ventilates the adjoining library from the home office as regulated by the gallery venturi roof stack.

3. Home Office. A home office fixed window with a lower ventilating awning section maximizes cross ventilation of the room diagonally through a door opening to the library or to the venturi roof stack.

4. Breakfast Nook. Lower screened louvers with operable insulated panel are located to provide diagonal cross ventilation to the solar gallery and the venturi ventilation stack.

5. Living Room. Ventilation is optimal. An exterior screened duct with operable panel is one option. Another is a powered duct system that can provide main-level pressurized cool nocturnal ventilation during warm and hot weather. It performs more effectively than an attic exhaust fan by using less horsepower, a self-actuating electrostatic filter, and operating more quietly.

Buttoning up the main residential area sustains daytime cool indoor temperatures. The cooling effect upon particular spaces is by the opening of outdoor vents and by means of the central gallery venturi ventilation stack.

6. West Bedroom Study. Screened louvers with an operable insulated panel in an outside corner diagonal to the door opening provide cross ventilation back to the gallery or to the master bedroom solar chimney. A side-sliding patio door with a narrow opening stop on a burglar alarm system can be used for direct ventilation of the space and optionally for the master bedroom.

7. Master Bedroom. Ventilation is by means of a metal plenum protected against rust located under the west earth berm (for earth warming of incoming air in cold weather and cooling it during hot weather). It is diagonal to a high vent to provide cross ventilation to a solar chimney. The dark metal solar chimney is designed with the broad side to the west and with eutectic salt tubes to sustain the heat in the chimney. The master bedroom is thus ventilated by temperature differential as night air becomes cooler. A self-actuating electrostatic filter is placed in the airstream entering the bedroom from the plenum.

The master bathroom is ventilated by air flow from the master bedroom and by other openings. Operable roof turbine and venturi ventilators exhaust air and odors from bathrooms of the facility. Powered exhaust fans and their noise are avoided.

8. Apartment Solar Greenhouse and Bedroom. Louvered screened outdoor air ventilation for this lower-level greenhouse and apartment is controlled by an inner insulated door. An inductive ventilation stack to the roof with a wind turbine exhausts air from the greenhouse and apartment. The master bedroom awning window section is located to optimize apartment cross ventilation to the greenhouse and its ventilation stack.

9. Solar Swimming Pool. The lower-level swimming pool area has an exterior security screened grille with an inner insulated door for ventilation control. Cross ventilation is regulated to the vertical ventilation venturi roof stack. During cold periods no ventilation is provided to retain central heat benefits of the 100% solar-heated pool. By using electrolytic disassociation of chlorine and sodium from salt (200 pounds for 11,000 gallons) for water purification, no residual chlorine odor is present in the air.

With the prevailing high relative humidity (usually exceeding 90%), mildew and mold are successfully inhibited by molecular adsorbing materials and a nontoxic surface coating. In an air test the bacteria, mold, and yeast plate count was no greater than that of an average home.

10. Passive Solar Greenhouse. This lower-level greenhouse offers multiple functions. It can be used to ventilate the guest apartment with an exterior screened louver, inner insulated door, and interior side-sliding glass doors. It is also used to ventilate and air-temper outdoor air for living areas of the main level above. For nocturnal summer cooling ductwork with a self-actuating electrostatic filter and blower are used to pressurize the main floor residential area above (see living room ventilation zone 5). By adjusting the opening of the main-level exterior wall ventilation louvers, the cool, pressurized night air can selectively cool interior spaces.

11. Guest Apartment Bedroom. The exterior grade level wood deck patio has a grilled opening to admit ventilation air and daylight to a lower-level guest apartment bedroom. Six-foot diameter corrugated metal half-section highway culverts arranged vertically in a cloverleaf pattern set into the earth below the patio deck can provide effective air tempering of ventilation air through all seasons.

Cross ventilation is provided to the passive solar greenhouse or to the main-level solar gallery vertical inductive venturi roof stack via the swimming pool area. An operable awning window of the apartment bedroom controls desired amounts of ventilation air.

PASSIVE SOLAR PARKWAY RESIDENCE

PROJECT

This 1961 project, the author's residence with his family for 10 years, was the third passive solar home designed by the author (the first was in 1946 and second in 1952) as an integrated holistic project. Primary issues of design were for solar and ecologic compatibility, economy of construction, low life-cycle energy use, nuclear fallout shelter protection, main floor multifunctional space use, and an upper level for entertainment and visiting guests (that separated them from main floor space use).

ENVIRONS

The location is on a principal landscaped residential parkway with many old "elegant" homes. The parkway was well-landscaped with large deciduous and evergreen trees. Flower bed landscaping through the central median was well kept.

CONSTRAINTS

The site was very narrow but a bit deeper than neighboring sites. It was zoned R-1 (single family), whereas the author had a strong preference for R-2 (two family) so that in frequent absence from the city the property would have more security. The street was composed of older traditional architecture. But the author in solar and ecologic concern with climate-responsive design proceeded more closely to a contemporary form in accord with the natural character of the site and parkway, with a due south front exposure. Privacy from the street was a consideration of importance.

ECOLOGIC CONCERNS

The tree-lined parkway with its median of landscaping that divided the traffic and an unusual central grassy commons for the homes that ringed the block were of great ecologic benefit. For the site itself there was a limited area for any landscaping.

Berms were landscaped on either side of a platform stepped entry walk with vinca major that proliferated as a dense ground cover. It remained largely green through the winter months and provided an admirable evaporative field with the sprinkler mist heads for summer cooling.

Large deciduous elms flanked the south front of the property providing shade in summer. Native plantings of mugho pines, pinons to cut wind on either side, and blue fescue made up added planting within a south solar courtyard. It was brick walled for privacy from the street at a height over which it was possible to see over when standing in the courtyard. A central open fence-like vertical wood grille and gate to match allowed a flow of outdoor air to the main entry door. The net result was minimum maintenance and a compatible ecologic setting.

EXPERIENTIAL

The parkway was delightful for evening strolls and the common to the rear of the homes brought neighbors together and a place for children at play. Everyone shared in its maintenance and upkeep.

The architecture was designed to optimize the visual and pleasurable correspondence between indoors and outdoors. Full glazing to the south of the living and dining room, the extension of the solar courtyard exterior brick walls into the interior, west ribbon windows of the dining room, and see through to the east outdoor screened and roof-covered patio provided visual relief and a connection to close-by verdancy and backdrop of parkway trees. A north roof deck over the garage overlooks the commons to the rear of the property.

SITE

The narrow site was situated between older and larger homes. From the street the property has a fortunate grade rise of about five feet to the north. This permitted the house to set into the grade three feet, thus being able to economically locate the footings directly under the concrete slab floors. Thus the frost line depth by code was met and an earth connection and a cost saving were realized.

It is rare to find a vacant site in a prosperous older residential parkway neighborhood.

ARCHITECTURE, FORM, AND SYSTEMS

The architectural form was derived from the conditions of the site, privacy, initial and life-cycle economy, solar, ecologic, climate-response functional and experiential factors. Insulated exterior brick cavity walls, interior brick thermal mass corridor wall, twin T prestressed exposed concrete second floor system (as a fallout shelter shield), heavily insulated second floor wood frame construction acting as a thermal bonnet over the interior thermal mass, and the earth connection were principal to the architecture as a thermal system. Large thermal interior masses are particularly advantageous in the often extreme thermal swings of the Colorado climate.

Setting the architecture into the grade and the east screened and covered patio likewise set in the grade (with an evaporative gravel-filled trough the length of its perimeter slab) and openings to a major portion of the main-level interior space led visitors to believe that in the heat of summer the 2600 sq.ft. main level was air conditioned.

During warm and hot weather the upper level stayed reasonably cool with nocturnal and sometimes daytime ventilation (depending upon outdoor temperatures) through a mechanical exhaust fan over the stairway, upper-level near-the-ceiling awning windows, and banks of awning windows below the fixed glazing of the main-level living and dining areas.

A screened main entry door designed for security with an inner security air flow control door provided cross ventilation as desired to the east patio, other

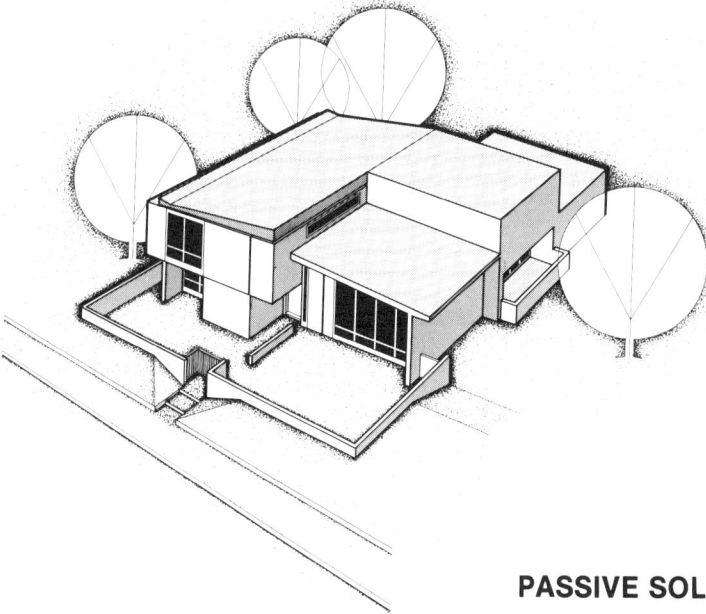

PASSIVE SOLAR PARKWAY RESIDENCE

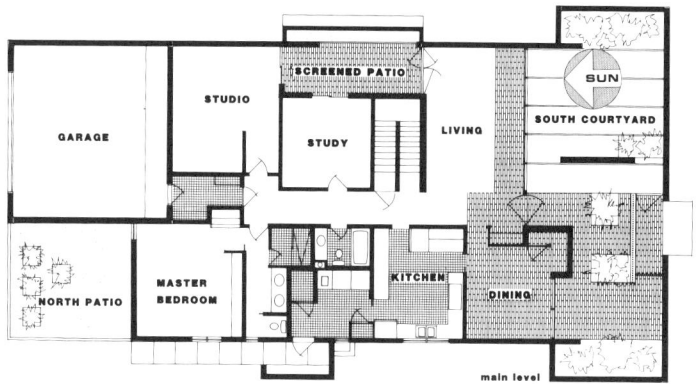

GARAGE	STUDIO	SCREENED PATIO			SUN
		STUDY	LIVING	SOUTH COURTYARD	
NORTH PATIO	MASTER BEDROOM		KITCHEN	DINING	

main level

NORTH DECK	GAME ROOM		SUN
	RECREATION ROOM		
	BEDROOM		

upper level

Holistic Ecologic Architecture/Case Studies   151

interior space, and also by means of the stairway, the venting of upper-level rooms.

The front solar patio was a pleasant place to relax even on a sunny day in winter. The recessed windows of the dining room with its brick floor and sidewall thermal masses received direct solar gain to these masses in winter but was shaded by the extension of the upper floor in summer. The living room with its high ceiling had a substantial roof overhang to provide summer shade but received direct solar radiation to an interior thermal mass sidewall and the floor during winter.

A sheer drapery was used to attenuate solar radiation as desired and a heavy thermal drape was separately employed to reduce re-radiative interior thermal losses during cold weather at night or on cloudy days. Within a period of time the author elected to eliminate the solar, maintenance, and stacking problems and cost of draperies in deference to high-performance glazing and useful blinds, as well as architectural solutions without draperies.

A small basement area had a fallout shelter designed to a 100 protection factor and a hydronic boiler for interior space heating that served seven thermal zones. The water from the hot water tank was devised to serve the fallout shelter in case of contingent need.

All of the detailing and surfaces of the interior of the contemporary architecture were designed for minimal maintenance and cleaning.

While enjoying privacy from the street and the neighbors, the interior had a well-daylighted and "open" feeling. A drawback of the narrow site was that the garage doors had to face north in access to the rear short stretch of alley. A few times in winter storms they did ice up and some boiling water was used to free them. But the garage acted as a good thermal buffer of the house against north and northwest winds and storms.

ST. PAUL STREET RESIDENCES

PROJECT

This 1974 project was to remodel and "solarize" an existing older home of approximately 1,000 square feet with a basement and to build an optimal conservation solar demonstration residence. The author chose to make the prototype demonstration project on a 28' by 28' foundation of 2,000 square feet with bedrooms, play space, utility, bath, and solar sublevel greenhouse and with living, dining, and gallery kitchen and bath main and a spacious loft level above open to the living areas below.

The total project was speculative and designed to promote the concept and value of solar energy and conservation strategies. The project was open to professionals, the public, and governmental officials for a period of over six months.

ENVIRONS

The site is in an older R-2 zoned neighborhood in which two <u>attached</u> residential units are permitted. The tree-lined street remains with well-kept properties.

The location retained some of the old aspects when it was a small town separate from Denver. On the corner was an old town hall converted to use by a Masonic lodge. The low-key middle class neighborhood had little activity with many older residents.

CONSTRAINTS

The tenant-occupied existing older home on the site was in less than acceptable condition. The arrangement of its rooms was decidedly undesirable, requiring going through an outdated kitchen to a rear-of-the-house bathroom and a main entry door in the middle of the living room.

A lower-level basement room that had been used as a bedroom had a leaking foundation wall and the utility facilities were antiquated. Budgetary considerations for both the remodelling and for the construction of a new residential unit were a basic constraint. Two large elm trees on the property complicated construction access to some degree.

ECOLOGIC CONCERNS

Retaining and protecting the large elms on the property was an issue. Inasmuch as the site was largely covered by the attached residences, landscaping was minimal. With the relocation of the entry to the remodelled residence, an east solar patio to the front of the house replaced an old porch. A protective and primary screen of bushes was planted around the patio.

EXPERIENTIAL

Eliminating the main porch entry of the unit being remodelled and providing a north protected airlock entry with door facing east and with egress between the living and dining rooms vastly improved the circulation pattern. The living room no longer functioned as a corridor to other spaces and conserved energy with the new unheated entry.

The new rear residence offered a greater opportunity for planning and design exploration. The resulting design with a small airlocked (unheated) entry to the east possessed a more enticing interior spatial experience. Entering the low ceiling entry to the two-story high living space with the open loft study space above, together with a circular window to the east harbored in a coherent in-depth reflective form (acting as a daylighting luminaire), large horizontal recessed window to the south, a glass door and window to a very small south deck, and some glazing to the north gave a sense of exhilaration and space expansion in so relatively small a home.

The angle-glazed greenhouse (set into the earth) added space and daylight to the lower-level bedrooms and central play space.

SITE

The site with its older home possessed value namely in the land. But the author desired to demonstrate a solar retrofit rather than tear down the existing structure. The tenant rental income did not even justify the value of the land.

A singular advantage of remodelling the older structure was that it was very close to the property line, allowing a wider and better approach to the new rear residence. The required zoning setback was five feet on the side lines, except when existing buildings were already closer to or on the property line.

Nevertheless, the existing home to the south was not high enough to shade the active air-type solar collectors mounted to the roof.

ARCHITECTURE, FORM, AND SYSTEMS

In addition to a focus on solar energy, the new architecture represented for demonstration four prototypes of construction:

1. *Stick Built.* On-site construction using lumber, materials, and products to optimal sizes and efficiency without waste and ready reference to the four-foot planning grid.

2. *Energy Core System.* For energy, practicality, and economics this is a preferred system. Structural manufactured energy core modules of bathrooms, utility rooms, and kitchens could be produced with integral thermal and electric connections for distribution.

3. *Panelized System.* The four-foot grid planning is directly aligned with the use of a four-foot wide panelized system.

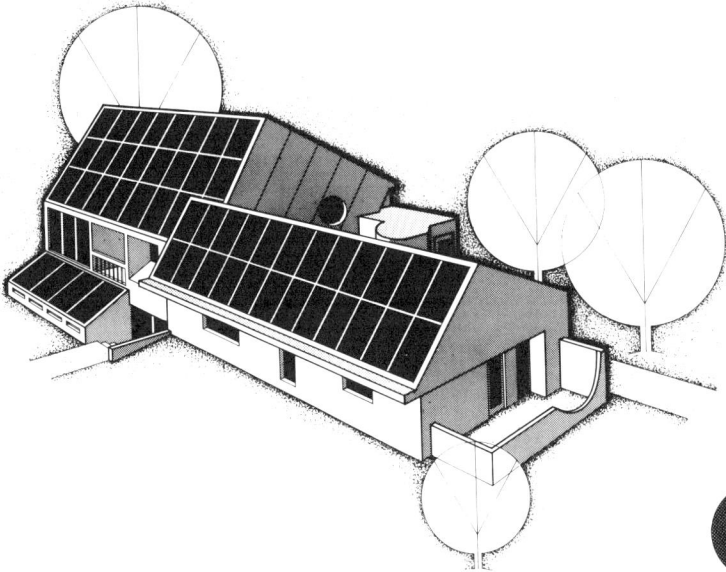

ST. PAUL STREET RESIDENCES

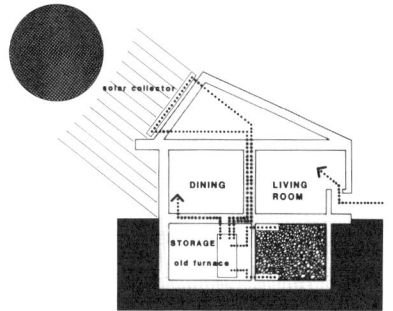

Renovation unit section

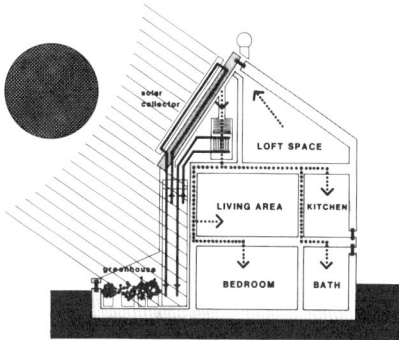

Section new unit

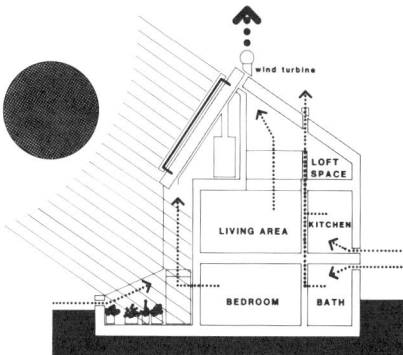

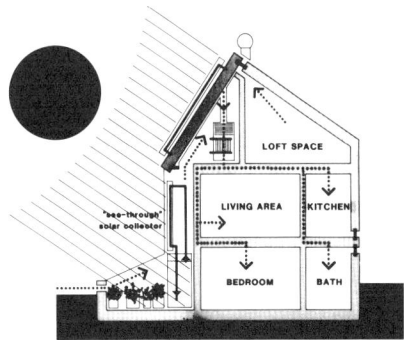

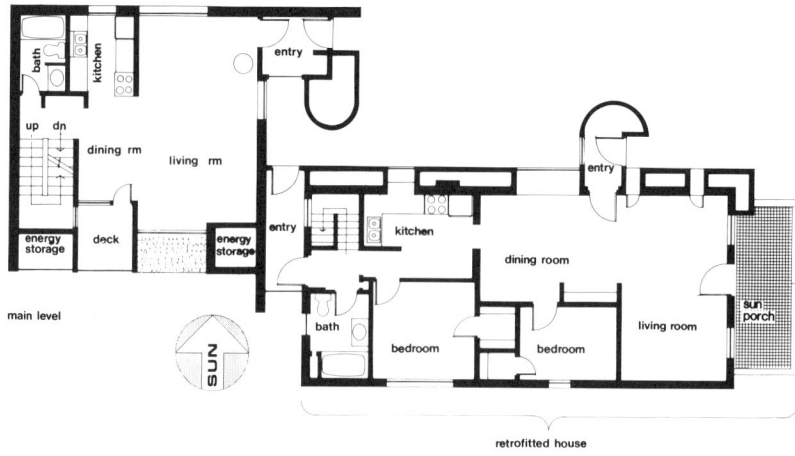

bath

kitchen

up   dn

dining rm

living rm

energy storage

deck

main level

entry

entry

energy storage

kitchen

dining room

living room

bath

bedroom

bedroom

sun porch

SUN

retrofitted house

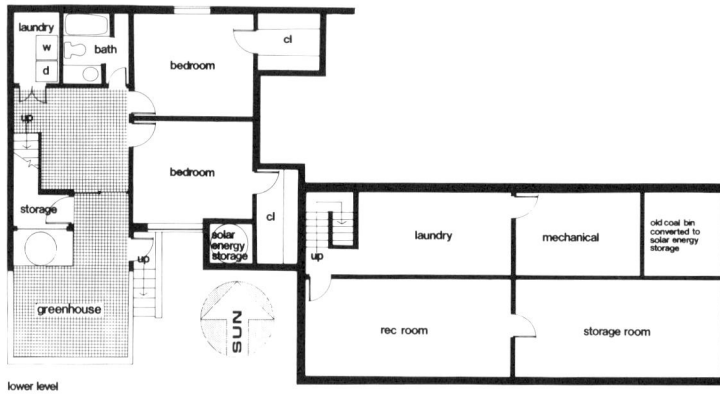

laundry

w

d

bath

bedroom

cl

up

storage

bedroom

cl

solar energy storage

up

up

laundry

mechanical

old coal bin converted to solar energy storage

greenhouse

rec room

storage room

SUN

lower level

156   Holistic Ecologic Architecture/Case Studies

4. *Modular System.* Using 14-foot wide modular manufactured sections would fit the 28' by 28' foundation. The distance factor from point of manufacture should be considered in ecologic and economic terms.

Planning and space planning on a four-foot grid would accommodate any of the foregoing construction systems. Emphasis is given to the particular advantages of the energy core module systems, namely:

- core modules of 8' by 9' by 9' could be shipped anywhere as to bulk and weight.

- the existing modular and mobile home manufacturing industry could manufacture them.

- for very large projects on-site facilities could be set up to make the core modules.

- kitchens, baths, and utility rooms are the most energy-intensive elements of a residence.

- an energy core storage module could provide thermal storage for solar gains and internal thermal loads or solar electrolytically generated hydrogen (for use as a fuel).

- the core modules would be structural and extendable for electrical and mechanical systems.

- the core units would be complete to every finish detail (but not "open" to the trades during construction).

- the kitchen segment core module would be fully energy integrated between heating and cooling appliances and functions.

- the core module units would be their own packaged system for shipping.

- the units could be stacked as well as placed laterally within the architecture.

- the manufacturing process would reduce costs and expedite site construction.

- the architectural envelope of the residence should be computerized to site-specific solar and climate-response and all other conditions.

- they would have to meet national, state, and municipal codes.

- the homes in being site-specifically designed would each have their own individuality.

- the core modules would be fabricated without weather constraints that prevail in conventional construction.

- quality control could be more effectively exercised.

- ecologic, economic, and health factors could be more assured.

- the units in number could serve any size of single-family or multifamily housing.

- the core modules would encourage the use of solar energy.

Energy integration of appliances and equipment should be primal ecologic design. Range tops, ovens. refrigerators, dishwashers, small appliances, washers, dryers, and hot water tanks all produce heat. Instead of individual appliances et. al, thermal gain and loss can be most effectively used by the holistic inter-energy design of kitchens, utility rooms, appliances, bathrooms, and space heating, cooling, and ventilating elements.

The relationship of solar, atmospheric energy, and ventilation within architecture should not be lost. All of the natural and technologic systems should be wedded and be inter-effective within holistic ecologic architecture.

This prototype residence for various construction systems offers a conceptual approach to the most practical and effectual strategies that may be used in residential architecture and design of small commercial buildings.

Superinsulation of the roof (R-52) and of the north wall (R-46) and over R-30 for other exterior exposures. Rockwool was used as the principal insulation material. It has greater insulation value than a comparative thickness of Fiberglass and due to its density avoids micro-convective losses, has some thermal mass, and packs in better between framing members.

The main solar energy system for space heating and domestic hot water consisted of 560 square feet copper selective black chrome surface, fluid-type, drainback flat-plate solar collectors facing due south with a 1,000-gallon (4-foot diameter by 12 feet high) Fiberglass thermal storage tank and insulated piping to an oversized heat transfer coil in a downflow furnace. Distribution was through a conventional duct system to all interior spaces on the three levels. An electrostatic filtration plus activated charcoal filter (after the electrostatic filter to adsorb ozone, some gases, and odors) avoided the danger of levels of ozone harmful to the respiratory system that can be produced by the electrostatic filters.

The greenhouse acts as a direct passive solar collector and is further augmented with solar gain from a "see-through" collector at the stairway between floors. Acting as an "open" system, water is pumped on solar demand through the black fin tube collector and heats a dark 380-gallon thermal tank that also receives direct solar radiation. Some passive solar gain is also received through windows of the lower and main level and secondary passive solar gains through glass sliding doors to the greenhouse.

The net result is that this prototype project was 100-percent solar heated. The sectional drawings illustrate the different modes of solar heating and also the recovery of the upper study ceiling-level heated air for destratification to the lowest and coolest point of the dwelling. Internal loads generated from appliances, lighting, and people were thus also more compatibly and comfortably distributed throughout the interior spaces.

As a matter of outdoor air tempering, cooling by horizontal vent panels along the front of the greenhouse at grade level could be regulated as desired. When daytime and nocturnal outdoor temperatures were moderate to cool during the warmer and summertime of the year, the induction of air for comfort was aided by stack action and a large roof wind turbine. During very hot periods outdoor air was pressurized and cooled by a roof-mounted evaporative cooler.

The roof structure to the south was constructed with a fully accessible space behind the solar collectors for easy access to piping and other elements of the system. The intent also was to accommodate monitoring devices as might be decided, but such testing inquiry was not elected.

The cost of this project was well within moderate means. The flat-plate solar collection system was expensive but construction savings and a cost trade-off were achieved by frugal use of framing members, simple structural spans, optimal interior volume with minimal exterior surface of the 28' by 28' configuration of the building envelope, standard size glazing, minimal interior partitions, stacked plumbing, and other cost-saving measures. It should be noted that as a prototype it could be a most appropriate model for photovoltaic panels instead of use for space heating.

Due to economies in design and construction and stick-built minimization of materials and labor (which would be a greater economy with the use of manufactured elements), the time of start to finish construction was less than for an average project of equal size. Core module units combined with panelized construction would further reduce on-site construction time, interim financial costs, and in a speculative market allow the builder to be consistent with marketing demand.

The older front residence redesign and remodelling were focused on livability and energy conservation, with optimization of the solar advantage. The roof angle was changed by the reframing over the older roof to accommodate air-type solar collectors set at an angle of latitude plus 15 degrees for optimal winter solar collection.

The author had designed and had working models made for active air-type collectors. But Dr. George Lof, a pioneer of active solar collection, formed a company at the time to manufacture flat-plate air-type solar collectors. The author elected to use the Lof-designed collectors.

For solar energy thermal storage an old coal bin in the basement under the living room was used. With insulative construction and connecting ductwork, a blower delivers solar-heated air to the top plenum of river bottom gravel that filled the bin and a duct connection to a converted gas-fired forced air furnace duct distribution system. The furnace was programmed to "back up" the solar system. Inasmuch as the basement insulated solar thermal storage bin would lose some energy, the basement and living spaces above were benefitted by a warm floor.

To make the basement a heat sink and for stabilization by earth temperature, the floor was slotted in peripheral places (after cleaning up the basement). An air intake from the north side was provided to aid cooling and ventilation with summer day and nighttime temperatures.

The new roof structure built above the existing was well insulated. A north side structure was built over the north solid brick wall and heavily insulated with the brick wall becoming an inside thermal mass instead of being exposed to the exterior. New double glazed fixed and operable windows were provided. The general interior was upgraded and refurbished.

Heavy butt shakes were provided for the roofs and exterior of both residential units. But the retrofit residence's solid brick wall to solar due south (and for the most part not significantly winter shaded by the neighboring residence to the south) was stuccoed and painted a dark color to pick up solar gain.

BELLAIRE STREET RESIDENCE

PROJECT

This 1955 passive solar residence on South Bellaire Street in Denver, Colorado, is a contemporary single-family two-level home. The principal design was for a sculpture studio, a spacious solar gallery with an adjoining south outdoor patio, and living room to the front for entertaining and exhibiting the work.

ENVIRONS

The location is in a quiet, affluent neighborhood of larger older homes with some newer mixed styles of architecture. The location is convenient to urban amenities and principal highways.

CONSTRAINTS

The greatest concern was for privacy from adjoining residences on either side. The required large front zoning setback left little yard to the rear despite the relatively small size of the residence. The limited budget was a particular constraint.

ECOLOGIC CONCERNS

Landscaping was limited by the size of the site. Topsoil was saved and excavated earth was used to form large berms in the front for planting of small evergreens and other plants as a separation from the street. Surface water is largely retained by means of roof drainage, careful site planning, and earth forming.

Shade trees protect the patio. The construction is of simple, natural materials with wood post and beam construction, unglazed natural red clay hollow tile masonry units, and dark quarry tile over concrete slab on grade.

EXPERIENTIAL

Interior illuminance was extensive full glazing between the solar gallery and the south patio, rectangular skydomes over the gallery, northside glazing as the most desirable daylighting for sculpture and artwork, and full height sliding translucent shoji panels between the studio and gallery. The interior daylight luminosity was notable through all seasons of the year and provided an ever-changing ambience.

The visual and physical connection between the solar gallery and outdoor patio promoted experiential continuity. Other openings whether full glazing or upper windows were appropriately chosen for direct solar radiation, daylighting, and view.

From the living room a few stairs dropped to the solar gallery and a half flight of the stairs led up to the rear bedroom and study. The varying interior spatial volumes added to the perceptions of dimension and daylighting.

SITE

The site was relatively small compared to other sites of the block and neighborhood. At one time there was a tennis court on the site. The site was principally flat with a terrace to the street front.

ARCHITECTURE, FORM, AND SYSTEMS

The frugality in construction, small exterior surface to interior volume ratio, optimal daylighting, practicalities of function, and focus on solar and climatic advantages were determinant of form. Direct passive solar gain with the dark tile and thermal mass concrete floor centralized wintertime solar heating for all interior spaces connected to the gallery. The south roof overhang provided summer shading and a place to keep patio furniture out of the weather.

The front airlocked (unheated) entry had a sidelight to the south to benefit by passive solar gain in winter.

The northside garage entry was airlocked, preventing the intrusion of vehicular emissions and gasoline vapors into the gallery. The garage acts as a climatic buffer. The garage doors face west, and the west drive approach allows the winter sun to melt snow in the afternoon.

The insulated low pitched roofs have a wintertime benefit of retaining snow, which acts as a thermal buffer against colder air temperatures. The roof decking and interior beams extend out as roof overhangs.

All interior spaces are cross ventilated. A sub-slab air distribution heating system warms the floor areas and peripherally distributes the heated air. Mechanical air conditioning has not been necessary.

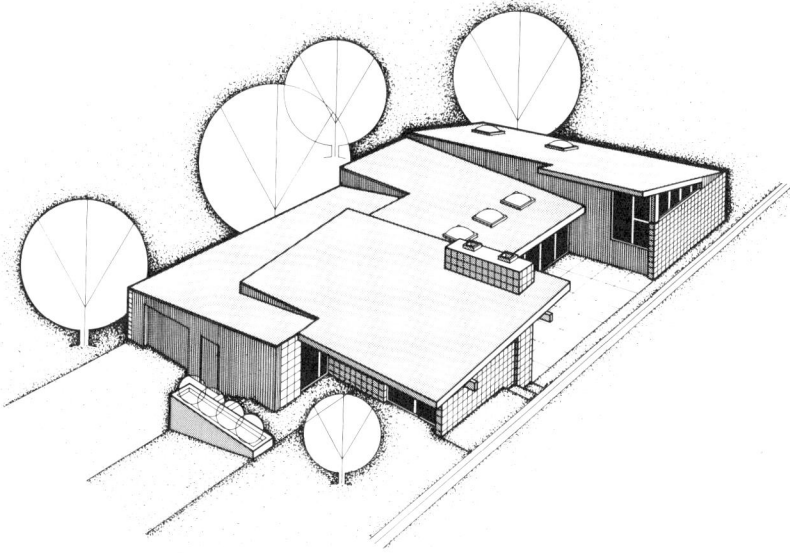

BELLAIRE STREET RESIDENCE

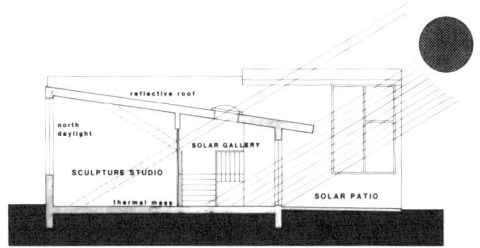

reflective roof

north daylight

SOLAR GALLERY

SCULPTURE STUDIO

thermal mass

SOLAR PATIO

Section

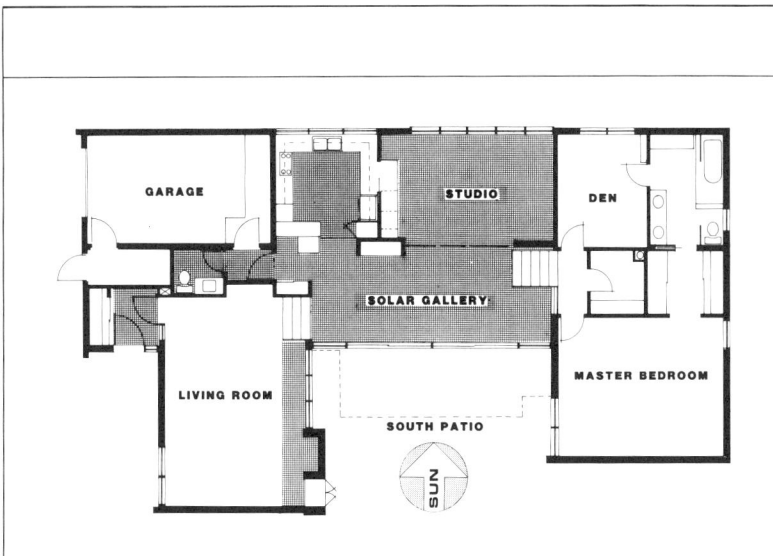

GARAGE

STUDIO

DEN

SOLAR GALLERY

LIVING ROOM

MASTER BEDROOM

SOUTH PATIO

SUN

Holistic Ecologic Architecture/Case Studies   163

ISOLATED WOODED LOCALE RESIDENCE

PROJECT

Located in a county dipping into metropolitan Denver, the property enjoys the urban amenities.

ENVIRONS

Located in a country-like neighborhood of open space, the environs are a curious mixture of older homes, barns, and outbuildings. Although close in, the lack of municipal sewer and water facilities left the area stagnated as to development. Since the building of this home in 1982 the general area has witnessed new development of some houses, apartment buildings, and commercial enterprise along the main highway to the north of the site.

CONSTRAINTS

The constraints were principally budgetary and acquiring utility access. The large site had no access problems for construction.

ECOLOGIC CONCERNS

The design intent was to minimize any impact upon the natural attributes of the site. Orientation and location of the house on the site was easily accomplished for full due south wintertime solar exposure. There was little to do in the matter of landscaping for the relatively flat site with the existing native vegetation providing an ideal setting. Natural wood materials were used for interior and exterior construction and finishing, together with an interior northside thermal mass brick wall. It should be noted, however, that persistent woodpeckers poking holes in the exterior siding resulted in the owners using a stucco finish over the wood to stop the aggravating assault when other methods failed.

EXPERIENTIAL

The design of the architecture is simple and straightforward. But with the predominantly glazed area of the south sunspaces and a clerestory above, and a two-story ceiling height atrium between the lower and upper levels, visual and psychoneural responses find a correspondence to the sky, to daylighting, and to direct solar radiation in winter of both the main and second floor level. The indoor/outdoor connection contrasts with the in-depth northside indoor protective spaces while leaving a visual and physical connection to the south unrestrained.

The planning of the home and the site lends toward bringing the family together. An upper-level central play space with a home study open to the atrium and bedrooms (one leading to a loft) and the general openness of planning between the levels provide a sensory contact. The inside-to-outside aspects of the sunspaces and the outer patio give places for play

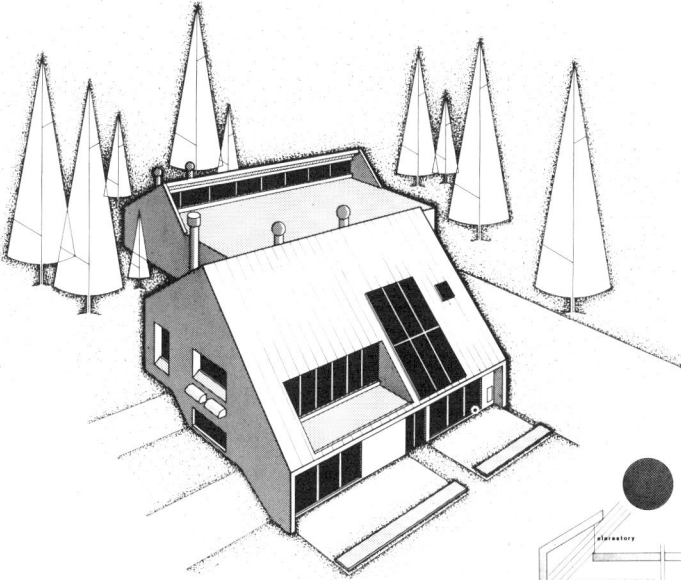

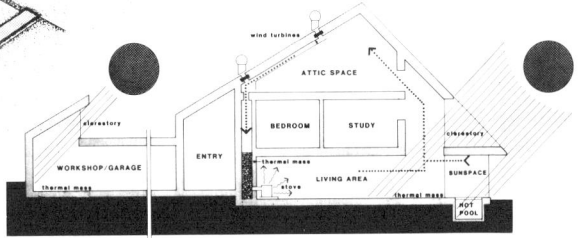

Section

ISOLATED WOODED LOCALE RESIDENCE

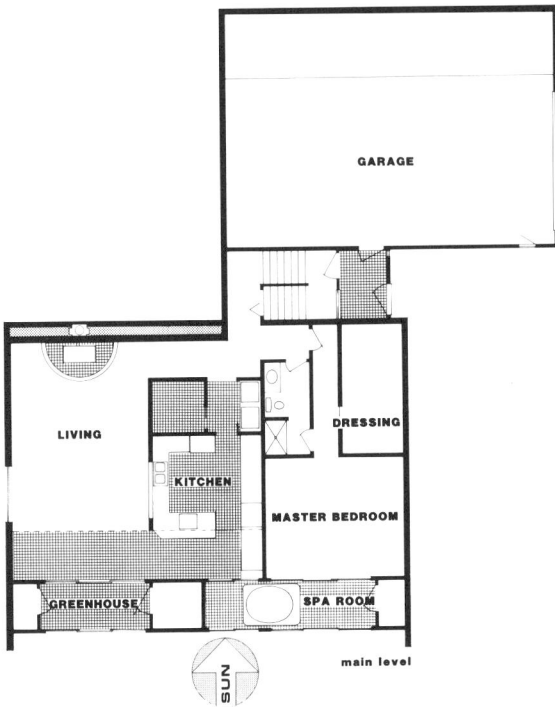

main level

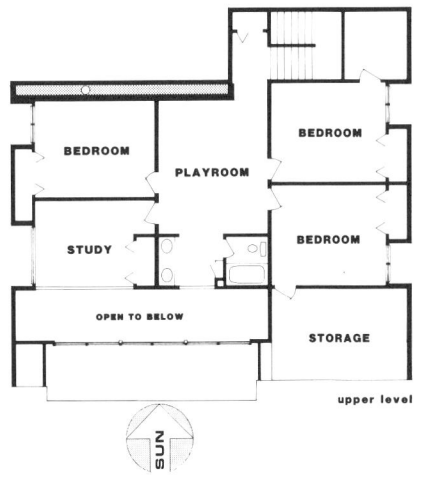

upper level

and activity. But the master bedroom on the main floor level with its sunspace with hot tub can be a haven for the parents.

ARCHITECTURE, FORM, AND SYSTEMS

From an economy in materials and labor, avoidance of waste, energy conservation, and an optimal advantage of solar energy and daylighting and view, the architecture acquired its form. *In the view of the author the architectural form and aesthetic are the end product of ecologic design.*

Standard patio door size clear double glazing is initially and in replacement most economical for fixed glazing. South windows and patio sliding doors from each sunspace and clerestory were so provided.

The depth of the sunspaces provided summertime shading and ventilation for heat removal for the comfort of interior living spaces. The master bedroom sunspace has a hot tub designed to be actively solar heated and receives direct passive solar gains. The sunspaces are designed with dark tile and concrete thermal mass floors. The solar gain from the sunspaces and the clerestory contribute thermal gain by an attic blower system (plus all internal thermal loads) that forces the heated air down through the northside gravel within and for heating the brick cavity walls.

The north exterior wall is heavily insulated and with a high-efficiency wood stove and its flue through the brick thermal mass. The cavity has return air at the bottom that compensates the south and northside thermal difference. The stove sits on a raised circular brick hearth.

Secondary solar gains through the outer and full interior glazing of the sunspaces add to winter solar gains. The sunspaces act as thermal buffers in such case in regard to the acquired secondary gains. The garage has a due-south clerestory that provides daylight and winter thermal gains to the workshop area of the garage.

The garage located to the north acts as a climatic thermal buffer. It has an east drive and garage doors for morning solar exposure in winter. It connects with a main (unheated) airlocked entry to the home interior.

With no windows to the north, few windows to east or west, and principal windows to the south with an energy-conserving exterior surface ratio to interior volume and a steep roof angle to the south for active solar collectors or photovoltaic the architecture is effectual in design.

The roof is white reflective standing seam metal and with the reflective relatively flat roof to the clerestory and of the garage reduce the summer solar heat impact. Wind turbines of the home and garage aid ventilation and summer cooling.

An earth berm around the east, north, and west elevations of the garage and house enhance the year-round thermal stability of indoor temperatures. The wooded areas around the project have a climatic moderating effect.

The design, passive systems, and the details were developed with initial and long-term energy conservation, frugality, and alignment with ecologic objectives.

RURAL SUBDIVISION RESIDENCE

PROJECT

This rural project located near Franktown, Colorado at an elevation of 6500 feet was completed in 1984. The design intent was to optimize energy conservation, daylighting, and solar gain during the winter months and to attenuate climatic extremes through all seasons of the year. The residence was set deeply into an existing earth berm for minimal exposed surface for winter wind protection with a 2000 sq.ft. lower level and 2000 sq.ft. upper level (total 4000 square feet). The upper level contains the main living area and bedrooms. The lower level has a greenhouse, utility area, guest room, fallout shelter, and large storage area.

ENVIRONS

The conversion of relatively pristine pasture land to a subdivision opens up many questions. This development benefitted by a developer sensitive to ecological preservation and the interrelevancies of development and roadways that were appropriate to topography. The large sites with concomitant low housing density result in infrequent auto traffic within the subdivision. From a meteorological study of the general area some years ago, air quality was determined to be the best between Denver and Colorado Springs by a leading ecologist.

CONSTRAINTS

A limited budget was the principal constraint. The topography and full solar access, earth sheltering, and the large site did not put any constraints upon location of the architecture on the site nor with design or construction.

EXPERIENTIAL

The quiet rural setting, magnificent mountain views of the Rocky Mountain front range, with a panoramic accord between the earth and the sky through diurnal and seasonal change provide an ever-changing delight. Extensive glass areas due south with clerestories bring daylight and wintertime in-depth solar gain to a central thermal mass of the main living area and to a northside bedroom.

THE SITE

The south sloping site with a subdivision road to the north on the fringes of a pine forest provides distant views to the south and mountains to the southwest. An existing group of pine trees creates a partial visual break between the road and placement of the architecture. The site was chosen by the qwners as a tranquil retreat from urbanization and as a place of connection with Nature. Vistas of the sky are unbroken, and the large sites have left extensive areas of native grasses.

Land forming and landscaping were planned with north and northside Austrian pines to turbulate cold winter winds. The self-sustaining native grasses of the site and additional landscaping of native materials require very little maintenance. A lower-level courtyard was excavated and land formed as a circular landscaped berm. The entrance driveway that circles to the garage is exposed to the south sun to melt snow.

ARCHITECTURE, FORM, AND SYSTEMS

The architecture is principally earth coupled, earth sheltered, solar, and climate responsive. The interior volume to exterior surface ratio is notably favorable to energy conservation. The north roof was sloped upward from the existing northside earth berm to deflect cold winter winds over the architecture. The south side has a large expanse of double glazing. The lower level has a direct gain passive solar greenhouse and guest room. A utility room behind the greenhouse receives daylight through the greenhouse and a glass sliding door.

Ventilation of the greenhouse with outside air is through a door-sized screened metal louvered section for security with an inside insulated door for air control. The greenhouse ceiling has vents through the floor above into a narrow upper (main) level sunspace. Designed as a solar-to-air transfer system, passive solar-heated air of the greenhouse is convected upward and further solar heated in the main-level sunspace.

This solar collection system, with its accumulated solar gain can with adequate plants perform as an air filtration and oxygenation system within the greenhouse. By a blower and duct system solar heat is conveyed to a central thermal mass. An energy-efficient fireplace built into the thermal mass wall is calculated to heat the central mass, as well as the solar gain received into the gravity-filled cavity between its brick walls. Return air flows out of the bottom of this central mass and back through the greenhouse and sunspace above.

The centralization of thermal gain from southside solar energy is more efficient (rather than thermal mass close to the glass that directly reradiates some of the gain) and more effectual in heating interior spaces. A side note is that with the low angle of the winter sun, secondary solar gain penetrates the main living area. The depth of the sunspace acts as a shading device to the high angle of the summer sun.

The cross-ventilated attic space is designed to vent the sunspaces during warm and hot weather. It is designed to be closed off with a counterweighted insulated panel in winter. All interior spaces have been planned with cross ventilation. Nocturnal cooling during cool Colorado summer nights is designed as a filtered pressurized air blower system located in the breakfast nook.

Northside bath areas are daylighted by energy-conserving skyshafts designed by the author. In-depth daylighting is through clerestories shaded by the upper roof overhang in summer.

The interior is not only light and airy but also with large glazed openings to the south and (door-height from the floor) the outdoor panorama fully

RURAL SUBDIVISION RESIDENCE

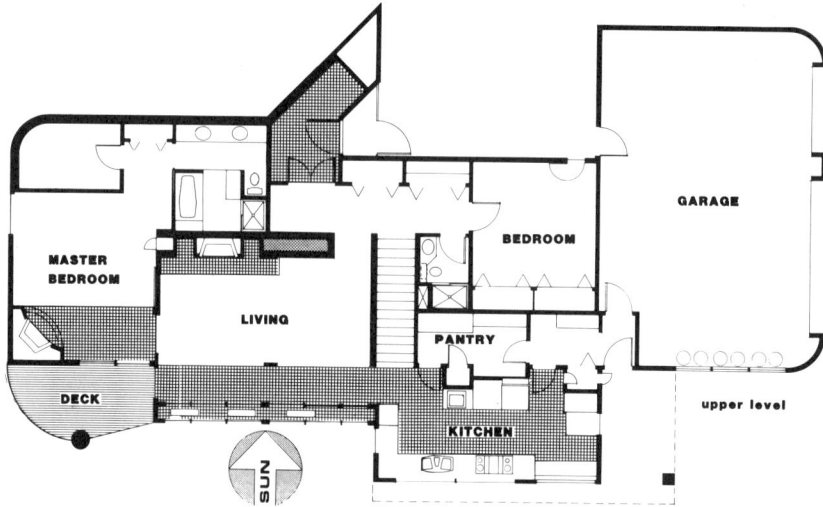

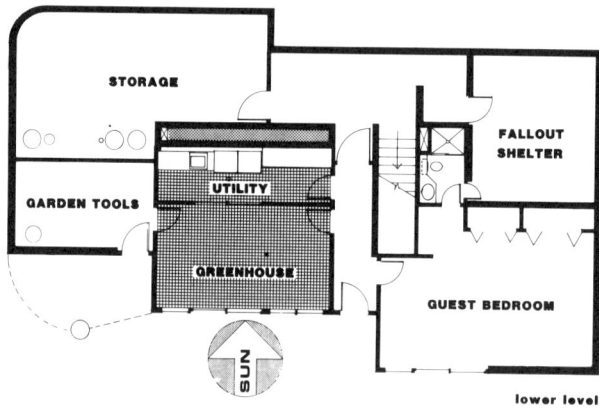

opens into the living areas. All interior spaces have flush details (no casings or trim) with slab doors to lessen cleaning.

The exterior monoacrylic stucco-like finish over polystyrene outsulation acts as a complete thermal break. With full thick batt insulation between the exterior wall studs, an effective climatic barrier is established. All plates are sealed as well as with foam sealer that stops infiltration around exterior doors and windows. Exterior surface maintenance of the walls and concrete tile roof is minimal. The exterior grey tone neutral colors compliment and do not compete with the natural setting.

The unheated airlocked front main entry is angled so as to have an east-facing door and to buffer the cold north and northwest winds. A large garage was needed to accommodate a truck and two passenger cars. It acts as a northside climatic buffer with insulated garage doors to the east. It has south glazing that allows direct solar gain in winter.

SECURITY

Being relatively far from urban populations, security was a concern but not a major consideration. Fixed sheets of double glazing provides a general discouragement to intruders. The full metal louvered panel in the greenhouse (not easily breached) provides ventilation and air tempering while also providing security. The unheated airlocked main entry provides thermal intervention and adds to interior security along with an exterior metal grillework door. The lower-level exterior door has a corridor with another door before access is gained to the upper level.

Skyshafts that serve to bring daylight to the northside bath and entry hall are of a size that does not allow human access.

RECYCLED URBAN ARCHITECTURE

PROJECT

This 1991 project was explorative. Renovation design of an existing two-level duplex was envisioned within an ecologic/biologic context and the prescriptions of zoning and building codes as:

- a single-family residence meeting marketing conditions of the area
- a single-family residence with a smaller guest house or an ancillary apartment
- a single-family residence and a separate ecologic prototype small, compact, and economical dwelling
- various other plan and developmental design configurations that cover a range of functional uses
- various volumetric and envelope configurations to accommodate solar photovoltaic cells or collectors
- single-family residence with studio, gallery, and home office
- duplex with studio and home office
- duplex, two levels, separately space zoned for guests and research; also designed to be two separate residential occupancies or be used as a single-family residence

This last option *without basic floor plan changes* was exercised as being most functional, ecologic, economic, and adaptable as an ongoing ecologic/biologic systems research facility. Additions to the east front, south side, and rear increased the square footage from the existing 1,700 to 3,000 square feet of occupiable space compact living. Flexibility in use, latitudes of experimentation, and potential of future marketability were deciding factors.

ENVIRONS

This property adjoins and extends to the north the architect/owner's Residential Research Facility completed in 1980. It extends and returns the original intent to explore, monitor, evaluate, and further research ecologic sun, earth, air, water, electromagnetic, and geopathic energies and biologic systemic response.

Within the last several years the older R-2 neighborhood has been under extensive redevelopment. Within a decade land values have increased over 400%. From older homes often less than 1,000 square feet, the latest grandiose multilevel 3,000 square foot plus single-family home or each of two residences on one 50-foot by 125-foot site separately sell in the range of $300,000 to $500,000.

A new high-end shopping center in the immediate area surrounding most affluent and parkway neighborhoods and proximity to major arterials and downtown has made this Cherry Creek North area of Denver a place of choice, only blocks from distinctive high-end shops, galleries, restaurants, banks, and other services and parkways that invite strolling and provide convenience. The site, being adjacent to the Residential Research Facility, was a practical and economic plus.

CONSTRAINTS

Comparative marketing value of new construction was a point of concern. In ecologic terms new oversized neighborhood projects with loaded amenities, profusion of windows (most often regardless of exposure), upscale materials, pretentious entries, and other motivational features set a distressing marketing norm. To a major extent older houses on a site are removed or demolished to make way for more opulent designs.

To compete and sell was one option seriously explored and to find a meeting ground between the ecologic and economic. A compromise exists in the duplex design concept chosen.

A developer who was considering redevelopment of the property proposed to tear down the existing structure with 12-inch thick brick walls, et al., and build a huge prevailing type single-family residence. Ecologic concern was the overriding factor in keeping the existing structure.

The existing 1947 structure was not without its problems. The constraints were its restrictive room arrangements, deterioration of exterior stairway, natural gas appliances and heating units in occupied space, foundation leaks, obsolete kitchens and bathrooms, tiny closets, old double-hung windows, and deteriorated asphalt shingles. Other constraints for any type of project were the roots of very large elm trees to the southeast (an ecologic plus) that limited new foundation lines for planned insulative and solar space additions to the east and south.

There is also a marketing stigma in substantially using an old residence as a main element of construction versus an entirely new structure. Using the majority of what exists was a more comfortable ecologic thought.

A constraint not usually thought about is the effect of electromagnetic fields upon our "body electric." High-voltage tower-supported power lines, alley and street power lines, and transformers produce strong electromagnetic fields attenuated by distance. Thus as a matter of prudence, using existing bedrooms and living spaces that were as far as possible from an alley pole transformer and power lines was a major consideration in planning and design.

ECOLOGIC CONCERNS

The site had the solar and climatic advantage in being an addition to the Research Facility site. The existing main floor level of the older duplex was approximately two feet below the average exterior grade. This provided a thermal advantage and was largely retained except for the front entry patio area and airlocked solar (otherwise unheated) entry that were made level to the interior floor.

The similar floor plans of each level were coincident with desirable daily and seasonal solar and climatic orientation. The one-above-another occupancies thermally benefitted by this arrangement.

Two towering elm trees to the southeast and a line of medium-sized elm trees that extended along the south property line from the middle of the property to the alley provide summer shade and allow winter solar exposure.

Reusing as much as possible of the existing on-site salvageable construction materials; reusing water and sewer connections; and minimizing machine time in excavation, earth handling, and other construction activities lessened ecologic impact and neighborhood disturbance. Fireplaces have no redeeming ecologic virtue. Although they have a gratifying appeal, they were not made part of the design.

To avoid dirt, grease, mud, bacteria, and mold from being carried to inside spaces, a switch to clean sandals is available at the entry. Direct solar radiation into the entry has a sanitizing effect on the sandals.

EXPERIENTIAL

The planned coordination between the present Residential Research Facility; relocation of the sidewalk to the curb; general treatment of the site; landscaping, cutting, and extending the front terrace; and controlling the approach provided an in-depth forefront to this rejuvenated duplex architecture. A front patio to the east and another to the south extends the interior to the exterior.

Renovated interior space on the original two levels is notably benefitted by the east and south addition. The east front bedrooms gained closet space and space for sitting, meditation, relaxation, and exercise. The south passive solar main entry and stairway (shaded in summer by an architectural canopy) provided a defined and luminous entry. This addition also provided a solar eating space extension of the upper-level kitchen and a luminous aperture for the lower-level dining room.

The west main-level addition at grade with south exposure and south walled patio has a luminous and private indoor/outdoor coherence and multiple use practicality. Full south glazing from the floor allows the reflected light from the concrete patio slab to penetrate deeply into the interior. An overhang and trees provide summer shading.

The relatively small divisions of interior space lack the lavish volumetric space of more pretentious homes being built. But the interior spaces take less to furnish, finish, and maintain and have less volumetric thermal demand.

Mean radiant interior temperatures are benefitted by the original brick thermal mass and the new heavily insulated envelope additions. Sound deadening between the main and upper levels was an essential element of the redesign. The winter greenhouse and outdoor summer garden provide an amenity for home-grown food.

Aesthetics are part of life, and the design for a solar sculpture garden on the premises is in process. Innovative ecologic furniture and lamps and sculptural elements are also in design and production for the interior.

SITE

Landscaped earth berms from construction excavation and regrading act as separation and backdrop to the south of the greenhouse. As an intent of the planning, the berms and high-walled south patio restrict outdoor activities that could be disturbing to the bedroom area of the Research Residence to the south. They also assure privacy.

Basement additions were avoided to avoid heavy machine time and earth removal with concomitant cost and air pollution. A better ecologic option if building codes and time had permitted would have been to use the excavated earth for construction.

Native low-water-demand trees and shrubs predominate in the landscape planning. Deciduous trees shade the early morning east sun and the west sun from the south patio. The tall southeast elms provide summer shade.

The large two car garage has storage space and a parking area for two additional cars and is accessed from the alley.

Roof water at the front is directed over a concrete slab to gravel-filled trenches that disperse water to irrigate the front planting. Southside roof water is channeled for irrigation. The garden area is watered by a louvered diffusion gutter along the fascia of the greenhouse roof.

Lawns were completely omitted from the planning to conserve water and avoid air pollution from lawn care (and the noise of powered mowers and blowers). The new sidewalk located at the curb allows for better natural and piped dispersion irrigation (without waste of water), easier maintenance, and a homogenous appearance. The extensive earth berming and height reduction of the front terrace using the earth in a more gentle grade to the curb sidewalk avoided the cost of surplus earth removal from the site.

Every tree, plant, and shrub has an ecologic significance. Land contouring and berming were designed to control natural irrigation and maximize the benefit of roof and surface water.

The site was treated as an extension of the architecture by its form and matching exterior patio walls.

ARCHITECTURE, FORM, AND SYSTEMS

The architectural strategy compensated for the space use deficits of the existing structure with ergometric replanning, optimizing efficiency and conservation, and creation of a more healthful environs. Energy self-sufficiency in the effective use of solar and other natural site-specific energies has remained a primary advantage. A number of alternative technologic ecologic innovations have been deferred until photovoltaic/hydrogen fuel cells for heating and cooling or other advanced technologic energy systems are available.

A commodious mechanical space was provided at the second floor level for alternative ecologic energy capability. The prevailing unoccupiable attic was also retained as an accessible space for thermal research in the heating and cooling of homes and buildings by electromagnetic, scalar, or other forms of energy conversion.

Encapsulation of the original building's large thermal mass (existing brick exterior walls) is with insulated additions to the east, west, and south and rigid foam outsulation of the entire structure including north and west portions

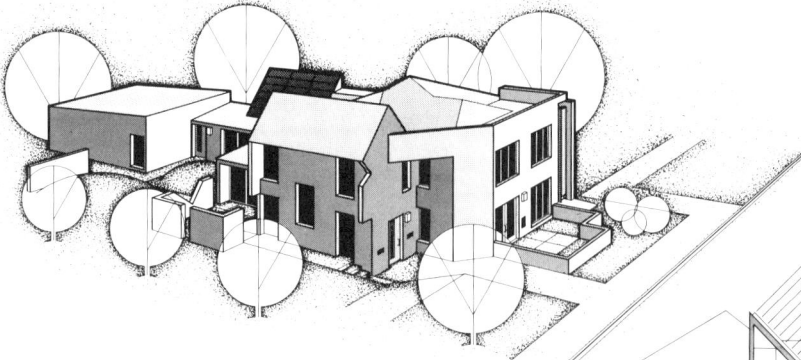

RECYCLED URBAN ARCHITECTURE

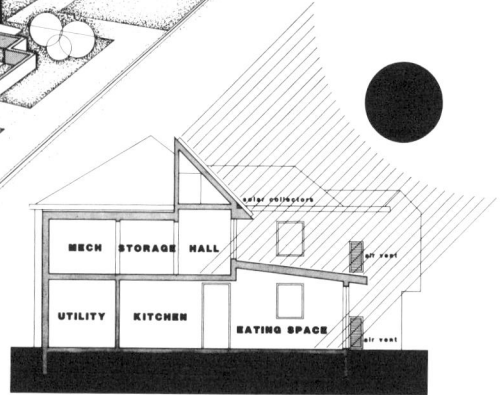

Section

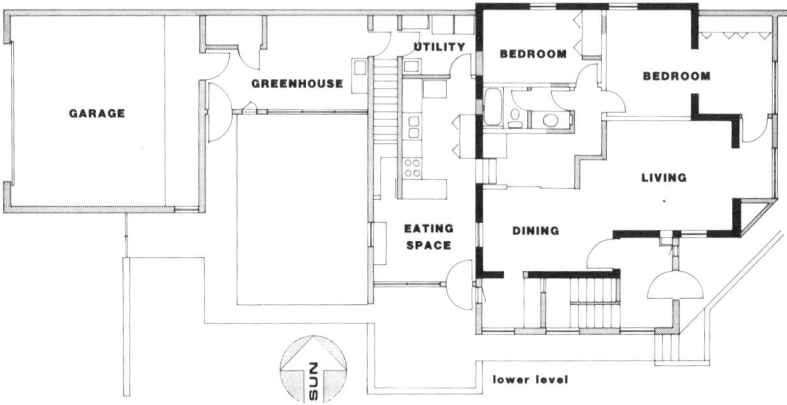

GARAGE

GREENHOUSE

UTILITY

BEDROOM

BEDROOM

LIVING

EATING SPACE

DINING

SUN

lower level

A "before" shot of the existing duplex. Note the high front embankment that was cut down to bring the main level to grade and create a more cohesive landscaped transition to the street.

MECHANICAL

BEDROOM

BEDROOM

SUN ROOM

STORAGE

UTILITY

LIVING

DINING

SUN

upper level

of the exterior. Insol-8 (R-8) glazing to the north, Heat Mirror 66 (47° reflectivity) for the east and west, Heat Mirror 88 glazing for the south casements, and low-iron Solite high solar transmissivity double glazing for the south entry and stairway enclosure and greenhouse provided an effectual use of daylighting, ventilation, and thermal advantage. Although benefitting by winter passive solar gain, the south entry stairway addition has a projecting architectural canopy over fixed glazing for summer shading to avoid overheating. Vertical casement reflective windows to the east were chosen to restrict solar thermal gain by the profusion of window frames and narrow restricted areas of glazing.

An initial biophysical concern was the presence of mold, yeast, and bacteria that in air tests was 10 times greater than that of an average house. Interceptive coating and a sealant were used to correct this condition. A nontoxic mildew control and penetration sealer were used to inhibit mold and bacteria and form a main level slab-on-grade radon barrier. Cracks and pipe penetrations were caulked with a nontoxic caulking compound against radon intrusion, plus an interceptive coating was used on the lower-level floor slab. Radon is vented from recycled under-slab aggregate.

An underlayment over the concrete was secured with a nontoxic adhesive sealer, and this recycled fiber board was sprayed with a plain, nontoxic water seal to prevent any outgassing of the recycled material from entering the room space.

All forms, openings, surfaces, land forming, landscaping, and exterior patios are integrally designed as elements of the climate-responsive architecture. Roof reflectivities were optimized to minimize summer solar gain, and the exterior color of the monoacrylic stucco (outsulation) accords with seasonal and diurnal solar radiation.

A heat destratification system of upper-level passive solar heat located under the entry stairway uses a blower for heating of the lower-level occupancy. It also serves for self-actuating electrostatic filters for pressurized nocturnal and daytime cooling. Filtered air for ventilation and cooling is separately provided for each level. Pressure relief is optional to achieve desired exhaust by reverse flow through intake air vents and operable windows. Natural cross ventilation is provided for all spaces.

With both conventional casement windows and louvered exterior vents, the option for cross ventilation can be by either means. Either under natural or pressurized ventilation and/or cooling, minimal energy is required for air exchange and indoor comfort.

An existing horizontal forced air unit was retained in the attic. If desired it could provide possible future air conditioning when CFC coolants are replaced by an environmentally safe product. A high-efficiency self-activating (nonelectric) electrostatic filter would keep the duct work clean and the interior air with less pervasive particulates. An optional roof-mounted active solar system with fluid-type flat-plate collectors can be installed as an energy source for heating the high-efficiency boiler in the mechanical room. It provides for space heating coil and for heating domestic hot water for both levels. Outside air for natural gas combustion and the venting of the insulated boiler supplementally serves the unit. All lines are insulated with nontoxic pipe insulation.

The lower level, with various occupancy use patterns, and upper level have fluid system hydronic European high-efficiency radiators with separate wall-mounted thermostats for temperature control of thermal space zoning. Due to the superinsulation, high-efficiency thermal glazing, earth connection of the lower level (more than two feet below grade), and solar energy, minimal heating was required. A duct system serving the west addition through the mechanical room was installed with connection to the greenhouse for air tempering, outdoor ventilation, solar heating, and natural cooling of air. This system serves for thermal experiments.

Preponderant glazing to the south of the south stairway addition, the kitchen eating space, and the greenhouse provides for wintertime passive solar gain. Architectural projections above glazed openings are selectively designed relative to effectiveness and use of interior space. The passive solar greenhouse with a thermal mass floor is not otherwise heated and acts as a connecting link between the two residence levels and the garage. It can be used for drying and heating of materials and items and outgassing when not used for ventilation and air tempering of occupied space. The greenhouse can be fully vented by inductive air flow through an opening to the rear stairwell vented by an operable upper-level casement window. The greenhouse can also function as a game room, for recreation, or as a workshop, studio, or gallery.

Provision was made for active flat-plate fluid-type solar collectors on the roof designed to serve an insulated storage tank that can act as a supplemental heat source for the boiler for selective thermal zoning and domestic hot water.

Bathrooms are separately vented by means of venturi roof stacks. The greenhouse is vented by means of an opening into the rear stairway and an operable window at the upper floor level. The garage is cross ventilated with a roof venturi exhaust stack and exterior operable panel through a screened louvered air intake.

Air tempering is accomplished by the entry and main stairway passive solar systems and also the greenhouse. A balance is struck between the incident solar radiation to thermal mass and the solar-to-air conversion of short wave photon to longer wave infrared energy in regard to the south stairway and entry sunspace and the "eating space" sunspace of the main floor kitchen area.

The project is superinsulated. The existing attic roof rafters were insulated with R-19 fiberglass batts with a cross-laminated low perm 3 mil vapor barrier holding it in place. The floor of the attic was insulated with R-19 foil-faced fiberglass. Existing attic space and insulation was fogged with an intervention sealer to avoid toxic outgassing and particulate emission. The insulated roof structure and attic floor system act as a thermal break and fully eliminate the need for attic ventilation. A very light colored roof, cross-laminated polyfilm on the attic side of the roof insulation, the attic as a air space, and the insulation of the ceiling provide an R factor above 45.

The east, south, and west additions have roof R factors of 38 and exterior walls of R-38. High-density R-30 fiberglass batts (low formaldehyde) were sprayed with a nontoxic sealer to intervene outgassing. The new monoacrylic stucco-coated exterior walls have thermal break outsulation (steam-expanded polystyrene) of R-8 as part of their total R factor. These additions have a low perm 3-mil cross-laminated polyfilm to seal in any emissions from the insulation, wood framing, or other elements of the outer wall assembly. Asphalt shingles of the roof were retained and received a monoacrylic coating for extended durability and weather protection in continuity with the additions.

Exterior grade plywood was placed over the existing and additional roofs plus steam-expanded polystyrene as a thermal break. The remaining original brick north and west exterior walls have 4" of high-density steam-expanded polystyrene and are finished with monoacrylic stucco. Elastomeric 100% acrylic nontoxic coating was used to coat the nontoxic sheathing of roofs and east and south additions pitched to assist drainage. Gutters have a "clean" square contemporary profile. A water dispersion gutter was installed along the greenhouse roof to water the summertime garden. The front down spout is 24 galvaneal stretcher level metal. Other down spouts are open front type.

In addition to fogging roof and exterior wall insulation with an interception sealant, the sealant was also used to coat the interior surface of drywall. Along with an interceptive, nontoxic, nonallergenic paint, it acts as a particulate and chemical outgassing interior barrier to the full assembly constituents of the interior and exterior walls.

In addition to the conservation of roof water for landscape and garden irrigation, all interior plumbing is water conserving. Low flush toilets, low water demand showerheads and faucets, and a small bath tub with shower minimize demand. Water is filtered for the kitchen sinks and an in-line magnet at the inside water main prevents mineral deposits in pipes and the hot water boiler and tank.

INTERIOR

Flush panel doors, flush surfaces, minimal trim, easy to clean surfaces, wall-to-wall hypoallergenic and chemical outgassing interception recycled carpeting treatment and underlayment, and durable contemporary "clean line" furniture minimize maintenance, repair, and replacement. With no draperies, nontoxic coated vertical blinds selected for insulative and solar properties control daylight, provide privacy, and minimize cleaning. All fabrics were selected for greatest durability, least maintenance, and as deemed prudent were made bio-protective with chemical interception treatment. All paints and finishes were nontoxic and nonallergenic. Minimal interior surfaces of the architecture require minimal materials and cost for maintenance and for repainting.

Custom made furniture and indirect lighting columns are functional, inter-adaptive, and designed by the author. The pieces were crafted by Colorado furniture makers using native Colorado woods and nontoxic, bio-compatible finishes and fabrics. Interior shoji doors and panels were custom made with translucent fiberglass and a nontoxic wood finish.

To effectively deaden sound between floor levels a clip-suspended drywall ceiling of the lower level; sound-deadening board; application of a sealant for interception of any outgassing of carpet underlayment of the upper and lower level; and recycled glass floor tiles for the lower east sun room, main entry, eating spaces, kitchen, and utility areas were provided. The stain-resistant dense cut-pile recycled carpeting over recycled pad and resilient underlayment relieves leg muscles and body tension. Nontoxic caulking around pipes and other penetrations ensures quietness for each occupancy.

Nontoxic caulking was also used around all framed openings. Fixed glazing was set directly into the structure with the monoacrylic stucco terminating against a metal stop at the glass. The fixed glass where concrete floor slabs occur was set within a thermally nonconductive channel with thermal break insulation extending through the slab to under-slab insulation that extends back four feet from the perimeter.

Existing electrical outlets were retained when possible within safety and purpose and in meeting code requirements. Porcelain electrical sockets with energy-conserving lamps, other energy-saving fixtures and lamps, and full-spectrum fluorescent lighting for the kitchen were used. A high-efficiency exterior lighting system activated by photoelectric cells was designed for any time conversion to photovoltaic power. Energy-efficient appliances were provided.

An initial issue of planning was to locate bedrooms and the general living areas as far as possible from electromagnetic fields produced by power lines in the alley. One residential unit above another helped to achieve this "distance from the alley" objective. Interior wiring was designed to reduce electromagnetic field proximity to persons in sleeping and prolonged exposure locations. A photovoltaic system was planned for research in effectual specific use.

This "recycled architecture" was planned and designed with a principal concern for research and experimentation as to materials (as the most important element for indoor air quality and vitality), products, and systems. An electrophoresis system (negative ions with Schumann positive pulse field) was installed in the dining/living area for controlled indoor air purification, vitalization, and bio-harmonic effect.

SECURITY

External high-efficiency lighting strategically placed, intercom systems to the main entry door from both levels, inner metal grilles for exterior security doors and for vulnerable exterior windows, insulated solid panel inner doors, internal security doors, and in-depth security planning act as multiple deterrents to entry.

The indoor greenhouse connection from the two residential occupancies to the garage and to the common front entry contributes to personal security. A horizontal slot opening from the greenhouse to the rear stairwell provides an overview observation of the greenhouse. Lighting on the alley and automatic-opening garage doors and steel-barred garage window accord with personal safety. The main lower level is designed for handicap access, including light switches, controls, and lever-type door hardware.

CONCLUSION

Setting the criteria of the project and a course of action from concept, planning, design, and construction required numerous trade-offs. A particular hurdle in any design equation are budgetary limitations, marketing potential, code limitations, and in this case somewhat vexing limitations as to the most effective use of the existing residential structure on the site and its interior space divisions.

Additions encapsulating the east and south elevations of the existing structure to an ecologic advantage formed a solar-responsive, insulative, air tempering shelter and acoustical intervention to external sound. The questions of the most coordinate connection with interior space, protective entries, and to have the design function either as a duplex or single-family residence were primary to the conceptual process.

Flexibility and adaptability for solar, thermal, light, the testing of materials, products, and systems and those that could be applied to the architecture were of the agenda. Biophysical, psychoneural, and behavioral factors as to harmony, harmfulness, or impairment were considered as equated with the site, the architecture, and the interiors.

Although there is not an attempt at this time to sell, the completed project fits into an untapped niche of marketing. The ongoing flexibility of this project allows it to function in a multiple number of ways as:

• a two-family residence
• a single-family residence
• single family with young, old, or any age persons living in defined, acoustically buffered separate space
• a residence with home office (as permitted by code), a studio, individual or cooperative use of the greenhouse and gardens
• an occupied residence (for security and economics) with ongoing research functions

The original 1947 duplex was adequate at that time with what would be deemed today as impossibly small closets, tight" galley kitchens, and cramped bathrooms. The main level and its entrance below grade also would be considered less than appealing. A principal point is that the change in perception of space, conveniences, and accommodations, colored with today's dreams of opulence and insatiable human expectation, is an index of gross environmental exploitation.

Palatial homes and buildings in size and amenities are springing up coast to coast that often claim to idealize energy conservation. But the bottom line is that on a *per capita* basis the magnitude of irreplaceable global resources and energies are being squandered in a headlong fashion.

Prestigious and unmindful consumption and a petro-economy are principal American ecologic penchants. But at best without significant ecologic and biologic materials and products, it is impossible to build without damage to the environment.

Some positive but mostly negative aspects were encountered within an ecologic/biologic paradigm. Local manufacture of gypsum board, steam-expanded polystyrene rigid insulation (no CFCs and in-process materials recycling), and cross-laminated polyfilm was a plus. Due to the brokerage of timber there was no assurance that Colorado lumber would be procured. Lodgepole pine (only lodgepole and spruce are cut in Colorado) was the only indicator.

The most difficult decision was in regard to "thermal break" roof insulation and that placed between wood member interspaces of the outer walls and roof. The final decision for the roofs was two exterior grade plywood sheets with a steam-expanded polystyrene board core (R-8) between them. The plywood was directly compatible to the application of a nontoxic 100% elastomeric acrylic water-based fluid-applied roofing. AirKrete, a completely nontoxic magnesium oxide (extracted from Gulf of Mexico sea water), was the best biologic candidate for insulation but was too costly, experimental, and difficult to install under prevailing conditions.

At the time of construction there were no materials or products that could *entirely* be called "ecologic" and "biologic." Designing and specifying within this pressing dilemma to ideally accord with an ecologic/biologic ethic can be frustrating. In the case of this project, intervention materials and means played a major part in the construction processes and finish work. Surface-applied intervention controls and coatings will have to be periodically reapplied as necessary. Intervention was largely anti-ecologic in the need of its use as an additional material but biologic in its intervening more toxic and allergenic materials.

The heavy air pollution of noisy earth-handling, demolition, and hauling equipment is intolerable but only can be eliminated by more gentle construction methodologies. Degrees of labor intensity needed to save salvageable demolition materials are too often disproportional to a salvage effort.

Renovations and additions do not usually lend well to the most efficient use of labor and material. Total benefits have to be specifically weighed for each project against the cost, space use effectiveness, and ecologic/biologic benefits of a new project.

When more ecologic products, systems, means, and methods are available and biologic/ecologic understanding is gained through research and experience, ecologic architecture could be less stressfully practiced.

ecologic design guidelines

Urban Design and Planning

Traditional urban design has embodied land planning, new developmental and existing urban contexts, pedestrian and traffic patterns, architectural and engineering elements, water courses, facilities and recreation, land forming, and landscaping.

Urban planning, as an intervention between the built environment and Nature, has had to consider in some degree the natural ecologic aspects of planning and design. However, urban planning is seldom pursued in a complete ecosystemic and ecologic context.

The intent of this ecologic guideline is to broaden the awareness and sharpen the concern of and sensitivities to Nature's ecologic vitalization, sustainability, and to the concurrent regeneration of the human mind, body, and spirit by a holistic paradigm of ecologic design. Every part and element of urban design and planning has an effect upon the whole. The whole has its effect upon the smallest parts and elements of the design.

Humanistic factors are now generally given a higher priority in urban planning than in the past. The accord generated in the development of space and place and the connections between spaces and the focal quality of place lie within today's comprehension of identity, relevance, human actions and interactions, aesthetic stimulation, and personal experience. Such is concordant to our personal impressions of place and self.

But the most comprehensive view of *ecologic design* makes paramount the issue of its *total impact upon local and global vitality and sustainability*. Nothing less than the dynamics of the space-time equation in full ecologic consequence can be credibly labelled ecologic design. Not to be forgotten is our position as a dynamic element of Nature's vital ecologic wholeness. In this light, the following guideline is presented.

Ecologic Paradigm

- plan and design within Nature's indigenous ecologic sustainability

- analyze objectives in terms of climate, seasonal change, and sun, earth, air, and water energies

- plan and design for intercorrespondence within our biologic, behavioral, and ecologic vitalities

- pedestrianism is important to urban vitality

- subsume our human ingenuity and decisions to ecologic viability, of which we are a dependent part

- use microorganic and total species planning as basic to ecologic design

- attenuate climatic extremes and create natural microclimates in accord with functional use

- site and design structures in accord with the energies of sun, earth, air, and water

- treat all design in the context of an energy dynamic

- effectively integrate a correspondence between residential, commercial, recreational, educational, and other facilities

- well planned urban growth can avoid energy waste of urban sprawl

- consider both the local and global ecologic effects of land planning decisions

- localized mini-parks within the urban fabric can relieve architectural density and ingrain ecologic elements

- water bodies and courses can be an important ecologic medium for aquatic species and wildlife

Land Planning

- how vital we can make public and private environments is the key to land planning, architecture, and interior design

- land forming and landscaping can not only attenuate climatic extremes and provide enclaves for gathering but also provide oxygenation of the air, vital negative ionization, and reduction of noise and air pollution

- summer shade, evaporative cooling, and wintertime interception and redirection of cold winter winds and turbulation to act as natural wind screens can reduce the climatic impact on both outdoor spaces and the architecture

- every blade of grass, every bush, every tree has an ecologic and climate-responsive function. When land forming and landscaping are adroitly used to achieve effective and protective enclaves and microclimates, an appealing aesthetic is the end product. Land planning with landscaping and architectural elements can bring people together or tend to separate them

- holistic planning in regard to the built and neighboring environs

- planning that reinforces the relevancy between buildings

- open space planning that enhances functional adaptability to buildings

Bio-sensory Response

- all environs condition and control our psychoneural responses and our course of action

- planned wooded areas, open areas, and water with places that allow for escape or for human connections, transactions, and socialization can enhance our accord with sensitive land planning

- planning that encompasses all seasons of the year, abides by the rhythm of day and night, and encourages safe and civilized behavior has a vitalizing biophysical and psychoneural effect

- land planning and architecture in a broad perspective provide the exercise of mind and body

- as we may choose to walk, stand, sit, run, and ascend or descend stairs or various elevations, we perceive our environment differently

- looking up at a high point or down from a high point, our perspective and perceptions are changed

- land planning and architecture are disciplines in practice of stress and stress release. Settings that we create can provide an ambience of composure or may lean towards action and exuberance

- from an ecologic standpoint we are earth creatures with a biologic and psychoneural affinity more with low-rise than high-rise structures

- focal elements within land planning provide mental guideposts and markers of distance

- architecture serves also to regulate our spatial comprehension and sense of place

- our relationship to the sky should not be forgotten. Its daytime vault of light and nighttime dark abyss are the backdrop of landscaping and architecture

Vehicles

- pedestrianism and bicycling are important to reduce dependence on petro-fueled vehicles

- all petro-fueled vehicles are hostile to the environment

- by size, speed, air pollution, and noise they are a serious hazard

- a prime concern is how to minimize the intrusion of the automobile on roadways and in parking

- separation of human activities, mobility, and pathway direction from vehicular traffic, with interventions to keep noxious fumes, noise, and the distracting automotive movement away from people, is highly desirable

- "green walls" of foliage along highway corridors can deaden sound, act as an air filtration system, and provide visual relief

- landscaped berms, land forming, and "green walls" can obscure the view of parking areas

- trees and placement of buildings relative to parking can provide welcome shade

- subsurface parking can have landscaping above, but careful planning is essential for personal safety

- adequate ventilation is imperative for subsurface parking and admission of vehicles

- open-block parking can be attractive for low traffic driveways

- automotive vehicles composed of energy-intensive materials and using polluting fuels damage the ecologic viability of our planet

- transportation alternatives include walking, biking, solar-powered electric vehicles, jogging, etc. that produce no pollution

- small people-powered and solar-electric-powered lightweight vehicles should be developed. These can also be used to move light loads from place to place

Amenities and Process

- solar photovoltaics can provide energy for street lighting and other public places

- high-efficiency lighting fixtures and lamps and their effectual placement should accord with safety and energy conservation

- all electrical power and feeder lines should be underground, although hopefully more and more *in situ* solar electric systems will be incorporated into homes and buildings

- land contouring, selection of landscape materials, and conservation of surface and roof water can conserve our municipal water supply

- careful planning can minimize machine time, cut and fill, and other earth handling

- concrete is a better ecologic choice for roadways and walks than more polluting bituminous materials

- total land planning and architecture should be integrated in ecologic, energy, and aesthetic terms

- resource recycling should be incorporated into all urban design and land planning decisions

- seasonal outdoor cultural, recreational, transactional, and societal activities appropriate to all ages can effectively be optimized with outdoor space planning and design

- architecture can benefit by a visual and actual continuity of Nature brought into the interior and the interior extended into the outdoor setting

- both underground architecture and roofscaping can add a practical and ecologic dimension to urban design and land planning

- physical safety as a high priority encourages the use of public spaces. Daytime as well as nighttime planning is critical to this end

- public restrooms and other facilities that pose a risk of molestation should be located, designed, and monitored with special concern

- plan for fire, police, ambulance, and other emergency services

- phone and emergency call boxes should be located for personal and collective safety and convenience

- safety should be a planning concern as to the water hazards of fountains, ponds, pools, streams, and larger water bodies. Ecologic factors should be prime to design

- bridges of ecologic design can provide access and add a measure of delight. Stepping stones across shallow water can be a challenging pleasure but a liability risk.

- liability risks are an element of planning and design

- locate people places away from power lines, microwave towers, and other electromagnetic hazards

- cognizance of air flight patterns and concomitant noise is important in planning

- plan for ease in servicing within minimal maintenance design

Residential Architecture

In the construction of a new home, various considerations in planning and design can conserve on energy and the cost of utilities and provide greater indoor comfort and an indoor environment more conducive to health.

Less waste of construction materials and labor, climate-responsive design, and making the best use of site-specific sun, earth, air, and water energies can conserve Nature's ecosystemic vitality. As Nature's vitality is sustained, we sustain our own vitality.

Duplexes, townhomes, and other forms of attached housing benefit by the commonality of wall and volume that reduces energy loss. The planning and design of attached and multilevel housing can usually circumvent the implied architectural limitations in use of solar and other natural energy alternatives.

Site development and architecture can be responsibly guided by an ecologic ethic. Community water purification, solar and hydrogen power generation, and property maintenance with possible gardening and other conservation activities within an aggregation of housing can be economic as well as ecologic.

Using finite resources and petro-energy for residential architecture contributes to "global warming," "acid rain" (from power plants), and depletion of the stratospheric ozone layer. Homes pollute the air on a life-cycle basis by their consumption of utility energy. By frugal design but with an emphasis on quality materials, workmanship, and building methods, features can be incorporated that conserve energy while not increasing the budget. Other features and concepts should also be considered that create a more livable and healthful environment and that save energy on a payback basis. You can spend something more initially to save energy over a period of years and have a more delightful home.

The Site

The best use of the site is to orient the home for the best solar and climatic advantages, to gain the best use of indoor and outdoor space, and to use land forming and vegetation to create privacy and protect the site and architecture from climatic extremes. Within the objectives of ecologic design, site-specific electives can achieve practical, ecologic, economic, and energy benefits.

- south slopes with unobstructed solar access are preferable

- a most effectual priority is to orient and locate the building or buildings to optimize solar energy

- calculating and designing to perpetuate solar access

- preserving solar access to adjoining properties

- locating the architecture as to the topography and existing vegetation and structures can secure a solar and climatic advantage

- seasonal use of outdoor space can be optimized with landscaping and architecture and to an extent compensate for reductions in architectural square footage

- when so located, driveways and parking areas can benefit by the winter sun

- saving topsoil with its teeming microorganisms and native vegetation is a primary step in ecologic planning

- excavated earth for sheltering and protective berms around the architecture can also be formed to extend seasonal use of outdoor spaces

- carefully calculated cut and fill can minimize the cost and environmental impact of earth handling

- land forming and landscaping can control wind and solar radiation, minimize irrigation by retaining roof and surface water, and provide privacy and noise control

- responding to the prevailing diurnal and seasonal conditions of adjacent properties

- locating electric power lines underground and transformers away from sleeping and living areas will reduce exposure to harmful electromagnetic fields

- using concrete for paved areas can avoid the odor and toxic fumes of blacktopping

- providing drainage away from all foundations is a good assurance against water intrusion

- using evergreens to the north and northwest and deciduous trees to the west, southwest, and southeast for summer shading will attenuate cold climatic extremes

Architecture

Architectural Basics

- orientation and location are critical to optimize the benefit of solar radiation, daylighting, controlled air movement, and thermal efficiency

- architectural climate-responsive forms, surfaces, and openings require site-specific analysis to most effectively accord with microclimatic sun, earth, air, and water energies

- small, adaptable, ergometrically planned homes conserve space and energy demand

- multiple types of housing need adroit planning to optimize solar, climatic, and interrelevant daylighting, thermal, and ventilation advantages

- exterior patios, courtyards, decks, and balconies benefit by privacy and quietness

- the entrances to duplexes and connected housing can be planned to avoid confrontation

- a construction-efficient planning module can conserve the use of materials (putting a 4-foot [1.2-meter] grid on plans to simplify layout provides a ready reference), minimize waste, and conserve labor

- maximizing the interior volume to exterior surface ratio conserves energy and materials

- thermal efficiency relates to climatic and solar north/south and east/west orientation

- for a northern climate, the east-to-west axis when greater than the north-to-south axis can effectively favor solar exposure

- avoidance of energy-intensive materials benefits Nature's ecosystemic sustainability

- keeping simple foundation lines with minimal "breaks" in plan or elevation saves materials, energy, and cost

- simple climatic orientation roof forms save materials, energy, and cost

- maximizing ecologic concerns includes our biophysical and psychoneural well-being and our behavioral dynamics

- treating outdoor spaces as part of the architectural scheme and indoor spaces as a continuity of the outdoors provides a vital connection

- we benefit in our physiologic and psychoneural responses by developing the floor plan, openings, and architectural envelope in accord with the seasonal sun and climate

- providing cross-ventilation of all interior rooms and spaces is most effective for ventilation and natural cooling

- windows located adjacent to interior partitions rather than in the center of the room provide for better daylighting, furniture arrangements, and for cross ventilation

- roof gardens, roof terraces, and roof greenhouses can add an ecological and functional delight and practicality to otherwise conventional architecture

- unusable attic and crawl spaces can cause infiltration and thermal problems

- energy self-sufficiency should be the bottom line

- ergometric interior planning and design can result in efficient, labor- and energy-saving environments

- basements are preferable to crawl spaces. Slab-on-grade floors can avoid dampness, mold, and radon problems of basements

Gaining the Solar Advantage

- the majority of homes can thermally benefit by passive and hybrid solar design. A substantial number can benefit by active solar design for domestic hot water heating and space heating

- solar collection systems can effectively use air, water, and other fluids to store heat for space heating, air tempering, and heating of water, concrete, masonry, and other forms of thermal mass

- passive and hybrid solar subsystems can be most beneficially suited to space function, economy, and efficiency

- the centralization of solar energy from all solar subsystems or other forms of passive and hybrid solar strategies provides an optimal opportunity for most effective energy utilization

- maximum glass to south, moderate amount to east, and minimum to west and north corresponds best for the south solar advantage within solar and climatic constraints

- living spaces and sunspaces benefit by maximized southern exposure in cold climates

- as a general guide for cold climate passive solar, about 15% of living space floor area can be allowed for glass to the south

- specific solar data for a specific location and passive solar methodology should be used for an optimal benefit

- shading should not be neglected for spring, summer, and particularly fall (when passive solar is prone to excess heat). Fixed versus movable forms of shading and solar attenuation are factors for consideration

- solar access, insolation, degree day considerations, all external and internal factors of solar direct gain, transmissivity, reflectivity, conductivity, air convection, and biologic and heat retention effects are pertinent

- orientation to "true" north, not magnetic north, is used to correctly determine the south elevation

- the type, configuration, amount, and location of the thermal mass for solar collection should respond to all conditions of space use and interior arrangements

- interior thermal mass exposed to the sun and by reflection received by all architectural and interior elements has a proportional relationship to glazing

- sunspaces can be useful as space, for greenhouses, or for a spa pool with separation by glass and glass doors to prevent undue moisture intrusion into living spaces

- attached sunspaces and greenhouses with sloping glass roofs invite problems (cold weather losses to sky, overheating with direct solar radiation, possibilities of leakage and breakage, surface dirt accumulation, difficult to provide shading)

- instead, standard vertical 34" x 76" (86.4 cm x 193 cm) or 46" x 90" (116.8 cm x 228.6 cm) double glazed (preferably argon filled) panels with a well-insulated roof or living space above are less expensive, practical, and avoid the aforementioned disadvantages

- a concrete slab on grade (edge insulated and with 4-foot [1.2-meter] wide under-slab R-8 more or less perimeter insulation, depending upon cold climate conditions) with dark tile is practical, functional, and relatively inexpensive (but rugs over the tile or heavy upholstered furniture can block the sun's direct radiation)

- an alternative that should be designed by a solar engineer or architect is to use dark vertical blinds or other surface that rapidly converts the direct solar radiation to heated air. Then this heated air can be relocated by a blower and duct system to a concrete basement or other internal thermal mass. This concept considerably improves solar efficiency due to diminished thermal loss and better solar utilization

• solar collectors for heating domestic hot water and a hot spa tub will save energy but may not under prevailing utility rates be cost effective

• a roof overhang for sunspaces can largely exclude the summer sun while fully receiving the winter sun

• skylights are energy losers, but south-facing clerestory windows correctly designed to receive full winter sun and shaded in summer can be a plus in energy terms, as well as the enjoyment of interior daylighting

• central and northside interior spaces can greatly benefit by daylighting and solar thermal wintertime gains through appropriately designed south-facing clerestories

• except for due south, all glazing selected as argon-filled, low-E double or triple pane and west-facing glass being reflective provides an important thermal advantage

• the interseasonal use of outdoor spaces can be extended by wintertime direct solar gains and summertime shading by trees, arbors, architectural devices, or canopies

• to the extent that daylighting is most effectually employed for indoor task needs, the greater is the visual and psychophysical benefit

• as daylighting reduces the need for electric illumination, the concomitant heat reduction will save on air conditioning energy

- planned "borrowed light" by interior spaces and "see-through" capability to other interior spaces and to the outdoors provides visual relief and reduction of tension

Earth Coupling

- the earth provides year-round more stabilized temperatures than outdoor air, and basements surrounded by earth are an example of effective earth coupling (they tend to remain at a more uniform temperature than above-grade portions of a home)

- as earth may be embanked against above-grade portions of a home (particularly northside), an earth-coupled stabilizing temperature can be accomplished with well-placed climate intervention insulation

- for on-grade construction (without a basement) the south elevation can be left at grade; other elevations can be bermed against footings and stem wall insulated foundation (to a frost line depth)

- the result is economy, use of displaced earth, and energy savings with slab on grade (edge vented for radon). Framing then starts from the stem wall foundation height upward

- garages can benefit by earth sheltering and insulating the garage

- maximum use of excavated earth for berms, embankments, and topographic contouring saves energy and money

Controlling Radon

- track-etch radon tests made prior to planning and design are important so that effective intervention and ventilation means can be applied to reduce respiratory risk

- since radon concentrations in the soil increase at a depth of 8' to 10' (2.4 meters to 3.0 meters), the design of a basement (R-8 or more insulation on earth side to depth of about 6' [1.8 meters]) and elimination of crawl spaces with slab on grade (edge and perimeter insulated) is advisable

- strategies for intervention, ventilation, and control can be used to reduce radon below 4 picocuries per liter

- a perimeter perforated drain around the bottom of foundation walls with sump and pump or daylighted is a wise precaution against subsurface water and can possibly reduce radon intrusion

- guidelines for radon reduction are available from EPA, the Concrete Masonry Association, and *Energy Design Update*

Ventilation and Openings

- screened ventilation air intakes sized, detailed with insulated closure panels or doors, and located to maximize cross ventilation can be more effective than operable window ventilation. Window locations relate to view, light, and privacy control and interior space functions

- windows best serve for daylighting, thermal gain, and view

- fixed windows with awning or casement window ventilation are advised over double hung. It is best to *cross-ventilate* interior spaces from low outdoor air intake to high exhaust

- interior doors properly located can aid and control cross ventilation of rooms and *all* interior spaces

- to minimize maintenance, all flush panel doors and elimination of or minimal door casings and all interior moldings leaves less to clean

- 36" (91.4 cm) wide or wider interior doors improve interior air ventilation, daylighting, and view from space to space and are well suited to handicap possibilities. Simple, durable, lever-type hardware located lower (about 34" [86.4 cm] high from floor) will better serve handicapped persons

- ventilation is most easily provided by screened patio glass sliding doors or awning-type or casement double-glazed windows (should be located opposite in sunspace from entry into living areas, thereby can be best used for ventilation and air tempering of living spaces)

- greater security is accomplished by fixed glazing of sunspaces with appropriately sized screened exterior intake air louvers or grilles with insulated control panels or doors

- insulated exterior entry doors at a 42" (1.06 m) width serve well for bringing in larger pieces of furniture

- security exterior screen doors that can act as insulated storm doors in winter can provide summer ventilation and winter thermal protection

- screened louvered exterior doors with inner insulated doors to control ventilation can provide security and egress for bedrooms and other rooms

- entries are best located to the south, east, or west and not to the north in a northern climate

- airlocked (unheated) entries are advisable for cold weather climate residential projects

- a roof-protected outdoor entry is desirable and appreciated by visitors, guests, and everyone else

- stack action, venturi, wind turbine, and solar inductive ventilation can effectively ventilate an entire residence, a bathroom, spa pool area, swimming pool, or other portion thereof, including an attic

- cooling towers, roof monitors, and exterior and interior architectural configurations, fins, and other interceptors can effectively control ventilation

- see "Mechanical Systems" for pressurized ventilation and cooling systems

Insulation and Vapor Barriers

- the author has not been enthusiastic about truss roof unusable attics; they have to be ventilated (including in winter), creating energy loss problems and possible air infiltration with accumulations of dust, dirt, and microorganisms

- cathedral ceilings, roof/ceiling framing in common, and usable attic solutions appear to be a better option for pleasurable and useful space

- roof/ceiling insulation in a cold climate needs to be determined, but should be not less than R-36, including thermal break sheathing to reduce energy loss through framing members or an insulative thermal break of rigid insulation under interior drywall

- a "tight" ceiling with "tight" cross-laminated vapor barrier under the drywall completely sealed should avoid any moisture intrusion into exterior wall and ceiling roof systems

- light fixtures or other items are advised not to penetrate into a ceiling/roof system. Electrical outlet boxes should be sealed

- exterior walls benefit by "tight" construction, a *complete* vapor barrier under drywall, and not less than R-24 insulation, including a thermal break

- a thermal-break rigid insulation is a benefit under exterior wood siding. An alternative is "outsulation" of 1-1/2" to 2" (3.8 cm to 5.1 cm) rigid polystyrene board (manufactured without CFCs) and exterior Dryvit, Sto, Settef, or other similar monoacrylic stucco-like finish (cement board or concrete sills with such finish will avoid possible deterioration of sills exposed to weather and sun)

Garages

- while north-facing garage doors are not advised, an attached garage can act as a good buffer to cold north winter winds

- garage air is improved with cross ventilation. A low vent with operable panel for incoming air should be cross-ventilated to a high vent (can be with roof stack or wind turbine) to vent gasoline and other fumes away from entry into the house

- 1 hour fire code drywall for the garage interior and insulated exterior walls and roof will provide fire and thermal protection

- not opening attached garages directly into living areas can avoid the intrusion of automotive fumes

- a weather-protected breezeway or vented airlocked vestibule between garage and house can avoid such intrusion

- completely detached garages have the disadvantages of lack of personal safety and exposure to the weather of persons and carried items but can greatly lessen exposure to fumes

Mechanical Systems

- mechanical systems should be subservient to and in phase with solar and natural energy systems

- the site, the architecture, the interior, and the type of space use should be regarded as an ecologic holistic energy system

- daily and seasonal thermodynamics and comfort zone conditions equate with state of mind and physiologic response

- high-efficiency systems for heating domestic hot water (can include solar) and for hydronic interior space heating provide comfort and economy

- mechanical ductwork distribution systems are subject to particulate and bacterial contamination, grounding off of negative ions, and noise.

- duct cleaning can be a difficult to impossible task

- filters generally installed are inadequate and inefficient in the removal of small particulates and airborne gases

- radiant baseboard zoned hydronic heat is a good option for zoned comfort, space-by-space energy control, and conservation

- air-to-air, water-to-air, and ground-to-air heat pumps are energy-saving options

- where air conditioning for hot summers is desired, a forced-air duct distribution system with high-efficiency furnace can be employed. A substitute for Freon is much needed as it contributes to destruction of our planet's ozone layer

- the use of natural nocturnal cooling in a well-insulated home and using earth cooling through plenums or a basement (without evidence of radon) can be evaluated as possibilities of reasonable comfort and economy without refrigerated air conditioning

- filtered *pressurized* nighttime and daytime cooling and ventilation air can be selectively designed to cool a portion or the entire indoor space (cleaner, quieter, and more effective and energy saving than an attic fan)

- evaporative cooling in dry climates can cool more economically than refrigerated systems (with no CFCs)

- mold formation in evaporative cooling systems should be avoided

- stack action and venturi temperature differential ventilation can effectively exhaust indoor space with outdoor air intakes, as opposed to mechanical means

- radiant floor heating systems unless under a surface temperature of about 82°F (27.8°C) are not good for the leg muscles

- the heating boiler or furnace and hot water tank should derive combustion air directly from outside and directly exhaust outside (not take combustion air from inside space)

- it is well to provide a 1-hour minimum fire protection enclosure around gas-fired equipment

- it is advisable not to cook with gas due to toxic fumes entering the air

- plumbing stacks favor economy and function when coordinated to minimize plumbing and also water service to bathrooms, kitchen, and utility room

- water-saving showerheads, faucets, and other devices will also save energy to heat the water

- locate solar and energy-conserving domestic hot water tanks near the point of use and with insulated hot water lines

- all plumbing lines in copper with waste lines in cast iron or copper exposed or in cabinetry avoids PVC outgassing

- exposed plumbing and pipe insulation should be nontoxic

- water purification aligns with health protection when provided for potable uses

- lead-free solder should be used for soldering copper water line pipes

- it should be noted that radon can be present in well water and potentially harmful to breathe at showers and other flowing outlets

Filtration

- electrostatic, activated charcoal, negative ionizing, and high-efficiency particulate air (HEPA) filters can greatly improve indoor air quality

- filters that remove particulates down to 0.03 microns are advisable

- molecular adsorbing filters and materials can be used to remove odors and toxic gases

- filter changes and maintenance should be a specification instruction. Proper filter maintenance should be a high priority

- self-actuating electrostatic filters avoid the electrical demand and ozone production of electrical electrostatic filters

- electrical electrostatic filters should have a charcoal filter downstream to capture ozone

- an electrophoresis effect of negative ionization and positive pulse 7.83 Hertz Schumann resonance properly installed can provide unparalleled vital air quality

- smoking should be relegated to the outdoors or to a very isolated and well-ventilated space

Electrical Systems

- underground electrical service

- main entrance feed and panel located on back of garage or away from living areas is prudent in avoidance of electromagnetic fields

- wiring for bedrooms in grounded conduit will remove the electrical field (but not the magnetic field)

- ground fault wiring near any plumbing fixtures is a precaution

- bedrooms should be wired so that "in the wall" or exposed electrical wiring is not directly behind or otherwise close to a bed (avoiding close proximity to electromagnetic fields)

- selecting the most energy-efficient light fixtures, lamps, appliances, and equipment will reduce energy demand but can introduce undesired electromagnetic fields

- be aware that close proximity to table, floor, and desk halogen, fluorescent, and other high-efficiency fixtures and lamps can cause an exposure to harmful electromagnetic fields

- using exposed radiant heat coils for baseboard or other heating devices removes desirable negative ions from the air

- hydronic electric baseboard heating units or radiators do not devitalize the air (radiant heat coils and heating elements ground off beneficial negative ions)

Cabinetry and Wood

- any exposed hardwood cabinetry, floors, or paneling using white oak contaminates the air with less terpenes

- all interior and exterior surfaces of kitchen, bath, or other cabinets covered with hard plastic laminate can act as a barrier to the outgassing from plywood and particle boards

- a hardboard without formaldehyde is available for cabinetry and laminate applications

- nontoxic finishes are available but expensive; selecting the least toxic finishes is advised

Finishes

- water-based interior nontoxic, nonallergenic paint for drywall or plaster surfaces is preferable to latex or oil-based paints from a respiratory health standpoint

- any enamel coating for doors or other surfaces that require a more durable finish is advised to be applied away from interior spaces and be fully outgassed for over a month before installation

- indoor space should not be occupied until odor and toxins of the paint or finish have been adequately outgassed

- not permitting smoking at any time during construction and finishing avoids interior contamination

Carpeting and Flooring

- carpeting and pad are easier on the legs and body than tile or wood floors and have an important acoustical advantage

- wall-to-wall carpeting reduces cleaning maintenance, but the toxic and allergenic materials of most carpeting and vinyl floor coverings can be irritating or harmful to the respiratory system

- carpet harbors bacteria and dust mites. For carpet cleaning, a central vacuum system or highly efficient micro-filtration power vacuum machine is advisable

- a nontoxic treatment for nylon carpeting is available to stop chemical outgassing

- continuous filament nylon greatly reduces shedding of irritating fibers

- a wood floor with nontoxic finish and untreated cotton throw rugs is another option

- dense, cut pile, tightly woven commercial grade carpeting with nontoxic primary and secondary backing with little or no odor is desirable

- maintenance is reduced by not having too many different flooring or floor covering materials in one project

- linoleum is not likely to cause allergic reactions, but it is imported and has a somewhat disagreeable odor

- adhesive used for carpeting or resilient floor materials installation should be nontoxic and relatively odor free

- nontoxic coatings are available to intervene toxic emissions from vinyl floor coverings

- tile, marble, stone, and slate floors can be maintenance demanding and hard to stand and walk upon but have legendary durability. Nontoxic grouts and methods of installation should be used

- terrazzo floors are another hard surface and expensive option that compromise acoustics and the physical body

- standing for a period of time on a hard floor (as in a kitchen) is tiring and stresses the body

- concrete trowelled to a hard finish can be coated with nontoxic materials

Window Treatments

- passive solar gain south windows are best without draperies. Vertical blinds that provide privacy while allowing for wintertime solar gains are a better option

- various duo-pleated and other movable insulative window coverings can be most appropriate to other glazed exposures

- in general draperies have an acoustical and "softening" effect but lack definitive light control and advantageous thermal benefit. They require considerable stacking room or in degree cover the glazing, obscure the view, and have a considerable need for maintenance

- insulative movable shutters and thermal covers can also be used but have a notable stacking space requirement

- a primary problem with movable insulation for windows is the time of day factor for its appropriate use

- exterior rolling shutters or screening operable from the interior are more effective than interior solar interventions

Exterior and Interior Colors

- in climates that have hot summers, reflective roofs provide a cooling advantage

- when cold seasons occur, darker-colored exterior walls will benefit by low-angle winter solar gains but be less heated by the high angle of the summer sun

- the reflectivity of exterior earth and paving surfaces should be considered year-round in their interior thermal influence where exterior glazing prevails

- white or very light-colored ceilings and interior sidewalls allow for the deeper reflective penetration of natural light

- doors between interior room spaces can act as reflectors. Gloss white lacquer or enamel doors in the path of incoming daylight can lighten adjoining spaces

- whether floors or walls should be a darker-colored thermal mass surface is germane to angles of seasonal solar penetration

- every interior space has its unique interseasonal climatic relationship

- the lightness or darkness, color, and texture of interior surfaces become the denominators of our visual response

- designing interiors responsive to daily and interseasonal daylighting is regarding the interior as a spatial luminaire

- all colors have an effect upon our psychoneural system

- exterior and interior reflectivity of surfaces, color, and hues has much to do with our level of psychoneural stimulation or attenuation

- forms, textures, and colors within daylighting or artificial light set our moods and attitudes

- interior paints and finishes can affect us directly. Outdoor finishes with odorous and toxic emissions can also have an effect upon us through window, door, and other openings

Commercial Architecture

In new commercial construction, planning and design can conserve on energy and utility costs and provide an effectual environment for the health of building occupants. Resources and energy intensities required for construction have an environmental effect from *source* to completion of the building. Everything is energy. Not only is the initial energy investment critical in ecologic terms and energy demand, but also the life-cycle investment.

Commercial projects vary greatly as to site conditions, occupancy type, and criteria for development. Every project has the uniqueness of its location, the perceptions for its need, its operational structure, and its economic parameters.

Even within occupancy types, great dissimilarities can exist. Within this context this outline for energy conservation by planning and design can only address common generalities. Within the broad range of basic considerations, factors common to most commercial projects are herein set forth. But adjunct category and sub-category types are also defined.

Commercial, institutional, and other nonresidential projects by size, scale, and occupancy type can more clearly have the attributes of residential architecture. Location also has its effect. An urban site overdominated by the relative size and scale of the architecture will impose ecologic design limitations.

When the solar access is limited or nonexistent, the site is in a location of considerable air pollution, and little if any landscape area is available, options for ecologic planning and design are accordingly limited.

Not to be excluded from energy concerns are the transitional and revolutionary forces of our society. The concept of office buildings as citadels of business with hordes of employees in a work day is melting away in the face of new perceptions and rapid technologic change. Architecture is a reflection of society, its needs, its processes, and its functional organization. So concept, planning, and design must acquire a new architectural reality that aligns with change.

The technology of architecture has preempted and caused serious repercussions upon Nature's ecosystemic and ecologic vitality. We have reached a crisis in which our global habitability is at stake. *Every* decision we make has a degree of effect upon the sustainability of our living planet for *human life*.

Primary Considerations

- architectural design can enhance the context of its urban setting without slavishly mimicking stylistic and eclectic form and details

- ecologic solar, climate-responsive, and health-aligned architectural design acquires a timeless aesthetic and credibility

- the ecologic discipline of design need not be counter to creativity but by its dynamic be a creative motivator

The Site

Every site has its conditions and neighboring conditions that either benefit or are contrary to the proposed commercial use. Regulatory zoning and building codes have an impositional effect of opportunity or constraint upon the proposed project, its functions, and its economic vitality.

Parking demands often are the major impediment to practical and economic site and architectural development. Cars are cumbersome, space-demanding, and polluting elements that can restrict the position, posture, and orientation of the architecture.

Inasmuch as "tight" or "generous" site dimensions may prevail and the opportunities and constraints of every site are unique, only common denominators that may more or less apply are herein set forth.

- saving topsoil and any native vegetation aligns with ecologic viability

- using excavated earth for protective berms can benefit outdoor space use and act as a beneficial microclimatic and acoustical intervention

- orienting and locating the building to optimize solar energy is an effective primary step in planning

- land forming and landscaping can control wind and solar radiation, minimize irrigation by retaining roof and surface water, and provide privacy and noise control

- locating the architecture as to the topography and existing vegetation and structures can secure a solar and climatic advantage

- seasonal use of outdoor space can be optimized with landscaping and architecture

- when so located, driveways and parking areas can benefit by the winter sun

- the architecture and the site benefit by responding to the prevailing diurnal and seasonal conditions of adjacent properties

- locating electric power lines underground and transformers away from occupied areas is a biophysical precaution

- providing drainage away from all foundations is a good assurance against water intrusion

- using evergreens to the north and northwest and deciduous trees to the west, southwest, and southeast for summer shading will attenuate cold climatic extremes

- every architectural project has an effect upon neighboring properties and architecture of these properties

- highly reflective glass and architectural surfaces can have an unfavorable impact on neighboring sites and structures

Architecture

Architectural Basics

- orientation and location are critical to optimize the benefit of winter solar radiation

- each elevation has its specific characteristics relative to solar radiation

- architectural climate-responsive forms, surfaces, and openings require site-specific analysis to most effectively accord with microclimatic sun, earth, air, and water energies

- site development and the architecture should not intervene solar access to neighboring structures nor reflect strongly upon them

- maximizing ecologic concerns includes our biophysical and psychoneural well-being and our behavioral dynamics

- treating outdoor spaces as part of the architectural scheme and indoor spaces as a continuity of the outdoors provides a vital connection

- avoidance of energy-intensive materials benefits Nature's ecosystemic sustainability

- keeping simple foundation lines with minimal "breaks" in plan or elevation saves materials, energy, and cost

- keeping simple climate- and solar-oriented roof forms and surfaces has an ecologic and economic advantage

- planning with the most appropriate module can minimize the use of materials (putting such a grid on plans can simplify layout and provide a ready reference during construction)

- providing the most favorable usable interior volume to external surface ratio conserves energy

- optimizing interior and exterior planning to effectively accommodate to change is economically prudent

- favoring natural ventilation when possible over mechanical ventilation is an economic measure and, depending upon location, a health advantage

- planning for efficiency but with a concern for functional flexibility serves both immediate and future needs

- eliminating the source or fully containing indoor spaces where smoking, noxious fumes, or undue noise compromise physiologic and psychoneural well-being

- thinking of functions and operational elements as a "dynamic" rather than a "steady-state" condition addresses reality

- avoiding noise sources, isolation, and acoustical control are of great psychoneural importance

- the condition of indoor air is benefitted by the use of effectual indoor plants, molecular adsorbers, and electrophoresis

- of considerable importance is the use of non-energy-intensive materials and construction processes

- quality and durability can dominate, in economics served with frugality

Daylighting and Solar Radiation

- location and design of atria and sunspaces can most sensibly accord with seasonal solar radiation, conditions of climate, effectual space use, and effect of neighboring structures

- optimizing daylighting with a corresponding reduction in artificial illumination and providing controls over direct solar radiation can economize on mechanical cooling and benefit our biologic vitality

- lateral daylighting (and lateral artificial lighting) benefits visual acuity even at relatively low footcandle levels of light

- secondary and adjacent interior space can considerably benefit by "borrowed" lighting

- optimizing solar, daylighting, and climatic orientation regarding all elements of architectural and interior design agrees with an ecologic ethic

- orienting south elevation to within 15 degrees of "true" north, not magnetic north, accords with optimal passive and active solar opportunities

- well-designed clerestories offer a maximum opportunity for daylighting and control over direct solar radiation and thermal gains

- north daylighting can provide relatively sustained, uniform levels of interior light for specific occupant purposes

- a roof overhang for sunspaces can largely exclude the summer sun and appropriate to occupancy, control direct winter radiation by external or internal means

- skylights are energy losers, but south-facing clerestory windows designed to architecturally control winter sun and shade in summer can provide appropriate year-round interior daylighting

- except for due south, all glazing selected as Heat Mirror, argon or krypton filled, low-E double or triple pane and west-facing glass being reflective provides an important thermal advantage

- framed windows have greater energy loss than fixed glazing set directly into an insulated surround of the architecture

Controlling Radon

- track-etch radon tests made prior to planning and design are important so that effective intervention and ventilation means can be applied to reduce respiratory risk

- radon concentrations in the soil increase at a depth of 8' to 10'(2.4 m to 3.0 m). The design of a basement or lower occupancy level is subject to dangerous levels of radon. A concrete floor tightly sealed can avoid intrusion into occupied space and be under-vented to the exterior

- crawl spaces are particularly vulnerable to radon intrusion. Slab-on-grade construction can more readily prevent radon intrusion and simplify construction as soils conditions may allow

- strategies for intervention, ventilation, and control can be used to reduce radon below 4 picocuries per liter

- a perimeter perforated drain around the bottom exterior of foundation walls with sump and pump or daylighted is a wise precaution against subsurface water and can possibly reduce radon intrusion

- guidelines for radon reduction are available from EPA, the Concrete Masonry Association, and *Energy Design Update*

Ventilation and Openings

- natural ventilation can be energy conserving and appropriate for small office and other buildings and other medium to high-rise occupancies. Plants can provide oxygen and absorb CO_2

- in such case, the location of incoming outdoor air and venting of indoor air by inductive stacks, wind turbines, or venturi applications should optimize cross-ventilation of interior spaces

- airflow thermal dynamics within and between interior spatial volumes equates with *architecture as a natural energy system*

- interior space planning and location of interior doors or other openings can be critical to good natural ventilation

- interior doors or other openings should be located to optimize cross ventilation of rooms and interior spaces

- air can be effectively and naturally tempered by the use of earth-tempered plenums, sunspaces, and a greenhouse or planted atrium to act as a solar gain and oxygenation system

- in various larger and more complex occupancies, a mechanical economizer cycle HVAC system, air-to-air heat exchanger, or solar-to-air thermal transfer system can be evaluated

- to minimize maintenance, all flush panel doors and elimination of door casings and all interior moldings leaves less to clean

- 36" (91.4 cm) wide or wider interior doors improve interior air ventilation and are well suited to handicap possibilities. Simple, durable, lever-type hardware located lower (about 34" [86.4 cm] high from floor) will better serve handicapped persons

- insulated exterior entry doors at a 42" (1.06 m) width serve well for bringing in larger pieces of furniture

- security exterior screen doors that can act as insulated storm doors in winter can provide summer ventilation and winter protection

- openings between floors can be used as an advantage for natural ventilation

- entries are best located to the south, east, or west and not to the north in a northern climate

- airlocked (unheated) entries are imperative. The heating and cooling of enclosed entries to buildings is a major energy and economic waste

- protected outdoor entries with canopies, roofs, or other protective means are desirable and appreciated by visitors

- canopies and architectural structures under which vehicles drive at building entrances, drive-up windows, and for loading and unloading should be designed to naturally expedite the rapid removal of gaseous fumes to prevent their entrance into the building and in heavily polluting breathable air

- the vehicular fumes of parking lots and spaces can invade interior space through air vents, windows, and other exterior openings

Insulation and Vapor Barriers

- for most commercial buildings, cooling is a greater thermal need than heating, therefore isolating a building from the exterior climate with adequate insulation saves energy

- a reflective roof will reflect the sun's energy, reducing the thermal impact upon the roof insulation

- the characteristic of a specific insulation material should be appropriate to its use

- an insulative thermal break (in addition to insulation) is most desirable in roof and outer wall sections

- insulation should be tailored to the seasonal impacts of climate, internal thermal load, and characteristics of exposure

- specification of proper installation of insulation is critical to realize its rated R-value

- "outsulation" is more effective than insulation. Steam-expanded polystyrene foam rigid insulation (without CFCs) is now available with partial recycled material. It is available for low-density above-grade and high-density below-grade applications

- vapor barriers should prevent moisture intrusion in the roof insulation and outer wall cavities. Cross-laminated polyfilms are less permeable than conventional types

- light fixtures or other items should not penetrate into the ceiling roof insulation

Garages

- garages that are subsurface or earth bermed enjoy year-round earth-moderated temperatures (adequate ventilation is critical)

- garage space should be located and designed to prevent intrusion of automotive fumes into the architectural interior

- fireproofing and fire safety should be a major consideration

- ventilation should be adequate. Carbon monoxide sensors to activate a mechanical ventilation system can be employed to ensure breathable air

- when natural ventilation is acceptable to code, stack action venturi ventilation can be employed to accelerate air exhausting of vehicular fumes from partially enclosed parking and loading areas

Mechanical Systems

• HVAC zoning should be for optimized energy conservation and most appropriate to need

• HVAC systems subservient to and supportive of natural thermal energy dynamics align with ecologic architecture

• active solar systems can be effectively used for air tempering during periods when the building is not occupied and for space heating (as appropriate)

• duct systems are prone to microorganic contamination and ground off beneficial negative ionization

• mechanical systems with the least life-cycle petro-demand cause less air pollution

• air-to-air, water-to-air, and ground-to-air heat pumps can be an efficient choice

• Freon used for mechanical refrigeration destroys the ozone layer. An ecologic substitute should be demanded

• economizer cycles reduce demand on heating and cooling

• pressurized and air-to-air heat exchange nocturnal and daytime cooling can also save on mechanical refrigeration

• high-efficiency equipment saves energy

• commercial buildings tend to have significant internal heat loads. Exhausting air can bring some relief

- design and install gas-fired equipment to be directly supplied with outside combustion air and directly exhaust outside

- providing a one-hour minimum fire protection around gas-fired equipment aligns with safety

- radiant electrical ceiling and floor heating systems are not advised due to the electromagnetic field they produce

- thermally zoned hydronic hot water or electrical baseboard or radiators favor comfort and economy. Adjunct ventilation and cooling are required

- location of radiators under or heated air distribution across exterior glazing in cold weather (that disturbs the thin air film) increases energy loss

- locate radiators and air supply away from windows and other glazed exterior openings (thermally efficient glazing reduces downdrafting)

- as appropriate, nocturnal or earth cooling can be employed

- radiant floor systems unless under a surface temperature of about 82°F are not good for the leg muscles

- centralizing mechanical equipment reduces distribution runs

- acoustically isolated equipment can avoid or reduce intrusive noise

- safe and convenient access for mechanical equipment is advised

- stacking all plumbing favors economy and reduction of problems

- specify energy-conserving plumbing fixtures and fittings

- all plumbing lines in copper with drain and waste lines in cast iron or copper exposed or in cabinetry avoids PVC outgassing

- lead-free solder used for copper pipe soldering avoids lead in potable water

- water filtration provided for potable use is a recommended health measure

Filtration

- electrostatic, activated charcoal, and high-efficiency filters can greatly improve indoor air quality

- filters that remove particulates down to 0.3 microns are advisable

- pressurized and air-to-air heat exchange systems can remove some outdoor air contaminants by filtration

- molecular adsorbing filters can be used to remove toxic gases that can originate from external and internal sources

- filter change and maintenance should be to specification instruction

- electrical electrostatic filters are cleanable but particularly subject to a short-term reduction in efficiency. Self-actuating electrostatic filters are cleanable, less expensive, and use no electricity

- electrical electrostatic filters should have an activated charcoal filter to subsequently remove ozone that can be generated by the particles on the filter

- sequential filtering for primary particles, HEPA (high efficiency particulate air) filtration, charcoal, potassium permanganate, or other molecular adsorbers plus negative ionization at the delivery point of distribution are desirable

- Schumann resonance (7.83 Hertz) positive charged plates correctly located can effectively receive deposits of negative-ion-system-charged particles that soil interior surfaces (electrophoresis effect). The most effective way to clean and vitalize indoor air

- areas smoking is permitted or where other fumes are produced need to be separately ventilated, heated, and cooled

- smoking areas or rooms should be isolated by partitions with outside exhaust that creates a negative pressure in the space

- copy machines and other reproduction equipment should be in separately ventilated space to remove their particulates and gases

- maintenance, including duct cleaning, filter cleaning and changes, and cleaning positive plate receivers and ionizing tips, should be routine

Destratification/Stratification

- using the upper strata of heated air at the highest ceiling level in winter for distribution to the lowest level of indoor space conserves energy

- using an air return at the lowest level of indoor space and supplying cool air at such level provides summer comfort for the occupants without cooling the full volume of indoor air

- destratification for winter and stratification for summer require the appropriate location of supply and returns, including effect upon the type of occupancy

- Casa Blanca and vortex fans can aid the process of destratification and summer cooling

Electrical Systems

- main electrical entrance and main and subpanels generate strong adverse electromagnetic fields. All service and electrical panels should be located away from occupied spaces

- locating electrical transformers and other electromagnetic-field-producing equipment away from occupied areas is biologically prudent. Equipment used for therapy is included

- commercial wiring by code is required to be in grounded metal conduit. Electrical fields are grounded off but magnetic fields are not

- ground fault wiring near any plumbing fixtures ensures safety

- the vast majority of commercial buildings have unnecessarily high levels of artificial illumination

- use definitive task lighting for effectual visual acuity and reduced electric demand

- fixtures with low ceiling brightness that deliver light *across* the work surface without glare or high reflectivity aid acuity

- a light source ahead of rather than from the side or above can be visually disturbing

- consider whether indirect lighting, low level, or more intense sidewall, ceiling, or other types and locations of lighting are most appropriate

- properly locate and select lighting for indoor and outdoor security
- provide well-placed safety and emergency lighting and exit signs

- lighting should be appropriate for computer, audiovisual, and other visual imaging equipment

- color index (Kelvin rating) of light and color surface correspondence can have a potent perceptive, mood, and attitude effect

- selecting the most energy-efficient light fixtures, lamps, appliances, and equipment that will reduce energy demand and the effect of undesired electromagnetic fields

- energy conservation lighting aligns with daylighting optimization

- provide incremental switching of light fixtures to accord with reduced lighting need and unoccupied space

- be aware that table, floor, and desk halogen, fluorescent, and other high-efficiency fixtures and lamps can emit harmful electromagnetic fields

- fixtures, equipment, and devices that emit electromagnetic fields should be located so that persons are not in sustained magnetic fields above 1 milligauss (100 nanoTeslas)

- using exposed radiant heat coils for baseboard or other heating devices removes desirable negative ions from the air

- hydronic electric baseboard heating units or radiators do not devitalize the air

- specify the most efficient and reliable electrical equipment, devices, appliance, and fixtures

- computers and other equipment emit electromagnetic fields to the side, from their rear, and through partitions that can be harmful to the operator or other persons with sustained exposure to the field

- negative ionization correctly installed with 7.83 Hertz positive pulse field locations can vitalize indoor air. Pure air is not enough; it is most beneficial when negative ions predominate

Finishes

- water-based interior nontoxic paint for drywall or plaster surfaces is preferable to latex or oil-based paints from a respiratory health standpoint

- any enamel coating for doors or other surfaces that require a more durable finish is advised to be applied away from interior spaces and be fully outgassed for over a month before installation

- various nonallergenic, nontoxic coatings are made for numerous types of applications. Their use in the intervention of toxic outgassing is often the most practical and least costly option

- not permitting smoking during construction and finishing avoids interior contamination and fire risk

Carpeting and Flooring

- carpeting and pad are easier on the legs and less fatiguing than hard surface floors and have an important acoustical advantage

- wall-to-wall carpeting reduces cleaning maintenance, but toxic and allergenic materials of carpeting, pad, and vinyl floor coverings can be irritating or harmful to the respiratory system

- dense cut pile wall-to-wall carpeting with little or no odor and nontoxic backing is desirable. Continuous filament nylons considerably reduce the shedding of carpet fibers

- nylon carpeting is amenable to a treatment when laid that intervenes chemical outgassing

- "glue down" installations should be without odoriferous and toxic adhesives

- carpeting for hospitals, nursing homes, and other bacteria-laden environments is made with a bactericide that intercepts chemical outgassing

- hard surface flooring such as marble, stone, brick, slate, tile, and terrazzo can cause physical fatigue

- wood floors can be maintenance demanding and more subject to wear depending upon finish. Nontoxic finishing is advised

- floor covering materials pose the greatest interior specification problem. Each project has to be evaluated as to factors of appropriateness, maintenance, sustained appearance, and longevity

Window Treatments

- vertical blinds provide light control, are easy to maintain, and require minimal stacking room

- horizontal blinds can with a white or light ceiling reflect daylight more deeply into a room

- exterior roller blinds or louvers operable from the interior are particularly effective in controlling solar thermal gain and interior heat loss and give the benefit of security

- direct solar radiation can be attenuated by fabric mesh

- thermal shutters and other coverings can be automated to control the incidence of daylight

Exterior and Interior Colors

- in climates that have hot summers, reflective roofs provide a cooling advantage

- when cold seasons occur, darker-colored exterior walls will benefit by low-angle winter solar gains but be less heated by the high angle of the summer sun

- the reflectivity of exterior ground surfaces should also be considered year-round in their thermal influence where exterior glazing prevails

- white or very light-colored ceilings and interior sidewalls allow for the deeper reflective penetration of natural light

- doors between interior room spaces can act as reflectors. Gloss lacquer or enamel doors in the path of incoming daylight can lighten adjoining spaces

- whether floors or walls should be darker-colored thermal mass surfaces is germane to seasonal solar penetration

- every interior space has its unique interseasonal climatic relationship

- the lightness or darkness, color, and texture of interior surfaces become the denominators of our visual response

- designing interiors responsive to daily and interseasonal daylighting is regarding the interior as a spatial luminaire

- all colors have an effect upon our psychoneural system

- exterior and interior reflectivity of surfaces, colors, and hues has much to do with our level of psychoneural stimulation or attenuation

- forms, textures, and colors within daylighting or artificial light set our moods and attitudes

- artificial illumination should be automated in phase with the penetration of daylight and its variant intensity

Interior Design

Most of our time is spent within indoor spaces. Every indoor space, be it home, a place of work, shopping, recreation, or entertainment, is beset with less than fortuitous microorganisms, toxic chemistry, aggravating particulates, harmful electromagnetism, and radioactivity. We can see some of what assails us, but much is invisible and not ordinarily detected by our senses.

Outdoor air, often polluted, is the source of indoor air. To outdoor air the indoor environs suffers to a larger or lesser degree from further pollution. The biophysical assault can in consequence lessen our immune response, provoke distressing reactions, and cause a state of environmental illness.

"Sick building syndrome" is well known. But many new and older homes and buildings can initiate and cause temporary or chronic symptoms and dysfunctions. New interiors can threaten our well-being by the effect of new materials, products, and finishes. Old interiors are likely to harbor dust mites, mold, and other microorganisms that can result in minor distress or major debility. Newly applied or very old paint can have an adverse biologic effect.

What may confidently be regarded as "environmentally safe" includes a relatively small number of certainties. From a selection and specification standpoint, the field of interior design has an extreme paucity of information. Manufacturers and material suppliers are not required to label their products. Carpeting, upholstery, and drapery fabrics may be labelled or designated as to the fibers of which they are composed. But a mystery remains as to how they may be chemically or otherwise treated with substances that may be toxic or provoke physical reactions. Even materials such as cotton, wool, and linen may be treated with potentially harmful chemicals.

The human nose is a remarkably sensitive instrument. Although some harmful substances may have no detectable odor, the nose can detect infinitesimally small increments of undesirable chemical substances. Inquiry and using the nose as a detector can give the value of some protection.

Interior ventilation, heating, and cooling can be aided or abetted by furniture and furnishings. Draperies over heating and cooling elements or interfering furniture can reduce thermal comfort. Indoor air quality can be improved by room-type air-cleaning devices with HEPA (high-efficiency particulate air) filtration, molecular adsorbers (such as activated charcoal), and a last negative ionizing stage to invigorate the air. Humidifiers should be selected with great caution to avoid air contamination with mold or bacteria. Free-standing molecular adsorbers or low cfm (cubic feet per minute) units can reduce mildew and adsorb numerous toxic chemical emissions.

It is best to paint or repaint interiors during periods of warm or hot weather with natural outdoor ventilation to dry out the solvents and help stabilize the paint solids. Paint from natural ingredients is available that is less likely to cause adverse reactions. The warm season approach is also a bit of health insurance as to when new carpeting, upholstering, or other fabrics and materials might be installed and fully ventilated.

Computers, stereos, televisions, and other electronic equipment can emit toxic gases for a period of time as well as produce adverse electromagnetic fields. Protective radiation shields are available for the computer screen, but in this country shielded computer transformers are not available. In the opinion of the author, neither children nor pregnant women should use computers unless they are a nonmagnetic-radiating laptop type with a liquid crystal display. TV viewing should be at least 8 feet (2.4 meters) or more from the screen. Halogen quartz table, floor, and desk lamps put out biologically excessive electromagnetic fields. It is not advisable to sit within 4 feet (1.2 meters) of the transformer or the bulb. For a position remote from people, quartz halogen torchieres are energy efficient and safe. It is best not to spend much time close to the ballasts of fluorescent light fixtures. Incandescent fixtures, unless equipped with dimming switches, are no problem. But they are not energy efficient. Energy-efficient lamps when located and used with an electromagnetic field of 1 milligauss or less (3 milligauss and more is particularly at a level of risk) are reasonably acceptable. Kitchen appliances and electric clocks in most cases will exceed 3 milligauss. Battery-operated clocks in close proximity to people solve this problem. Avoid the use of ionizing smoke detectors; photoelectric types are alright.

Built-in cabinetry that closes up to avoid dust accumulation can reduce routine cleaning. But all cabinet surfaces (including edges) can avoid formaldehyde outgassing by using regular "hard" plastic laminate materials or an inert hardboard. The absence of molding, trim, and the use of flush surfaces on all cabinetry and for interior doors, walls, and other surfaces will conserve on cleaning.

Nonallergenic padding and the least allergenic carpeting with tight short cut pile simplifies cleaning, has an acoustical advantage, and is easy on the legs but may not be tolerated by very sensitive individuals. A central vacuum system is preferable. But a high-efficiency vacuum with a HEPA filter and multilayer dust bag is available that does not emit dust back into the room. Avoiding dust-collecting and high maintenance surfaces is economical and leads to a cleaner indoor environment. The following guideline covers other factors that accord with health and an ecologic perspective. For residential interior design projects, refer also to "A Guideline for Ecologic Residential Architecture." For commercial interior design projects, refer to "A Guideline for Ecologic Commercial Architecture." (Note - From an ecologic interior design standpoint, special attention should be paid to these topics within the architectural guidelines: The Site, Architecture, Gaining the Solar Advantage, Controlling Radon, Ventilation and Openings, Mechanical Systems, Electrical Systems, Cabinetry and

Wood, Finishes, Carpeting, Window Treatments, and Exterior and Interior Colors.)

Materials and Products

- The intent of ecologic interior design is to avoid energy-intensive, allergenic, and toxic materials and products.

- 80 to 90% of our time is spent indoors subject to an assault of toxic chemicals, irritating particulates, questionable electromagnetic fields, radon emitted from the earth, and invasive petro-energy fuels.

- Interior space is product oriented with furniture, furnishings, appliances, devices, household and other products, and the clothes we wear.

- Kitchen appliances, televisions, lamps (designed to conserve energy), and other electrical items emit provocative electromagnetic fields. Human proximity can be harmful.

- Products produced from afar by nations that have few natural resources have from source to place of use a "pollution trail" that includes product packaging and transportation.

- There are no standards as to toxic outgassing from materials and substances of products and finishes.

- But imported products are more apt without manufacturing controls to emit toxic outgassing. Domestic manufactured products reduce the "pollution trail."

- Untreated natural fiber materials such as wool, linen, and flax may be allergenic to some sensitive individuals but avoid toxic outgassing.

- Carpeting is the most pervasive floor covering and can emit disturbing odors and toxic outgassing. Definitive controls are needed in its manufacturing.

- The toxic chemistry of synthetic materials, substances, and finishes leaves them open to question as to their respiratory and biologic effect within the indoor environment.

- Vinyl floor, wall, and upholstery coverings are a case in point. Thorough outgassing by the manufacturer should be a minimal requirement.

- The author uses a ventilated sunspace (closed to indoor living spaces) to outgas (sometimes for weeks or months) any product that exhibits the smell of toxic chemistry.

- Products, materials, objects, and anything that requires outgassing and might be subject to fading are shaded within the sunspace. New electronic equipment most often needs to be so treated.

- An outdoor screened porch or a balcony (for security) can serve for outgassing in the warmth of the sun and in the outdoor air. Magazines, books, and personal belongings can be so treated.

- Furniture is the largest space-consuming element of indoor space and can thus be a major contributor to indoor air pollution.

- It should be noted that in our toxic society, more and more persons (at any age) have become more sensitive to the concentrated indoor pollutants of our homes and buildings.

- Thus if we value our well-being, health, and vitality, the most prudent and cautious selections we can make in materials, substances, and finishes is in the interest of everyone.

- Leather is a natural product, but the aniline dyes or other treatment and finishes applied to it can be adverse to our respiratory system and body contact.

- Unfortunately, manufacturers of carpeting, floor coverings, furniture, furnishings, and equipment do not advertise the energy intensity nor toxic or electromagnetic effects of their products.

- Persistence by design professionals is *essential* to root out the truth of the "pollution quotient," energy intensity, toxic chemistry, and adverse electromagnetic fields inherent from source to delivery of every material and product.

- Our responsible ecologic stewardship and sustaining Nature's vitality that keeps us vital can be titled "*ecologic design.*"

- How we use furniture and furnishings with concern, frugality, effectual purpose, durability, and lack of maintenance equates with the parameters of ecologic concern.

- Urethane upholstery and pillow fillings tend to be more allergenic and toxic than other types of fillings.

- Before covering and being placed in a home or building, the basic materials of construction, fillings, and finishes of furniture should have no tell-tale toxic odor.

- A sensitive nose is a marvelous instrument of detection. But keep in mind that numerous toxic substances have little or no detectable odor.

- Our human ecology of health and vitality can suffer by "bad" choices.

- Another ecological consideration of importance is the relative energy intensity of materials. Aluminum in manufacture is an energy-intensive material but is energy-conserving when recycled. Steel, particularly with chrome plating, is energy intensive but has low maintenance and long-term durability. In comparison, wood (depending upon source and variety) is less energy intensive as a material and for the most part in a manufacturing process. Steel and aluminum can have coatings and elements and certain woods can have finishes that can affect sensitive individuals.

The Solar and Daylighted Interior

- Solar radiation is a clean source of energy. Its most effectual and efficient use is within architecture and its interior spaces.

- The colder the climate, the more that the wintertime sun can be welcome. But solar energy can not only heat space and temper incoming air, but also it can aid summertime ventilation and cooling by temperature differentials. It can heat domestic hot water but also be the initiator of physiologic well-being and psychologic relaxation with its direct warming rays.

- In sunspaces with thermal mass floors, walls, or thermal storage elements, furniture and furnishings and floor coverings should not block the sun's direct radiation. But highly reflective surfaces of furniture or furnishings with absolute minimal intervention are acceptable.

- Direct solar radiation can be less of a problem for some interior spaces than others. Architecture and interiors should go hand in hand.

- Draperies are an anathema due to their likelihood of being over south-sun-receiving glazing, requiring considerable stacking room, not controlling privacy or daylighting effectively, being a cumbersome bulk subject to sun damage and fading, and in initial and life-cycle terms rather costly. Their singular advantage is acoustical. The aesthetic is in the perceptions of the beholder.

- Sunspaces can not only be an energy system for the architectural interior but also a place for drying food, clothes, or whatever.

- Vertical metal blinds, if they are dark on one side and highly reflective on the other, can act (with the dark side to the sun) as air-type solar collectors and conversely in summer reflect the sun's radiation.

- Daylighting and direct solar radiation will have warming effects upon the interior through each day and season.

- Daylighting as a prime consideration for indoor light can conserve on air conditioning.

- The most energy-efficient lighting fixtures and lamps are best employed on a task lighting basis. Electromagnetic source proximity to people should be a concern.

- Borrowed light in interior spaces can be effectual for various tasks.

- Seeing through from space to space and to the outside relieves eyestrain and tension.

- The changing ambient field of daylighting and direct solar indoor illumination is beneficial to our vision and psychoneural system.

- Solar skyshafts (invented by the author) can serve well for light and with thermal efficiency for specific areas, while a roof monitor or oculus can bring daylight into a larger area.

Ecologic Ethic and Policy

- Adaptable, flexible, and ergometric planning that agrees most well with our mobility, body mechanics, articulations, and our interactions, communication, and transactions with others is consistent with effective ecologic economy.

• An *ecologic ethic* is how we do the most with the least, not sumptuous, gilded overtones of opulence. But we do not have to abandon the human spirit, the ecstasy of life, nor the enrichment of perception.

• Creativity need not be stilted nor lose its edge over ecologic platitudes. Ostentatious design can be interesting, but can we afford the ecologic price?

• There is no national energy policy nor one among designers. In the interest of Nature's sustainability, we greatly need an *international* energy policy.

• Designers can demand that manufacturers reveal all of their sources of materials and all substances toxic or otherwise within their materials and products.

• More information is needed about what exists or can be made within an ecologic ethic.

The Ecologic Aesthetic

• Aesthetics are important to our composure, psychoneural stimulation, and emotional well-being.

• Color, form, texture, and how light reflects or is absorbed by surfaces affect our state of mind.

• Our psychologic and physiologic responses are constantly programmed by the changing nuances of light.

• Our perceptual viewpoint (lying down, seated, or standing) and our mobility within space continually exercises our mind, body, and attitudes.

- The dynamics of Nature, the sky, changes of weather, the wind, aromas, and temperatures as a sensory experience provide a contrast to and relief from the steady-state conditions of the architectural interior and its furnishings.

- A "true" ecologic aesthetic evolves out of the harmony of architecture and its interior with the dynamics of Nature's ecosystems and vital living ecology.

- Every day, night, and season when experienced within the interior as from view and changing ambience of daylight and direct solar radiation conditions and vitalizes us.

- Everything we choose and plan in concept, design, and realization has an effect upon the habitability of our planet, as well as upon ourselves.

Landscape Design

The native landscape is a primal element of Nature's ecologic design. But for the most part, the *primal ecosystems* of trees, plants, and the organisms that correspond with native vegetation have been altered and sometimes largely displaced by the introduction of nonindigenous species. Centuries of human manipulation have changed the primordial aspect of indigenous native ecosystems.

How well Nature's ecologic balance fares in being altered is a matter of subsequent observation and judgment. In the main, *native* plants and organisms in a dynamically balanced setting are more compatible to prevailing conditions of solar radiation, climate, and natural ecosystems. As species of native plants and organisms die off or are suppressed, a certain vulnerability is created. Non-native plants and organisms introduced as "controls" for human objectives have often created problems in natural sustainability or through unexpected dominance.

Every blade of grass, tree, or bush, and microorganisms of the soil that sustain them, have site-specific solar and microclimatic implications. In arid and semiarid areas the challenge is how to retain moisture and reduce water demands. In areas with abundant precipitation the challenge is more one of how to control drainage and minimize soil erosion.

In any case, the more that vegetation and indigenous sustainable practicalities can be adhered to, as well as the reduction of solar and climatic extremes, the more usable the site becomes during seasonal periods. Treating the garden or landscape as a series of outdoor functional spaces and climatically organized pathways can align with and effectively benefit functional use.

Land forming, architecture, and construction features planned and designed around the principles of xeriscaping, the most sustainable vegetation, and most appropriate site use should accord with water conservation and ecologic vitality. To equate with ecologic design, the following guidelines are given.

- analyze all ecologic conditions of the site and adjoining sites

- determine the site-specific interseasonal profile of solar and microclimatic energies as to location and latitude

- determine the neighboring effects upon solar access, air quality, wind, temperature, and precipitation

- determine strategies against the effects of automotive and other air pollution

- determine the use and construction-period protection of existing trees and other vegetation

- implement strategies that can be used to preserve fertile soil and its microorganisms

- develop strategies for the retention of surface and roof water for effective irrigation (preferably by gravity)

- consider the selection and most appropriate location of shade trees for respective south, west, and east exposures

- use evergreens for attenuation of cold north, northwest, and northeast winds by relative density and air turbulation

- provide ground cover and bushes with consideration of minimal maintenance demand, least water for dry climates, and effect upon ground air movement

- consider relative oxygenation and CO_2 absorption during primary selection of plant materials

- use berms for effective vegetative summer evaporative cooling, noise attenuation, and protective wind turbulence in winter

- use enclaves, pathways, and the architecture for effectual solar and climatic protection of outdoor space

- use earth cut-and-fill for earth and vegetative sheltering of the architecture and outdoor spaces

- consider the time-related growth and scale of trees, bushes, other plants, and grasses

- do not neglect the growth factor and comparative scale of landscape elements to architecture or other construction features

- organic food grown on a site is most nutritious and energy conserving. Commercial food has a high energy and pollution "quotient" from field to consumer

- on-site organic gardens, fruit and nut trees, and fruit-bearing vines and bushes can be outdoor or indoor greenhouse ventures

- aquaculture is coming into its own and again, the more you raise and eat on the same site, the more that health and energy conservation are served

- by creating outdoor livable climates and conditions, one can in many cases conserve on the need for indoor space

- "biotecture" can itself become a living and growing architectural protection and architectural form

- various herbs, flowers, and plants that have medicinal and culinary properties can be cultivated in very little space

- birds in particular can be encouraged to nest and feed as both a delight and for control over various insects

- architectural elements, arbors, gazebos, pavilions, earth sculpturing, and other sculptural elements can provide relief and focal interest

- fountains, waterfalls (provide beneficial negative ionization), and pools or ponds can promote a cooling environs

- epidemiological methods can prevail to effectively avoid the use of toxic chemicals for insect, disease, and weed control

- paving materials that are energy intensive can be avoided. Concrete is a better choice than hydrocarbon materials Aggregate finish concrete, stone, and gravel can blend with a natural setting

- all methods and means that have the least ecosystemic and ecologic effect compliment our health and well-being

- roof gardens and landscaping can provide an opportunity for verdancy on limited sites

- indoor landscaping of attached greenhouses, sunspaces, atria, and other indoor areas can be for edible food and air purification

- NASA research studies have revealed that certain plants are particularly effective as air purifiers

  - spider plants and golden pathos for formaldehyde released from insulation, plywood, and carpeting

  - english ivy for benzene (a carcinogen) from tobacco smoke, gasoline, inks, paints, and plastics

- chrysanthemum, peace lily, and gerbera daisy for trichloroethy-lene adhesives, varnishes, lacquers, and dry cleaning

• the plant - with roots, soil, and microorganisms - forms a miniature ecosystem

• the plants not only absorb CO_2 and provide oxygen but split-leaf philodendron, spider plants, bamboo, ficus, and other common plants are literal air purification machines

• how many plants to use for space and conditions is under further study

Products

Products are intimate to our lives. In our daylong activities we use a multitude of products. All of these products represent an energy investment. From their sources to the energy they require for maintenance and operation, and in replacement, they have an effect upon the environment. Each product has its total initial and life-cycle energy demand in our fossil fuel, technologic society.

Where there should be a global policy, there is not even a national policy on resources, products, and energy. Except for some health and safety codes, products can be manufactured from any resource using any amount of energy. This applies to basic resources, the energy intensity invested in the product, (including transportation), and all steps of handling until it is in the hands of the consumer. Our fossil fuel economy promotes pollution and environmental denigration.

The ultimate depletion of environmentally damaging fossil fuels in several decades will force us to alternatives. As oil, the dominant mainstay of global energy, becomes ever less available in a rising tide of world population and energy demand, national and global economies will have to shift to less waste, higher efficiencies, and alternative fuels.

Fuels from biomass to solar-electrolytic-produced hydrogen; more efficient motors, lighting, and processes; and strict avoidance of waste and effectual recycling will hold sway. There are directions now that entertain these desirable goals, but they are meager in comparison to the magnitude of national and global need.

Proactive rather than reactive attitudes and efforts are essential. Time is against us. National and global resources and energies require international policies with sustained and equitable cooperation.

Decision makers, entrepreneurs, and designers of every ilk and persuasion by concept, design, and choice of resource and energies have a critical position to help us *now* move into a new age of *ecologic design.* A sorting out needs to be accomplished of those technical processes in extraction, processing, assembling, transporting, and storing substances, materials, and products that have either no or minimal adverse effects upon Nature's ecosystemic and ecologic domain. Financial and constructive policies require an environmental responsibility and an ecologic ethic.

The vast scientific and technologic experience we have gained in energy and resource exploitation can serve us well in the realization of effectual ecologic alternatives. We urgently need a national and global technologic information base. Technology has determined our lifestyles, expectations, and economies. A responsible *ecologic technology* can redeem our wayward and dissolute course of environmental exploitation.

Coupled with technologic misdirection is marketing. Advertising, promotion, and other marketing strategies to increase consumer desire, expectation, and product sales are ingrained in what we call "free enterprise." Marketing creates product awareness, real or illusory benefits, and seeks to capture consumer interest and dollars. Unfortunately, the scions of psychographic and demographic strategy rarely have an ecologic conscience or adequate humanistic concern. Most promotion overrates what is being sold, and environmental impact statements do not appear in advertising copy.

Thus "ecologic design" is pitted against the existing monolith of business practice, promotion, and its incessant fossil fuel demand, toxic chemistry, anti-ecologic processes, and colossal waste. In-place capitalization of machinery, equipment, and the buildings that house them also is a formidable impediment to ecologically concerned procedures and processes.

But regardless of these imposing obstacles, if we don't change to an *ecologic consciousness* in *all* things, we seriously undermine our well-being and Nature's regenerative powers.

Consumers usually buy what they perceive for need or desire at the lowest price. The effect of what they buy upon the environment is somewhat gaining in public consciousness. But while recycling has had a fortunate advocacy and public response, the more important issue of *choice in the first place* does not enjoy a comparative concern. What we do not buy of that which is harmful to the environment, to ourselves, or results in needless waste should be our priority concern. Recycling requires effort and energy. What we *do not buy* requires only restraint.

Education remains the key in public and professional life as to what choices are consistent with an ecologic ethic. Inquiry into every aspect of resource and energy demand in extraction, processing, and distribution is critical to make intelligent choices. Every individual, group, and organization directly or indirectly involved with design and materials selection should be active and proactively demanding of materials vendors, manufacturers, and marketing people to furnish information regarding *every detail* in the concept, design, manufacture, and distribution of products. Hopefully a cooperative ecologic attitude and constructive information will be provided by the various trades and enterprises.

Obsolescence

Planned obsolescence and unintended obsolescence through poor design, faulty materials, and lack of quality control of products comprises a notable amount of energy waste and concomitant environmental denigration. In sustaining an industrial society for profit and employment, short-term *planned obsolescence* is an attractive option in the design and manufacture of a product and its components.

For the most part the longevity of a product or its components in our technologic society is an unnecessarily short time. The failure of even a minor part or a product can either render it useless or be too labor intensive to be worth repair. The lack of quality control of products and their components has been a growing issue of obsolescence.

The design of products that makes them difficult to service and repair can hasten their day of obsolescence. Products that are essential to the function of a product such as disposable filters are dependent upon their continuing supply. Not only is the disposable item that serves the product a waste (unless it has a secondary use), but also the continued usefulness of the product itself is at stake.

In the common marketing process, the design of products has been acculturated to reach definable market segments. This segmentation in design and promotion has resulted in innumerable variations that have an anti-ecologic effect by their diversity in manufacture, packaging, and handling on their way to the consumer. The lack of standardization of many things breeds waste.

On the other side of the coin is the impact that ecologic design and specification will have on source materials, production machinery, distribution, capital investment, organizational structure, and management. Depending on product and all of the factors that contribute to it, the structure, character, operation, and economics of a business are likely to be changed. Our economy will have to change when a market becomes both ecologically minded and has a productive ecologic ethic demand.

The present structure of most business and manufacturing enterprises is less than optimally efficient, environmentally concerned, and socially responsible. Market share, success, and profit are principal driving forces.

But the time has come, the public is aware, and it has a growing environmental consciousness. While not acting in ecologic but a partial accord with an ecologic consciousness, the movement is gaining momentum. Architects, designers, planners, and the makers, vendors, and promoters of products in response to the "necessity" have a direct social responsibility to the biologic and ecologic effect of products.

Guidelines

- the total "embodied energy" of a material or product is from its source, to use, the duration of its usefulness, and final disposition

- only by this total equation is ecologic design meaningful

- the ecologic connection with all resources and energies employed for a material or product is fundamental to ecologic design

- the efficiency and effectual nonpolluting means of extraction, processing, and finishing of materials and products equate with ecologic design

- ancillary factors of materials and product protection, warehousing, shipping, marketing, and selling are elements germane to the ecologic economics and total energy quotient

- durability, functional maximization, and material and product reliability relate to time-frame conservation and satisfaction

- long-term durability is a preference over a "throw-away" axiom and short-term obsolescence

- multiple use design paradigms can lessen resource and energy demand

- the waste from any material, product, process, or system can be advantageously used

- standardization of parts, pieces, and all product components can result in ecologic and financial economy

- products designed to act as the package can minimize packaging requirements

- packages can be designed to act as secondary products

- packages can be designed for numerous uses and be most suitable for energy and resource conservation

- the avoidance of allergenic effects, toxic outgassing, electromagnetic anomalies, and radioactivity from materials and products (including the finish and all components of a product) can avoid distressing health problems

- a harmful bio-synergistic effect should be avoided when a multiple number of products are used together

- fail-safe components in product design can avoid greater problems in product failure

- petrochemical and other ecologically harmful energies should be avoided in material and product manufacture or use

- designing for either no or minimal maintenance, repair, or replacement of parts during the lifetime of the product favors conservation

- products designed for ease and clarity of use are "consumer friendly"

- products that deliver an "ecologic message" align with an ecologic ethic

- because products are made from "natural" materials does not mean their processing, manufacture, delivery, or use is environmentally benign

- specific nontoxic, nonallergenic synthetic products can serve better than (and conserve the sources of) natural materials

- synthetic products made from renewable resources are preferred

- claims that materials and products are "ecologic" or "environmentally safe" require close scrutiny and verification

- what is the final vote on health and safety of <u>any</u> material or product?

- choose and use biodegradable products

- *every option and choice in design has ecologic consequences*

- the vast scope of basic resources and nonpolluting energies offers a broad range of opportunity for ecologic responsibility and design

- recycled materials and products have an ecologic advantage but often can have a biologic disadvantage

- check factors of adequate appropriateness, durability, and maintenance of recycled products

- avoid the use of recycled products that emit harmful gases and particulates

- select recycled products that have relatively low intensity recycling embodied energy demand

- use interception methodologies and biologically safe interception products that provide sustained healthful environments

Systems

Ecologic systems can be defined as having the least environmental impact and the highest level of effectiveness and efficiency for the purpose intended. Systems are structures of order and functional modes, with operational integrity.

Systems are lifelines and support mechanisms of society. They function within their own integrity. In addition, how effectively and efficiently they serve urban design, architecture, transportation, and the making and use of products is critical to Nature's ecosystemic and ecologic sustainability.

Ecosystems and ecology are Nature's systems. The effectual relevancy and redundancy of natural or technologic systems is germane to their time-frame appropriate and effectual crucial viability. Fail-safe factors inherent in Nature's systems benefit the continuity of their performance.

In systems using sun, earth, air, water, electric, magnetic, gravity, fossil fuels, nuclear, or any other energy, the bottom line is: *What is the total (holistic) ecosystemic, ecologic, and human effect?* How to get the most productivity, mileage, and reliability out of any system is a matter of concept, design, and conservation. While energy-intensive *fossil fuel and nuclear source energies are moderately to grossly anti-ecologic*, natural energy systems despite a degree of ingenuity and energy control needed to effectively use them do not impose distressing adverse effects upon the environment.

In our technologic society systems often control systems. Thermostats control mechanical heating and cooling systems. The more that the spaces within architecture are thermally zoned and controlled relative to indoor task and activity needs, to solar and climatic intervals, and to occupant thermal loads, the greater can be the conservation of energy. The more that the air-to-fuel mixture and ignition of an internal combustion engine is controlled relative to load, altitude, and temperature, the greater is effectual use of energy. The more that a product can operate within its highest efficiency level, the greater are the energy savings.

We live in an information age that has and still is evolving from information to integrated technologic production. Robotics integrated to systems information has displaced manual labor. But the optimal ecologic realization is reached when the greatest efficiency is achieved from initial idea, to completed product, to distribution to place of use with the least environmental impact. To what extent the technologic sophistication of a worker-less factory is ecologically sound should be open to scrutiny. The highest technical solutions have specific categorical limitations that should be recognized within any system.

On the other hand, information, diagnosis, analysis, and cognitive structuring can be accomplished with computers and by other technologic means. The smallest energy inputs can provide the greatest informational outputs, as well as provide control over the processes that structure the urban scape, architecture, servo-systems, interiors, products, and equipment.

Without a holistic perspective that is devoted to an ecologic ethic that includes our own state of health, well-being, and vitality, sophisticated ingenuity can be misapplied. Such most often is the case in our prevailing accepted technologic framework of concept, design, systems, process, and product.

To escape our continuing ecologic injustice within our multitudinous technology and its systems, a fresh approach can often be more effective than our tendency towards gradualistic "improvements." Economic as well as ecologic benefits cannot be ignored. Gradualism generally appears safer on the economic course and equates with evolutionary change. But revolutionary change in the design and scheme of systems and production is the needed reality faced with the degree of our technologic misdirection.

The rate of change depends upon disparity between a polluting and environmentally destructive system and its replacement by or modification to a constructive one. Each categorical system must be examined within its own context. It also must be weighed in societal terms and as to ecologic benefit as well as cost benefit. To seriously entertain options as to the most effective choice, most logical ecologic choice, and societal effects and possible repercussions is a task that must address short-term as well as long-term life-cycle aspects. It is essential that our short-term technologies and economic shortsightedness not preempt more important long-term ecologic considerations.

All systems relate to time. They function relevant to the dynamics of human perception, evolving lifestyles, and technologic change. To break out of our present mind-sets, systems are a potent key to how we are viewing and will view the world. To ride the ecologic evolutionary and revolutionary tide requires patience but not procrastination. Our own human biologic system and cerebral acuity are remarkable. It is the most personal model of ecologic wisdom and power. As we heed ourselves, we can heed ecologic and technologic decisions.

Guidelines

- design technologic systems that align with Nature's ecosystems and ecology

- optimize the use of solar, earth, air, and water energies

- small energy inputs can maximize and produce the greatest energy outputs

- entropy and waste can be used for energy advantage

- earth electromagnetic fields and gravity can foster energy economy and conservation

- the efficiency and ecologic compatibility of vortexian energies are inherent in Nature's systems

- control systems can manage with minimal energy greater operational systems

- displace finite energy systems with renewable energy systems

- urgently phase out environmentally aberrant systems

- technologic design that equates with time-frame durability, self-sustainability, and avoidance of maintenance favors energy conservation

- a critical point is to select systems most appropriate, efficient, and effectual for each specific use

- organic regenerative systems can often effectively displace immutable technologic systems

- planned coherence with Nature, daylight, and sun favors ecologic and our physiologic, psychoneural, and responsive vitalities

- the scale and magnitude of systems can equate with risk and means of safe control

- systems that proliferate production can benefit or be counter to health and well-being

- all systems have resource and energy consequences

- all systems have societal and economic consequences

- avoid systems that are in conflict with each other

- our well-being depends on ecologic systems economics rather than our prevailing anti-ecologic economics

- systems can be self-generating as well as planned

- a holistic perspective in systems, concept, design, and realization is critical to ecologic consequences

- the interdependency and redundancy of systems should not be overlooked

- the use of ecologic systems is essential to every phase of design regardless of scale or application

- systems can function on natural energies and require little or no manual attention

- as we design systems that are not compromised by human neglect, we favor effectual operation

- computers are needed that do not emit adverse radiation and electromagnetic fields

- the integrity of a system depends upon the integrity of its subsystems

- redundancy can save a system from failure

The Ultimate Reality

The greater the world population and the more that we design, make, and construct to serve that population, the greater is the increment of environmental harm. Industrial nations lead the world in the exploitation of finite global resources and energy. The United States with 6% of the world's population is the leading exploiter of the world's resources and energy.

Even with an ecologic conscience, ecologic intent, and ecologic design it is impossible to completely avoid a degree of impact upon the local and global environment. Our prevailing fossil fuel economy and electromagnetic and toxic chemical technologies will not disappear overnight.

The huge in-place commercial and industrial investment in facilities, equipment, processes, organization structures, marketing, and distribution will not suddenly change. The corporate mind, its perceptions, and its ways are deeply ingrained in our total society.

Designers have an edge over most of society. Within their creative domain they can abide by a responsible philosophic ethic and modus that guides their work. An ecologic ethic and credo can immediately and without fanfare be accepted by a designer and "ecologic design" be principal to the designer's work.

Perceptual and economic constraints will hamper the ecologic design intent. But with ardor, persistence, ingenuity, and influence on principal decision makers, the course of ecologic design can be set.

In many commercial and industrial operations the resources and energies used are not easily nor economically replaced by more benign and less ecologically damaging materials, processes, and energies. The pressing question is, what should a designer or other person in a design decision position do?

Many products and materials that are anti-ecologic should not even exist. Industry is quick to cry when faced with an economic impact of much less consequence than abandonment of their venture. In defense they often voice warnings of unemployment.

But we are in revolutionary technologic, societal, political, and economic times. Hardships are bound to occur. *Drastic changes are needed to significantly embrace an ecologic ethic and ecologic design.* But like voices of freedom now ringing around the world, Nature's ecosystemic sustainability and ecologic viability and our own measure of health and vitality require their freedom from technologic exploitation and productive misdirection.

The ultimate fate of our species lies within our hands at this critical time. We worship personal power, prestige, and wealth. The designs of vehicles, architecture, interiors, and products are too often aimed at personal visions of unabated luxury, status, or personal power than at an ecologic state of mind.

As a designer I admire the sophistication of the high-tech look. But I do not believe that we have to abandon technologic sophistication. Rather, it should accord with natural ecologic forces and optimal conservation of finite resources and energies. The contemporary design perspective aligns with basic functions, simplicity of statement, honesty in materials and methods, and freedom to express within a highly disciplined design vocabulary.

The clean lines and functional simplicity of contemporary design are more adapted to materials and labor frugality, ease of maintenance, and ecologic economics. Contemporary design in its broadest sense should not be envisioned as any particular style, but rather the freedom to design, specify, and construct what is most appropriate to the intended purpose, consistent with ecologic and health-giving objectives, frugality in use of resources, and avoidance of deprecating and harmful energies.

It is of note that the most ancient of architecture abided more closely to what we can claim as ecologic design than the architecture of today. Structure, form, and materials choice and correspondence to the locale and climate distinguished this architecture. While not-so-ancient Greek, Roman, and other historic architectural styles still persist, they now exist as inappropriate stylism or humorous anecdotes mostly without an ecologic accord.

It is best to take Nature more seriously. We are part and parcel and at the top of the ecologic chain. As we by design destroy the ecologic links, we undermine our own well-being and future. The ultimate reality is upon us: to what degree and how well we respond determine our fate.

Informational Base for Ecologic Design

An ardent concern, search, gathering, evaluation, and documentation of methodologies, materials, and products is critically needed to encompass ecologic design. Within architecture this was a directional role played by the American Institute of Architects Research Corporation during the late 1970s and early 1980s. It is most regrettable that this organization and this impetus lost continuity as a solar, energy conservation, and environmental ethic. In the light of today's scientific, technologic, and societal knowledge, a biologic concern is recognized as well as the ecologic necessity.

Within an in-depth research and evaluative process, the *Environmental Resource Guide* prepared by the Committee on the Environment of the American Institute of Architects is being developed by category. It is imperatively needed as an essential part of the informational base.

The full implication of every choice made by urban planners, architects, and interior, industrial, and marketing designers of basic resources and energy and all of the process and distribution systems that attend design and its realization is critical. Much can be done within conceptualization and design development as outlined within the guidelines of the American Institute of Architects, of this book, and other sources. But basically to date the unknown components of energy intensities, measures of concomitant pollution and environmental denigration, and ecologic and biologic repercussions are considerably greater than those known.

As the urban planner may contemplate the built environment, further land development, and the redesign of urban areas, what serves best for human need, relevant context, and effectual ecologic time-frame considerations? As the architect may contemplate the site, the criteria for planning and design, regulatory codes, context of the setting, and aesthetic concerns, what serves best in ecologic terms and human vitality? As the interior designer may contemplate the architectural reality, functional needs, ambience, and human responses to all attributes of the interior, what serves best in accord with health, ecologic lifestyle, and aesthetic pleasure? How many industrial and marketing designers equate electronic, mechanical, product, packaging, and promotional design with ecologic and biologic concern?

Since the 1970s regulatory codes, building and automotive conservation standards, and the general desire to reduce energy demand have reduced the use of polluting energies. But with more people, more cars on the road, global trade, and national and global expectations, the ecologic picture is not a bright one. The images we have that project affluence, wealth, power, and status are a dismal prophecy in terms of ecologic sustainability, ultimate global equity, and well-being and survival of people. *We all cannot have it all!*

As individual design professionals we can demand more information where it is lacking. Basic information in our complex and multidimensional society is so often difficult to obtain. Manufacturers are often loath to reveal the substances and processing inherent in their products. Professional organizations carry a greater weight in the "demand to know" than an individual. Time is passing rapidly with a never-ending proliferation of toxic, particulate, electromagnetic, radioactive, and other bio-antagonists. Unless we arrest the vastly prevalent design that is anti-ecologic and decreases our collective well-being, our fate but mainly that of our progeny will be less than fortuitous.

Our professional organizations (and ourselves) have a responsibility to research and specify the products of ecologically and biologically oriented manufacturing processes and products and methods of construction. The more support that designers give through design and specification of materials and products most suited to ecologic and biologic design, the more that the environment and ourselves are benefitted.

The magnitude of the informational base needed for discrete and intelligent design is somewhat staggering. But present choices within concept, planning, and design for the most part are blindly made without regard for their *full negative initial and life-cycle ecologic effects.* Designers have to adhere and be responsible for legal codes and regulations in the interest of public safety. But present choices without a reasonable and accurate information base relative to the risk to people and the environment have no responsible foundation. To the extent that harmful choices are made, to what extent is the designer legally liable? Suits have already been instituted in regard to the "sick building syndrome."

The greater issue is professional responsibility to collective human well-being and ecologic viability.

Expanding Design Practice

Ecologic design opens up new creative and innovative opportunities for the designer. In urban design the process of concept and planning can be viewed as creating the most healthful and vital ecologic environment. How best may outdoor spaces serve within vitalizing and rejuvenating ecologic settings? Land forming and vegetative and architectural elements of control over urban patterns of air movement, oxygenation, CO_2 absorption, and ventilation and the interplay of sun, earth, air, and water are critical to ecologic and human vitalization. There are notable concerns to save energy in architecture and concerns directed towards healthier homes and buildings. A consolidation of these attitudes plus an abiding *global ecologic concern* are needed.

Architectural design to save energy has been almost entirely directed towards operational energy conservation and has not focused on the *initial energy factors* of materials and construction methods. This oversight is critical in ecologic terms. The initial energy intensities, including extraction, processing, transportation, and distribution of materials and products, account for a massive effect in pollution and denigration of global ecosystems. Despite this magnitude of impact, no extensive informational base exists as to the ecologic and health benefits of materials, products, and energy choices that are made in design and specification.

As design professionals, the more we become informed, the more service we can offer to a client. The more an informational base can be developed, acquire credibility, and act as a ready reference, the more that designers can confidently incorporate effectual and assured ecologic choices into their designs and specifications. Expanding the base of service is most important when securing architectural commissions is most competitive and difficult.

Ecologic design equates with frugality, with efficiency, and with effectual design to purpose. All of these values increase the potential of work. Home owners and business owners alike subscribe to these objectives.

More and more persons at home and work are exhibiting sensitivities to allergens, toxins, and electromagnetic fields, as well as to noise and other stressors. Environmental illness can at any age be symptomatic or be more seriously incapacitating. Computers and electronic gear and more intense fields from energy-conserving lighting pose particular problems, as well as the indoor environments where we spend most of our time.

The side effects of our technologic society demand greater attention. This consideration falls within urban planning, architecture, and interior, industrial, and marketing design. Indoor and outdoor urban and often rural environments are fraught with psychoneural and physiologic peril. As designers in our technologic world, we can beneficially provide less stressful and more healthful environs. It is a professional opportunity within a societal responsibility.

Product design covers such a broad base of materials and energy use, the meeting of human needs and desires, and related energy demands from source to use that "ecologic design" has variant categorical implications. The making of a toothpick has vastly different implications for wood than as a material for construction lumber or when used in fine cabinetry.

Only within a total assessment of resource, energy, and production demands can any specific product be evalued as to its ecologic effect. Alternatives, modifications, or remedies that can result in a product with no (or at least minimal) risk to the environment lie within the province of ecologic design.

Industrial design covers all aspects of commercial products which can include machines that make products or other machines. The automobile is a case in point. Marketing design can be an overlap with industrial design as to packaging. But psycho graphic and demographic parameters of design are entirely within the field of marketing, promotional, and advertising efforts and presentations.

Ecologic design would vastly change the marketing and promotional perspective. "Truth in advertising" might become a reality or at least would have a credible power upon consumer attention and acceptance. Inasmuch as most products are anti-ecologic, a 180° swing in the conceptual, productive, and marketing perspective is necessary.

Within an ecologic ethic, new attitudes toward executive and personal employment will evolve. Under ecologic design new opportunities in the ecologic use of the earth's energies and resources would predominate. Most products now on the shelves would be obsolete. Only by rapid revolutionary rather than slow evolutionary change can the interest of the environment and the consumer be best served. The more our present modus of design, production, and marketing remains what it is, the more ecologic and human sustainability remains at risk.

Time is of the essence. The public is well aware of environmental consequences. However, *each* person is part and parcel of local and global atmospheric pollution and the denigration of Nature's planetary domain. Our species has lasted for millennia, but its continuance is threatened by our overt lifestyle modes and habits, our incessant expectations, and our inexorable per capita energy demands. It is a personal as well as collective problem.

All of this spells opportunity for the designer well versed in ecologic concerns and the power of ecologic design. Our individual directions require education and persistence in following a *true road* within ecologic concern.

A shift in perception to these expanded views of concept, design, and realization is the first step towards a professional ecologic design practice. Professional and public ecologic education is essential based on the most credible information.

The public is affirmatively for the environment. But on the one hand, our society gives concern and caring and love to its children, while on the other hand individually and collectively we poison the atmosphere, increase environmental electromagnetic fields, and otherwise undermine their vitality and health. An *ecologic ethic* can lessen and eradicate this inconsistency.

Ecologic Design Precepts

- *We are a part of Nature's ecologic design.*

- *Our undisciplined ingenuity has exploited rather than aligned with Nature's design.*

- *Our moment of "truth" is here. As we destroy Nature's ecologic design, we destroy ourselves.*

- *Science, technology, and design must accord with Nature's ecosystems and living ecology.*

- *An ecologic ethic, responsibility, discipline, and realization are essential to human vitality and survival.*

- *If we profess to be members of and designers within Nature's ecologic reality, we are in a key position to implement responsible Ecologic Design.*

- *This responsibility is a creative, conceptual, design, and economic opportunity for the design professions.*

- *Ecologic education is a public, private, and professional key to an ecologic conscience and ecologic ethic.*

Ecologue

Our life is filled with technologic wizardry and gadgets that we can make or try to make work for us. But we seldom fully understand the inner workings and mechanisms of the incessant flow of new technologic wonders. We possess them but they are alien to us.

The secret truth is that the technologic reality possesses us. We are programmed by the divisive patterns and symbols of our technologic culture. They have appeared to liberate us but often by their complication and demanding presence we accede to their indoctrinated ways and messages.

This perceptual, undaunted, technologic wonderment has its benefits as long as we remain in control, but our mastery at times can be marginal.

The precepts and *necessity of ecologic design* can be programmed in our computer software and matriculated by a CAD system. But the essence of architecture is an art as well as an expression of science and technology. When *science and technology by necessity* become compatibly and comfortably aligned with ecosystemic energies and global ecologic sustainability, our society will have reached a turning point for human survivability.

While in historic tradition architecture has been more the handmaiden to the prevailing culture and its ways, the time has come when an ecologic ethic must be initiated within urban design, architecture, the interior, landscaping, and products and systems associated with architecture.

Clients are looking more and more to energy efficiency and conservation. The leadership in our profession, the practicing architect, group architecture, and designer effort and the architectural and design education system can formulate the study, evaluation, and processes of ecologic design.

Many ancient and vernacular concepts in architecture remain valid and fitting to an ecologic precept. But stylistic cosmetics and forms irrelevant to and that preempt ecologic coherence and sustainability are contrary to the precept.

The bottom line messages that our planet is delivering to us are that all design must follow our planet's ecologic design if the design of our human species is expected to continue. *Only as our planet's ecologic systems and ecology remain vital can we as part of it remain vital.*

"Green" is in. It is a rapidly growing element in public, political, institutional, and business sectors of our society. Only time and our individual commitment and effort against the counterforces of our local, national, and global imbedded institutionalization can give witness to an illusion or reality of provident change.

informational reference

Book References

Ecologic Architecture has centered around the principal and corollary elements of ecologic design. The focus has been on the *process of ecologic design*. As an informational and methodological base, other publications are referenced. Technical as well as nontechnical constructive information as listed contributes to the design process. Although most are in major agreement, some counter and diametric viewpoints will be found in this environmental literature.

ECOLOGIC AND BIOLOGIC PARADIGMS

BioLogic by David Wann. Johnson Books, 1990.

Circumscribes the biologic and ecologic aspects of design and alternatives within clarity, humor, and practicality.

Dwelling, Place and Environment Edited by David Seamon and Robert Mugerauer. Columbia University Press, 1989.

Essays by authors that explore the themes of environmental ethics, sacred place, sense of place, environmental behavior, and an intimate phenomenology of experiential architectural design.

The Natural House by Frank Lloyd Wright. Horizon Press, 1954.

Wright's discussion about the nature of form, function, materials, and concordance with Nature.

Survival Through Design by Richard Neutra. Oxford University Press, 1954.

A classic. Neutra's exposition of biorealism emphasizes our essential connection with Nature and bioresponses to architecture.

Biosphere Politics by Jeremy Rifkin. Crown Publishers, 1991.

Out of the dark ages and history emerges a vision of the "biospheric age" that deals with a new reality leading to a new earth-centered social consciousness. Rifkin foretells a sustainable biospheric personal and public ethics.

Places of the Soul: Architecture and Environmental Design as Healing Art by Christopher Day. The Aquarian Press, 1990.

A philosophic and visionary book that weds the spiritual with observations and practicalities of ecologic and biologic consequence.

ECOLOGIC PLANNING

Earthscape by John Ormsbee Simonds. McGraw-Hill Inc., 1978.

A comprehensive, analytical, evaluative, and advisory work that sets forth ecologic land planning and development strategies that sensitively respect Nature's sustainability.

Your Edible Landscape Naturally by Robert Kourik. Metamorphic Press, 1986.

An ecologically detailed account of what and how you can conserve and grow an edible landscape.

SOLAR AND CLIMATIC ARCHITECTURE

The Natural House Book by David Pearson. Simon and Schuster/Fireside, 1989.

In-depth considerations in "creating a healthy, harmonious and ecologically sound home environment." It offers a wealth of historic and native connections.

Climatic Design by Donald Watson, FAIA and Kenneth Labs. McGraw-Hill Inc., 1983.

Well-ordered information and documented procedures for climate, solar, and ventilation evaluation within the architectural design process.

Sun Spaces by Peter Clegg and Derry Watkins. Storey Communications, Inc., 1987.

A broad cross-section of attached sunspaces, owner discussions, and practical details.

Sunlighting as Formgiver for Architecture by William M.C. Lam. Van Nostrand Reinhold Co., 1986.

An impressive coverage of the sun's character, characteristics, and biologic and psychologic visual responses. It offers solar techniques and extensive case studies.

Natural Solar Architecture: The Passive Solar Primer, Third Edition, by David Wright, AIA. Van Nostrand Reinhold Co., 1984.

A rule-of-thumb solar book with a sense of humor. A handy, practical guide to the concepts of passive and active solar energy. Addresses solar and climatic architectural environs.

Passive Cooling edited by Jeffrey Cook. The MIT Press, 1989.

A literal compendium of passive cooling concepts and effectual strategies contributed by research, evaluative, and design professionals. Abundant points of information can assist designers in hot and arid climates as well as in locations with hot summers.

The Passive Solar Energy Book (Expanded Professional Edition) by Edward Mazria. Rodale Press, 1979.

A comprehensive book on the fundamentals of passive solar energy and design. Easy to follow charts, calculations, and appendices are a ready reference.

Passive-Active Solar Heating by Michael Meltzer. Prentice Hall, 1985.

A practical solar heating technology book, with presentation of solar basics.

Solar Interiors by Katherine Panchyk. Van Nostrand Reinhold Co., 1984.

Physiologic realities, responses, and recommendations for comfort and well-being. Daylighting, thermal gain, shading strategies, and insulation are evaluated.

Passive Solar Architecture: Logic & Beauty by David Wright and Dennis A. Andrejko. Van Nostrand Reinhold Co., 1982.

The innovative and aesthetic possibilities of solar and climate-repsonsive architecture are presented with conceptual emphasis and clarity. 36 regional projects give evidence of ecologic practicality.

EARTH ECOLOGY AND TECHNOLOGY

Gentle Architecture by Malcolm Wells. McGraw-Hill Inc., 1981.

An ardent ecologic and practical philosophy of architectural earth design that respects the primary and phenomenal aspects of Nature.

Earth Sheltered Housing by Max R. Terman. Van Nostrand Reinhold Co., 1985.

Locational, climatic effects, comprehensive planning and design solutions to earth sheltered housing.

Earth Sheltered Housing Design (2nd Edition) by John Carmody and Raymond Sterling, Underground Space Center, University of Minnesota. Van Nostrand Reinhold Co., 1985.

With comparative earth sheltering techniques, structural materials and system design, financing, code regulation aspects, a number of effectual case studies are presented.

Natural Architecture (2nd Revised Edition) by Charles G. Woods. Amity House, 1988.

A compendium of solar, earth sheltered residential designs with variety and aesthetic appeal.

Earthship by Michael Reynolds. Solar Survival Press, 1990.

Conceptual build-your-own-home planning with sun, earth, air, and water and recycled tires and cans is the forte of this book.

ATMOSPHERIC BIOEFFECTS

Atmospheric Ecology for Designers and Planners by William P. Lowry. Van Nostrand Reinhold, 1991.

Climatological analysis of cyclic atmospheric patterns in ecologic interresponse to site, planning, and design.

Biosphere 2 by John Allen. Penguin Books, 1991.

In controlled research the biosphere simulates our natural ecologic/climatic zone life-support systems within the isolation of a high-tech structural enclosure.

BIOELECTROMAGNETISM

The Body Electric by Robert O. Becker, M.D. and Gary Selden. William Morrow and Co., Inc., 1985.

Electricity is vital to the life process. The book deals with our bioelectric selves and Dr. Becker's pioneering research and study of the neural, brain, cardiovascular, tissue regeneration, and other biophysical effects of electromagnetic fields.

Cross Currents by Robert O. Becker, M.D. Jeremy P. Tarcher, Inc., 1990.

The evidence and adverse bioeffects of man-made electromagnetic fields are examined in light of research and case studies. Electromagnetic pollution and bioelectromagnetic risks contrast with the benefits of biologic therapy and physiologic regeneration. As electromagnetic beings, our proximity to adverse electrical and magnetic fields can cause hypersensitivities, pathogenic syndromes, and physical dysfunction.

SUSTAINABLE COMMUNITIES

Sustainable Communities by Sim Van der Ryn and Peter Calthorpe. Sierra Club Books, 1986.

An overview, evaluation, and environmental remedies for the urban and suburban fabric. Studies on the relevancies and strategies for urban and architectural developments and redevelopments within sustainability, a passive solar emphasis, and societal, economic, and ecologic viability.

Cohousing by Kathryn McCamant and Charles Durrett. Ten Speed Press, 1988.

Describes community living that shares the benefits of societal cooperation in food served in a common facility, adjunct amenities for children and adults, and shared resources. The social atmosphere and community structure with private dwellings are derived from Danish examples. American counterparts are being built.

ENVIRONMENTAL RESOURCES

Superinsulated Houses and Air-to-Air Heat Exchangers by William A. Shurcliff. Brick House Publishing Co., 1988.

A physicist's analysis of superinsulation, vapor barriers, radon, and air-to-air heat exchangers.

The Healthy House by John Bauer. Carol Communications, 1989.

A book that examines biophysical insults and offers an extendable evaluation of "safe" resources.

Man, Climate and Architecture by Baruch Givoni. Van Nostrand Reinhold, 1981.

A book that evolved through several editions has a fundamental environmental and technical base. It has a broad scope for review and design that includes physiological, physical, and architectural relevancies. Solar and natural energies applications, materials, openings, and shading are evaluated.

Solar Hydrogen: Moving Beyond Fossil Fuels by Joan M. Ogden and Robert H. Williams. World Resources Institute, 1989.

An architectural and vehicular perspective on the safety and practical environmental benefits of solar hydrogen technology.

Why Your House May Endanger Your Health by Alfred V. Zamm with Robert Gannon. Simon and Schuster, 1980.

A book with a fund of information consistent with clinical ecology. Practical considerations for a healthy home cover aspects of architecture and the interior including electromagnetic radiation.

Materials, Products, Systems

Relatively few materials, products, and systems are both *ecologic* and *biologic*. Claims can be greater than the reality. Trade-offs are inevitable. To design and specify with ecosystemic sustainability *only* in mind or biologic health *only* in mind falls short of an ideal reality. *Within the relevancies of choice lie the degree of biologic, ecologic, and economic consequence.*

Most homes and buildings are not designed to either bio-sensitivity or to ecologic accord. New projects spring up without regard to solar and climatic diurnal and seasonal orientation or inter-responsive effects or to biologic well-being.

From a materials, products, and systems standpoint, commercial and institutional projects should not be construed in the same light as residential projects. Acoustics, bio-fatigue factor (hard vs. soft materials), practicality, minimal maintenance, and life-cycle ecologic economics are all germane to selection and specification.

The most critical choices are best made within a holistic context. Intervention is often the most immediate, economic, and practical procedure for bio-protection and well-being. But often it does little to benefit the environment.

Natural as well as synthetic products can be a burden to our wellness. Allergenic, toxic, and other symptomatic responses can be triggered by singular or synergistic combinations of airborne, contact, or electromagnetic antagonists. The reactions of environmentally sensitive persons should be respected. Natural products can invite more allergenic and pathogenic microorganisms than synthetics. Synthetic chemistry, bioelectromagnetism, and noise can play their part in human distress. Products that originate, are processed, packaged, transported, and sold by techno-industry put people and the environment at varying degrees of risk.

As *ecologic/biologic design and specification* emerges more into the mainstream of architecture, urban planning, interiors, and product and system design, more business and industrial establishments will be encouraged and motivated towards increasing ecologic/biologic materials and products.

This process is becoming more evident. Ecologic and biologic materials and products are becoming more visible. The references herein of manufacturers, products, and distributors are not intended as an endorsement. Further in-depth research and confirmation of ecologic and biologic reality can more clearly define what is credible and what is not. Materials and products of very low toxicity may bother certain sensitive individuals but otherwise have no other contrary biologic effects.

Ecologic/Biologic or Biologic/Ecologic

"Whether an *ecologic/biologic* or *biologic/ecologic* emphasis is made, under which do materials, products, and systems have the greater benefit?" is a prime question. Trying to find an ecologic/-biologic perfect or satisfying answer is most often impossible.

Everything in our technologic petro-based society is contrary in one respect or another to ecologic or biologic vitality or both in well-being and vitality. Only what we may raise, process, or put together *in situ* might escape from a causation of ecologic or biologic harm. Our bio-exposure is not only in the home and workplace but everywhere we go on the street, in vehicles, and in places where we shop, travel, and find entertainment and leisure.

Until the basic sources of resources and energy are renewable, clean, environmentally and biologically compliant can we begin to accomplish meaningful change. *An ecologic/biologic economic is essential.* A most impending threat is destruction of our thin protective ozone layer, among other planetary deprecation. *Our collective global criticality of higher order weighs against the biologic well-being of the individual.*

Considering that ecologic factors are inscrutably complex and biologic factors are mainly obscure, the task of materials, products, and systems selection within the context of any project is difficult at best. Economics is no small factor. The items desired are likely to cost more, often because there is not a history of effectual use and durability.

The trade-off initial investment cost in items such as active solar systems compared to the cost of relatively cheap utility energy is a major constraint.

Life-cycle servicing and repair costs can also be a factor.

Environmentally sensitive individuals can test their respiratory/biologic response with small samples of any material before selecting it for a home or building. Such testing is not absolute but can be surprisingly accurate with some individuals.

Construction

Complying with building codes and institutionalized methods of construction can result in a tremendous waste of energy, materials, and time, as well as ecologic harm and pollution.

Drastic changes in building construction technology and attendant codes are essential. Digging wide trenches as access for footings and foundations often leads to excessive use of materials and heavy, noisy, air-polluting equipment. Then the demanding task of backfilling to prevent cracks and failure of interior concrete slabs and exterior walls, walks, or drives presents neighborhood disruption, time, along with ecologic loss.

Ecologic and economic advantages would be realized in conceptual and technologic engineering solutions in which architecture was successfully supported in all soils conditions and for all types of construction with an *absolute minimum of earth disturbance.*

Technology above the plane of the earth offers a greater range of selective construction options. The vast majority of projects, considering the uniqueness of every site, the criteria, and the design perspective, are custom, one-of-a-kind ventures in commercial architecture. Tract housing with its repetitive constancy provides a duplication not ecologically site specific. A marriage between energy-intensive manufactured modular baths, kitchens, and utility rooms with panelized or other systemic construction systems modified to the solar, climatic, and topographic realities of every site is the route to greater economy in construction time and financing within ecologic concern.

From a biologic and ecologic standpoint there is a question whether high rise buildings should even exist. Studies have not been conducted regarding the effect that high rise structures have on life-supportive earth energies and the internalized electromagnetic Faraday cage effects of the structure on people, whether such buildings may be steel framed or reinforced concrete.

Every class of building and its occupancy use should be more closely evaluated with bioelectromagnetic instruments and its relevancy to our electromagnetic body frequency. Computers should be regarded as part of the building electromagnetics. They need redesign to avoid the positive ionization and electrical and electromagnetic fields they now produce.

Solar Basics

LOCATION

Every home or building by its microclimate and occupancy relates in a special way to holistic factors in perception of need. Light of the sky-vault and of direct solar radiation are basic to ecologic design. Ecologic design should equate with location. In mild as well as locations of climatic extremes, concept and design should accord with an optimization of solar benefits. "Solar Basics" are predicated on predominant climatic location of the temperate and cold northern hemisphere. Tropical and semi-tropical areas require design congruent to location.

ORIENTATION

Orientation to due south or within a 20° angle of it is critical to effective use of passive solar collection. The most effective hours of the day for due south collection are from 9 a.m. in the morning to 3 p.m. in the afternoon. The incidence of solar radiation varies considerably throughout the United States. Cold northerly climates with abundant sunshine can benefit most by solar gain for appropriately designed solar architecture.

Orientation with glazed openings to the south can not only be a wintertime advantage, but also outdoor spaces can be made more useful. Solar patios, courtyards, porches, decks, and balconies can be made more useful during cool and colder weather.

For passive solar homes it is best to have most of the living areas to the south with closets, storage, and bedrooms to the north. Residential home spaces most practical for passive solar collection are sunspaces, attached greenhouses, and eating spaces. Care has to be exercised relative to fading and solar damage to furniture and other items. The more insulated a project is, the more passive, hybrid, and active solar collection can be economic and effective.

LATITUDE

The sun's daily and seasonal path equates with latitude. As a general factor for active solar systems (with fixed due south flat-plate collectors), the latitude plus 15 degrees serves best for the angle of solar collection when winter heating is a prime consideration. For year-round solar collection needed for heating domestic hot water, hot spas, swimming pools, industrial, and other residential and commercial needs (such as a car wash), the solar collectors should be set at the latitude plus five degrees. For passive and passive hybrid (mechanical assist) solar systems, the seasonal and diurnal sky position of the sun should be considered relative to latitude.

SOLAR GAIN

Unwanted solar gain can be as important as wanted solar gain. External attenuation or as may be desired particularly for west windows through all seasons of the year complete intervention can be more effectual to avoid west external sun gain and interior space overheating.

South solar gain can be most advantageously used for all types of architecture in which the sun's radiation can serve best relative to interior occupancy functions, daylighting, and thermal gain. Although solar gain can considerably to more fully provide cool and cold weather heating, the most appropriate type of glazing, external contributory solar reflection, luminosity of interior surfaces, degree of solar access, furniture, furnishing, and content of the interior and not least the purpose and time-related use of indoor space are part of the total solar thermal and lighting equation.

Interior space to a sunspace, greenhouse, or atrium can secondarily benefit as solar radiation penetrates through glazing to the inner space. The primary outer space will then act as a thermal buffer to the solar gain secondarily received by the inner space. The sun's radiation received by interior spaces through south-facing clerestories can provide light and thermal gain to such spaces. Thermal mass located to receive clerestory solar radiation can retain such warmth to central or northside portions of architecture.

THERMAL MASS

The simplest form of passive solar system is that in which glazing to the south can receive direct solar radiation and in which a thermal mass can thus directly gain in temperature. The closer the mass is located to the glazed surface, the more re-radiant long-wave thermal energy will be lost to colder temperatures outdoors.

The thermal mass can be a dark surface of concrete, tile over concrete, brick, or other mass. Trombe walls have been extensively used in solar projects. But they do block the south view and visual connection with nature and being close (in most cases) to the glazing can have significant thermal loss to cold outdoor temperatures. Walls close to glazing can present a cleaning problem. At the rear of a sunspace or attached greenhouse a thermal mass in receiving direct solar radiation can with consideration of the thickness and type of mass heat interior space by thermal lag. Large tubes and drums of water have been more efficiently used in deference to concrete or masonry.

Thermal mass is important as to location relative to use of space. Furniture, furnishings, equipment, and time of day use of space. The mass cannot perform its thermal reception and retention functions if it is covered or shaded to a significant extent. In occupied areas the thermal mass should be large enough to avoid discomfort. Everything within a space has some thermal mass contribution. Sunspaces for residential, commercial, educational, institutional, religious, or other applications should be specifically designed to time periods of use and the elements that accompany that use. Glazed sunspace pitched roofed areas present particular problems. Not only can direct solar radiant energy (particularly in summer with the sun much overhead) be intolerable, but also overhead glazing is prone to outdoor dirt, grime, weather etching, and leakage. Interposing shading devices inside is not nearly as effective as outside. But the weathering and solar effects upon an outside shading method can be considerable.

Dark vertical blinds or other interceptors located anywhere in the solar path will transform the shortwave of solar energy to longer thermal waves heating the air which can be naturally or mechanically convected to a thermal mass. This would usually be to a mass deeper in the structure where its thermal gain can be most efficiently utilized. Large internal thermal masses also stabilize indoor temperatures through all seasons. They provide a mean radiant temperature with the ambient air temperature for comfort. Active solar systems consist of either air or liquid type solar collectors with insulated ducts or pipeline connection to thermal storage. Air systems use gravel storage bins or plenums. Liquid systems use storage tanks that with heat exchangers can be used to heat internal water systems, hydronic space heating, hot spas, swimming pools, and other purposes.

Solar attics or conversions of attics to receive solar gain and also penthouses can receive direct solar gain that can mechanically be distributed for interior space heating and air tempering. The Hay Skytherm solar and clear-sky nocturnal cooling within a thermal mass water pond system can be adapted to southern or northern climates.

VENTILATION/AIR TEMPERING

Sunspaces and greenhouses can function as air tempering and ventilation elements of architecture. Air can be introduced into sunspaces, greenhouses, attics, or penthouses through controlled outdoor air intakes. The air can then be designed to convect naturally or be mechanically distributed as desired through interior space by means of ductwork or other transfer systems.

Homes and buildings can function as literal solar-activated heat pumps. As solar thermal gains occur at south glazing, cooling displacement air with rising currents of heated air from the sun's energy can produce an inductive interior space air flow. Solar plenums and chimneys can induce stack action air flow for ventilation and aiding interior cooling when outdoor temperatures are cooler than indoor temperatures.

Venturi ventilation aided by exterior air movement and earth temperature cooling in summer and heating in winter can be an advantage when combined with solar heating, ventilation, and cooling.

GLAZING

Glazing for passive solar architecture and elements of the architecture can be most effective as to location, glazing with minimal framing members, and using high transmissivity glazing with high insulative qualities. Solite is a low iron slightly patterned glass that for fixed glazing provides high

solar transmissivity (available in standard glazing sizes).

An extensive repertoire of technologic glazing represents broad options. Glazing to project-specific thermal, daylighting, view, and shading conditions, configurations, and design most appropriate to each elevation or other portions of the architecture equates with energy conservation and is a performance, ecologic, and biologic benefit. Tailoring the glazing with low-E, Heat Mirror, argon or krypton fill, control over edge and frame losses, and glazing proportions most suited to the conservation of energy along with optimal daylighting, solar, and climatic concerns lends to solar control and architectural thermal efficiency.

WINDOWS

Traditionally windows have been placed at the center of interior rooms and other spaces. From a functional standpoint this results in various shortcomings. The more that a material, product, or system is functional in bioresponse, composure, effective use of space, and in congruence with the natural thermodynamics of a home of building, the more it is ecologic.

Centrally located windows have the following disadvantages, depending upon skyvault and direct solar exposure:

• limit the best functional use of interior space.

• in commercial use are not likely to accord with the advantage of best daylighting for visual acuity, tasks, and activities.

• in residential use are not apt to be appropriate to best furniture and furnishings arrangements (particularly in bedrooms).

• are not likely to accord with the best scope of view to the outdoors (glazing to the floor improves the visual indoor-outdoor connection).

• cause visual glare by contrast to the relative darkening of the exterior wall.

• are in the poorest location for effective cross ventilation.

• the higher the window sill height, the less that daylight can reflect from floor surfaces into interior space.

- the traditional rigidity of center-of-the-wall window placement can limit privacy.

Instead of the relatively poor daylighting and ventilation of a single center-of-an-exterior-wall window, two windows located as far apart as interior partitions allow will provide greater in-depth interior illumination (with white or light-colored reflective walls) and considerably better ventilation. Exterior wing walls adjacent to windows will tend to enhance interior ventilation. The direction of prevailing winds should be considered in window type, outward projection of the window, and the "hand" of its opening.

Casement windows, depending upon direction of swing and the corresponding influence on ventilation, are usually a better candidate for effective ventilation when using operable windows for such purpose. Awning windows located close to the floor or high up to provide a desired ventilation pattern also give protection against rain. Double hung windows for the most part are the least efficient and have greater energy losses than the aforementioned types. In cold weather windows lose a greater amount of internal heat the closer they are to the ceiling. Skylights will lose the most. Clerestories, not subject to the same degree of clear-sky temperature losses, will lose less.

Windows without draperies or need for shades or blinds for privacy or direct sunlight control are an architectural idealization. The architectural depth, form, and other exterior and interior design elements can all play their part in diurnal and seasonal aspects of sun and daylight.

In general, windows in size and location that open the correspondence between interior and outdoor space, provide lateral daylighting for best visual acuity, and by alignment against interior partitions can optimize interior space use and functional and bioresponsive needs are preferred.

Windows and other glazed openings are critical to the optimization of daylighting, thermal performance, useful light with energy conservation, ambience of the interior, and connection with the outdoors. The more that the architecture as to form, details, and openings functions as a year-round site-specific daylighted internal luminaire, the less is the demand upon light control devices with their concomitant maintenance.

Hurd Insol-8 has at this time the greatest domestically produced center-of-the-glass R value (R-8). But glass edge and framing losses account for a lower total value of R-4. A window assembly from Switzerland has a somewhat better overall value of R-6.5 due to the careful detailing of the glass setting and frame.

At this time an Andersen Permashield window has an overall rating of R-2.9. Pella has Slimshade low-E windows with the benefit of daylight and privacy control with a no-cleaning-required horizontal blind between two panes of glass. Fixed glazing set into an insulative surround as part of the building avoids the edge and frame loss factors as well as avoiding the "crack" infiltration factor of any operable window.

SHADING

Solar reflective and heat absorbing glass can have a distinctive effect upon internal solar gain and usable light. Shading by the forms and details of the architecture can avoid the time period maintenance of exterior awnings, applied canopies, and external interposition of screening and other devices. Caution in the selection of glazing to avoid temperature differential glass breakage due to shading is advised.

Internal shading or closure blinds, shutters, movable panels, or draperies have the benefit of being out of the weather and require less cleaning but are for the most part less effective than external shading methods. Blinds and shades located between glazing members have the advantage of remaining clean and being more thermally effective than interior installations. Insulative blinds and other devices for thermal benefit can provide shading.

COMMERCIAL VERSUS RESIDENTIAL

Virtually every single-family home can enjoy some major to minor benefits depending upon the characteristics of climate, degree of insolation, volume to external surface ratio, glazing, thermal mass, earth sheltering, and connection with more or less passive, hybrid, or active systems of solar collection. Solar systems can singly or collectively be appropriate and economic. Townhomes and other attached and multiple forms of housing have for the most part due to proximity and housing density less opportunity for solar energy.

Commercial, institutional, religious, and educational buildings have to be specifically evaluated. Retail stores and shopping centers have large internal loads of lighting and people. The need for air tempered ventilation can be a major energy requirement in offices, and places of assemblage and congregations of people. Return air supplemented by the heat from lighting, equipment, and people can add usefully to solar heating. Commercial buildings often require cooling in midwinter.

But buildings are not always occupied and the air tempering need can be ably provided by air-type and in some cases by passive solar gain stored within a thermal mass for smaller projects. Nonresidential low rise buildings can often have more the attributes of residential rather than commercial architecture.

High rise buildings (depending upon solar access) are a natural for solar collection on the south side for heating of the interior north side as well as for general air tempering. Regardless of height the occupancy time periods and heat loads of lighting, people, and equipment are major to the effect upon interior comfort.

The more any home or building can be made comfortable, optimally daylighted within visual comfort, and most conducive to psychoneural and physiologic benefit, the more that an ecologic/biologic idiom is realized.

DAYLIGHTING AND LIGHT

Daylighting is important for people. Its constant variance provides a psycho-visual exercise. Steady-state overly bright indoor artificial lighting is conducive to psychoneural overstimulation and general fatigue. Surface brightness of a light source and glare are counter to visual comfort. Lateral daylighting with light *across* the page or work surface equates with visual acuity at low light levels.

Direct shafts of sunlight can be visually and thermally disturbing for various activities and tasks. External and internal reflectivity of direct sunlight and skyvault daylighting should be part of the design equation. Reflective daylighting and direct solar control by architectural design are exemplified by the central clerestory of the author's Residential Research Facility (see pages 128-138) that is a successful model for office and other nonresidential applications. In year-round light

meter monitoring the effectual light levels and acuity for reading, writing, and other tasks were surprising during cloudy, hazy, and overcast weather. The readings were generally somewhat to considerably *higher* under less than ideal sky conditions.

Bright downlighting from artificial illumination can reduce the visual contrast between the surface of writing, drawing, and reading and the darker impression, actually reducing acuity as the high footcandle level of light is intercepted. Common levels in offices of 50 footcandles without regard to the biophysics of eye and mind are grossly wasteful of electrical energy. Reflected light whether from skyvault, sun, or artificial sources has a softening and quieting effect within interior space. Optical means have been developed to selectively deliver natural light to interior spaces.

Large and small south-facing clerestories can be designed for optimal daylighting with adequate solar control. North windows and north-facing clerestories can provide uniform skyvault daylighting for commercial projects. Thermal balance should be considered with solar thermal strategies.

Daylighting design with a sensitivity to the uniformity of north skyvault light, the time sequences of solar radiation for diurnal and seasonal east, south, and west exposures can not only conserve on artificial lighting demand but also reduce air conditioning commonly needed more in commercial buildings than residences.

Earth

From ancient times humans have lived within the earth, within earthen dwellings and also sheltered by the earth. Adobe, rammed earth, and underground architecture provide a referable experience.

Principal constraints to more highly developed earth technologies have been preempted by codes, labor, time-demanding construction methodologies, stylistic cultural perceptions, construction and economic limitations, trade unfamiliarity and inexperience, and factors of finish and durability.

Earth is the most common material of any site that is removed rather than in some effective way used for construction, land forming and sheltering, for climate control, or as a thermal mass. It seems unreasonable that basic materials of construction should be procured, processed, and transported great distances when the earth of site or close vicinity might be effectively and economically used.

An advanced earth technology requires accurate classification, analysis, and securing code approval. Due to the greatly diverse constituents of earth and the structural, thermal, weather resistance, and other properties needed in architecture, an accurate analysis and formulated sample testing are needed. Machine or otherwise manufactured and tested adobe blocks may avert this foregoing involvement. The process is energy intensive but machine energy is less than for most other materials.

During the 1960s the author designed a very large adobe two-story and central courtyard Colorado ranch project. The adobe blocks were imported from Mexico. A higher technologic approach was undertaken by the author and an experienced soils engineer as a contemplated site-specific construction earth technology for the author's 1980 Residential Research Facility (see case study pages 128-138). The tests made of various admixtures of sawdust and other waste materials including various stabilizers were very encouraging. Compression tests of over 1,000 psi were reached with fractional amounts of cement in the earth mix.

Extensive research needs to be done to qualify and codify earth as a material, a structural medium, a stable element that can be tailored to be insulative, endowed with definable thermal properties, and other attributes that are most appropriate to architecture. Injection methods for soils stabilization could lessen demand on polluting heavy earth handling equipment. Avoidance of toxic and bituminous materials in earth technology can be prudent in terms of air quality.

Underground architecture has been explored in depth and design by architect Malcolm Wells. Earth berming and earth sheltering have become more common in relation to landscaping and architecture. Earth coupling primarily takes advantage of the year-round thermal stabilization of architecture in an earth connection. This connection being insulated or otherwise is an intervention that does not allow outdoor seasonal changes in temperature to have a significant thermal effect upon the interior space connection.

Underground architecture particularly accords with the "closed" aspects of shopping centers, industrial buildings, museums, and other nonresidential occupancies that have significant internal heat loads. With a central mall oriented to the sky, daylight and sun and other buildings with indoor and outdoor atria, clerestories, and other openings as appropriate to site-specific microclimate can be primarily and effectively illuminated and ventilated with the earth as both a connection and as a stabilizing temperature intervenor the architecture becomes more energy self-sustaining.

In our likely national direction toward societal and economic decentralization as partly escapism, instantaneous communication, concerns with intensifying violence and more verdant environment, opportunities for earth technology will increase. The urban context with its noisy, stressful arteries, polluted matrix, and high architectural density limits choice of a practical and economic urban earth technology.

Recycled and waste products in being carefully classified for use with earth and cementitious materials can in conservation be constituents of new earth technologies. Adobe and rammed earth classes under the auspices of the Southwest Solar Adobe School are held in Arizona and New Mexico. For their publication *Earthbuilders Encyclopedia* and information, write to Southwest Solar Adobe School, Sabrial Research Station, P.O. Box 153, Bosque, NM 87006.

Concrete

Concrete has innumerable uses. There are few projects that do not use it in one form or another. Concrete can bear compression but suffers in tensile strength without reinforcement. Steel is the most common reinforcement, but glass and plastic rovings and other metals can give it tensile properties.

Concrete of cement, sand, and gravel can also be formulated with sawdust, wood shavings, and other discarded materials and as may be suitable to use engineered with a certain amount of earth. Earth technologies should be more in ecologic favor as a material of the site or vicinity. Earth concrete is not a new technology.

Additives are used in concrete to facilitate its form, retard its hardening, improve its water resistance, to keep it from freezing in cold weather, and to improve its curing and hardening. Considerable petro-energy is employed to extract, transport, and process its constituents; to premix and transport it to a project; to pour, pump, or shovel the wet mix in place; and as to the case may be to finish its surface.

Once set and hardened the concrete becomes immobile. Considerable energy is used to remove nonreinforced and a greater amount reinforced concrete. Its monolithic immobility can be for years of benefit, but the immobility factor can be a minor to formidable impediment to renovation and remodelling. Initial planning can ecologically and economically benefit a renewal process to meet with a restatement of need, concept, and design.

Concrete can be panelized as precast, pre-stressed, or otherwise modular members that can align with architectural changes in purpose, expansion, and addition. Concrete flatwork unless in pavers or movable modules can practically negate its reuse as architectural component members. Commercial projects are most subject to change due to changing business conditions.

"Cast in concrete" can be in long-term durability an ecologic advantage or an ecologic disadvantage in its immobility.

Aggregate finish concrete as may be used for exposed surfaces for patios, walks, walls, driveways, and other purposes is attractive, durable, and easily maintained. Cement for concrete work should not come from a kiln that burns toxic waste due to possible contamination of the concrete. The constituents of concrete should not be toxic or radioactive.

Exposed interior concrete surfaces can be stained for practicality with AFM MaxiStain or finished with 100% acrylic All-Deck over a fiberglass mat for exterior or interior use.

Avoid additives to concrete used within indoor space. Sensitive persons may be affected by them. Concrete slabs can be cut and laid up like stonework for a pleasing appearance. Pieces of discarded concrete can be pulverized and used for gravel. Concrete must be cautiously used for fill or not at all due to earth cover that can sink between interspaces among the concrete.

Masonry

Masonry of brick, stone, or concrete block have respective advantages and disadvantages. The more "local" the stone, brick, or manufacture of the block, the better. The "embodied" energy and attendant pollution factor vary not only with the category of material but the total process from source to project.

These materials have a substantial thermal mass that aids the flywheel effect towards interior temperature stabilization. Relative porosity can be a factor in weathering. When the thermal mass is *within* the building as opposed to an exterior wall with exterior side insulation and the insulation is on the *outside* of the thermal mass exterior wall, performance can be improved about 30 percent. Outsulation is thus better than insulation. Outsulation can also bridge over dissimilar materials, providing a continuous thermal shield for the building.

Exposed brick, stone, and concrete blocks conventionally provide a fire-safe and durable exterior. Installed masonry veneers with insulation of the inner supporting wall or cavity insulation board or insulation fill can provide degrees of insulation. But if outsulation is not used then an adequate (relative to climate) continuous thermal break should be designed.

Brick and stone floors can be difficult to maintain, depending upon hardness of surface, texture, porosity, and mortar used for joints. Thickness, color, and thermal characteristics of brick or stone need to be considered in their use for floors or walls.

An aspect of brick, stone, and block is that they can be arched or vaulted forming domed roofs. Masonry materials are more *in situ* labor intensive than usual methods of building. However, low-tech labor-intensive construction has within a site-specific context an ecologic benefit. Sun-baked bricks made from on-site clays or earth-clay mixtures can be where codes permit a decided (labor intensive) ecologic benefit.

Metals

Aluminum is more energy intensive than steel in its original manufacture. But while steel is energy intensive, aluminum is less energy intensive in being recycled than steel.

Alloys added to basic metals, forming, anodizing, plating, welding, machining, or otherwise processing or finishing metals adds to their "embodied" energy. With unique tensile and compressive strength, metals serve for structural, reinforcement, and broad range of specific practicalities.

With electrical and electromagnetic properties not shared by other materials, metals have distinctive latitudes of application. A question in the minds of electromagnetic researchers (including the author) is, what are the biophysical electromagnetic implications of metal members used in buildings? The full answer is not in, but considering that we are electromagnetic beings living, working, and existing within electromagnetic architectural cages of unregulated electrical and magnetic frequency and intensity leaves unresolved the factor of bio-risk.

Prudence indicates that we examine the total aspects of building materials, products, and systems, not only upon airborne and contact effects but also those of harmonic and dissonant electromagnetic fields. The electro-conductive and magnetic propensities of all wiring, water piping, metal members, reinforcement screeds, lath, foil, or other metal elements whether grounded or not likely have a subtle or significant effect upon us.

As being most appropriate, durable, not exposed to corrosion, and most recoverable, metals have a place in ecologic architecture. Using metal framing for healthy homes has been touted as being an alternative that avoids the outgassing of wood framing. But wood framing can be sealed with AFM WaterSeal. A building enveloped with steel members results in an internalized Faraday cage with occupants subject to the collective electromagnetic field.

Wood

Wood is an ancient and most versatile building material. Used more extensively in the residential framing, cabinetry, and finish cabinetry than commercial it has some negative as well as salutary characteristics.

On the regrettable side, it is subject to decay, insect infestations, forays of woodpeckers, weathering, warping, moisture retention, shrinkage, and is combustible. In addition, the natural outgassing of the wood can adversely affect sensitive individuals.

On a global scale trees remain being ruthlessly cut. The cutting of old growth forests of our own country as well as the attrition upon tropical forests depletes atmospheric oxygen and is a loss in CO_2 absorption. Humankind has an affinity to the "tree of Life" but an unkindness to the regenerative forces of Nature.

What we may choose and specify of various species has a direct connection with forest sustainability. The end use of wood in architecture from the forest tree to cutting, hauling, milling, drying, handling, and distribution to the point of use should be considered. Specify domestic (preferably local), sustainable growth, preferably air dried, free of toxic wood treatments. Where subgrade wood requires treatment, copper chromated arsenate (CCA) is preferable to the relative risk of other more volatile methods.

Exterior weather-exposed solid wood beams, columns, and siding will stand up better with the texture of resawn rather than with smooth surface lumber in receiving a solid body stain. The textured surface absorbs and retains a greater amount of stain or paint.

Exterior grade plywood using phenol formaldehyde is reputed to be biologically acceptable for exterior and interior use. Interior plywood and particle board should be adequately sealed against outgassing of urea formaldehyde of their manufacture.

Certification of soft wood plywoods should be by the American Plywood Association (APA), for particle boards by the National Particleboard Association (NPA) and for hardwood plywoods by the Hardwood Plywood Association (HPA) in accordance with EPA test chamber outgassing standards.

Wood is regenerative and renewable within sustainable growth forests. There is heavy demand upon wood for construction for all of the interior needs of furniture, cabinetry, and other architectural and interior uses. In parts of the world it is blatantly exploited for firewood, and forests are decimated for agriculture and cattle raising.

The great number of species of wood with their indigenous characteristics and amenities of use are a human benefit by Nature. But until social and economic global equity can curtail the needless destruction of tropical and our own "old growth" forests, we are myopically ravaging Nature's ecologic sustainability. Some manufacturers have stopped using tropical woods.

Wood is a marvelous material and a most ecologic design resource. But as it is employed within form and use it bears a relevancy to the petro-energies used to fulfill a design or specification.

Urea formaldehyde common to use of interior hardwood plywood and various forms of particle board are noted as a biologic risk. Phenol formaldehyde used in the making of exterior grade plywoods is reputed not to be a significant respiratory risk according to the American Plywood Association's risk assessment.

AFM Water Seal can be applied as a sealant to contain the natural chemical outgassing of the wood. Dura Stain or other water-based finishes such as AFM Safecoat paint do not according to the manufacturer present a respiratory hazard. Livos and Auro natural plant resin finishes also are formulated to avoid harmful chemical outgassing.

Solid wood cabinets for kitchens and other purposes with bio-acceptable finishes can allay some of the apprehensions that persons with or conscious of environmental sensitivities might have.

Wood is not getting more plentiful. With the national volume demand and ever-needed environmental constraints, wood is not apt to be as available as in the past. Small, efficient, and affordable housing would put less demand on the total supply. Huge homes for few people with often cascades of roofs and dormers are far from frugal.

A new laser conservation technology is now being used that analyzes the most effective way of cutting each specific log to procure the most useful dimensional lumber. The computer laser process saves about 15 percent of the timber and is further used to determine the dimensional size demand.

Roofing

Roofing is one of the most problematic elements of architecture. Pitched roofs are less prone to leakage than flat roofs. Steeply pitched roofs to shed snow and winter in northern climates contrast with nearly flat or very low pitched roofs that retain snow. Snow on a roof in cold weather acts as a desirable thermal intervention. Flat and very low pitched roofs, however, can be more prone to leakage and a delay in repair during wet weather.

Asphalt shingles are neither ecologic nor biologic. Fiberglass shingles have less asphalt. Coal tar and asphalt roofs due to their source and outgassing are not advisable for sensitive persons.

Monoacrylic (100% acrylic) materials for roofs, exterior decks, and other uses are likely to be better tolerated by sensitive individuals. Standing seam meatal roofs with baked finishes are also unlikely to affect sensitive persons.

Wood shingles and shakes that are treated for fireproofing, stained, or otherwise sealed with petro-based materials are questionable as to biologic effect. Clay tile, natural slate, and concrete tile (subject to mold or mildew in a moist climate) require roofs of adequate structural strength.

Inasmuch as most commercial buildings are likely to be "sealed up" against outdoor conditions, various forms of least toxic single ply roofing may be selected. Leakage is most apt to occur around flashing and various intersections of roof surface and roof stacks. Metal flashing is inert, but non-toxic membranes can be used that are more compatible in coefficient of expansion to the roofing application than metal.

Rubberflex (a misleading name) is a 100% VOC compliant elastomeric acrylic seamless applied roofing material suitable for both pitched and flat roof applications. It is manufactured by Republic Powdered Metals, Inc., P.O. Box 724, Medina, OH 44258. All roofing materials should be applied strictly to manufacturer's instructions.

Plastics

Plastics derived from petro-sources and toxic chemicals that may be employed in their making have a counter ecologic effect. Hard plastic laminates, however, are a better biologic choice than soft plastics in regard to outgassing. Hard plastics are those that can fracture upon bending.

Hard or solid plastic laminates commonly used for countertops and cabinetry appear unlikely to have an effect upon persons with environmental sensitivities. In fact, such hard laminates when applied to materials that do outgas formaldehyde or other toxic emissions may by *completely* encasing plywood or particle board act as a shield against outgassing. This occurs when all surfaces including the ends and edges of material are so encased. Medex is a hardboard without formaldehyde appropriate for cabinetry.

Soybeans and other natural renewable plants could be a resource for plastic formulations. The question exists as to processing energy intensities, other constituents added to the formulation, and suitability to purpose. If *all* plastics were prohibited from use, the loss would be enormous. Certain polymers have little known effect upon health. The ecologic equation is more complex and each resource and its *total* impact is individual.

Determining which plastics may or may not be biologically safe can be a dilemma. Usually plastic materials and products that use no solvents and that give little or no odor are preferable. Plastics that have no or low levels of toxicity, do not shed particles, contain no volatile compounds, have been "baked" to remove outgassing, and are chemically stable are less likely to be a biologic problem.

Plastic used for glazing of windows, skylights, and other exterior building envelope openings can have properties more effectual for specific usage than glass. Polycarbonate plastic can offer a greater degree of safety than glass for protection against break-in or severe impact. It offers a particular advantage of safety against overhead shattering. It also can be bent as desired for architectural applications more readily than glass. The principal shortcoming of polycarbonate glazing is susceptibility to surface scratching. Coatings can acts as a means to protect the surface. But over a period of time the surface hardness of glass offers much greater resistance to scratching.

Recycling

Recycling is much in the public mind. Landfills and other dumping grounds for trash are filling to the hilt. The separation of the various categories of trash is critical to economic and ecologic effect.

Under the status quo most trash is "waste." What is made and packaged in the first place needs to be the prime concern. Design and marketing potential are primary to the effort of producing ecologic materials, products, and systems.

How we may *best* be able to reduce the infinite accumulation of trash that is burying us needs to be addressed from source, to use, to trash as a resource. The more that trash can be used at its point of discard without undue applied petro-energies and questionable and toxic additives, the more that our global ecosystems will remain sustainable.

The energy of sorting, collecting, processing, and ultimately reusing in a similar or quite different form the multifarious stockpiles of trash needs closer evaluation in ecologic terms. Imagination, design, and purpose are core elements of an ecologic ethic.

Architecture has been the direct and indirect recipient of a number of discarded products. Bottles, cans, paper, metal, wood, masonry, concrete, and other elements of discard have and continue to find their way into architecture. Automobile tires have been used but are more questionable as to their outgassing.

Used brick and old barn beams are often bought at a premium. Historically many materials including stone and marble in their original or altered form have been purloined from earlier architecture to serve that which is newer.

To recycle entire or notable portions of existing architecture can be accorded to historic preservation or may simply be encased or otherwise used within the design of a new, renovation, remodel, or addition project. It is not always as easy to weigh the total cost consequences of renewing or otherwise designing projects as that of a *totally* new project.

Meeting and matching to old conditions can unearth the unexpected. But nevertheless, the merit of preservation and the ingenuity employed can result to an ecologic advantage.

Within the scope of interior designs, furniture is often refurbished, antique pieces can be valued, classic items cherished, and multitudinous items of the interior of the past be reclaimed.

Recoverability

Usefulness, adaptability, and durability relate to recoverability when a project has reached a termination of purpose. As it may no longer be functional for its purpose, how can it be reclaimed or how can elements, parts, or components of the architecture be used as they are, be made adaptable, and still have a functional and economic durability?

Initial concepts and design can use construction materials and elements of the architecture and its systems after the demise of its purpose or to make way for new construction when properly planned. The more recoverable these entities for further use, the less ecologic and economic demand is made.

Dimensional lumber, doors, cabinetry, and other wood items can be recovered from houses and buildings when they retain useful value. Wooden beams such as microlams and other laminations of wood including plywoods can be recoverable depending upon condition. Adhesive applied or in which adhesive applied materials are attached to wood materials can cause them to be without further architectural value.

Poured-in-place concrete (unless used as originally poured) has doubtful architectural reusability. Post-tensioned concrete falls into this category. In contrast precast and prestressed concrete slabs can be recoverable. Modular sizes used for foundation, wall, stairway, and roof constructions may be particularly re-employed in new construction.

The modular building block constructions of children provide a model for full-scale architecture. Panelized and modular core systems that can be manufactured of wood, concrete, metal, or perhaps some environmental plastic can provide the adaptability for change. The more adaptable to answer the possibilities and probabilities of future use, the less is the demand on basic resources for new construction.

Steel that is bolted in place or otherwise fastened for easy demountability can be a recoverable asset. Welded in place steel members pose a greater problem. Steel has an impressive longevity and durability (if protected from rust). In compression and as to tensile strength it has occupied a principal position in building construction. As with other metals it is mined. Its process of manufacture is energy intensive.

Carpet

Carpeting is one of the most controversial of indoor products. Its propensity to gather dust and dirt, encourage microorganisms, and to flake off particles into the air justly invites criticism and advisable avoidance. Through exterior openings dust, dirt, pollen, and pathogenic organisms are tracked into interior floors and stairways on footwear. The Japanese custom of removing shoes upon entering would be a definite advantage to interior cleanliness.

But carpet is the most accommodating, adaptable, and acoustical of interior materials for residential and commercial use. It will accommodate to an entire floor of any size, configuration, or substrate material. It is adaptable to floor, wall, stairway, and ramp installations for which it provides safety and an aesthetic surface of texture and color. It is acoustical in deadening sound and footsteps within space and to spaces below. Carpeting is comforting to the leg muscles and can lessen fatigue of the body in standing and walking or in sitting upon it.

Depending upon selection for residential or commercial use, nylon carpet can provide a low demand upon maintenance and cleaning. Short, densely packed commercial grade continuous filament cut pile carpet can be prescribed for this objective and provide long-term durability. "Continuous filament" significantly reduces the flaking off of possibly irritating particulates. An appropriate resilient nonallergenic and nontoxic pad can add to comfort, acoustics, and durability. Recommended for "healthy homes," untreated wool and cotton rugs are considered naturally more "ecologic and biologic" but are subject to stairway and over wood floors harboring of soil requiring more maintenance than wall-to-wall nylon. These factors reflect in lifetime labor cost and ecologic effect.

The greatest shortcomings of carpeting are chemical odors and outgassing that may offend the nose and be counter to respiratory well-being. Chemicals in carpeting reported by one manufacturer (principal odor sources) are 4-phenylcyclohene as a byproduct of styrene, butadiene sodium polyacrilate, ground marble filler, and synthetic soap, which comprise the latex backing adhesive, with polypropylene for primary and secondary backing. the report states that no formaldehyde or asbestos is present in the carpeting. The question as to specification is, what is the respiratory effect of the chemistry and dyes on the respiratory system of people by any manufactured carpeting? Residual odor and toxic outgassing depending upon materials of manufacture may linger on for weeks, months, and for more than a year.

Bacteria, mold, and dust mites harbor in carpeting and rugs as well as in bedding and upholstered furniture. The application of antibacterial and antifungal chemicals to carpeting and making it stain resistant can have the added benefits of control advantage but a chemical outgassing respiratory disadvantage.

Adhesive applied methods (a release type of adhesive can be used) can be provocative in laying carpet and outgassing toxic fumes for a period of time. A nontoxic adhesive by AFM Products is available as well as a coating that can be applied to nylon carpeting and rugs to contain inherent chemicals from outgassing. After four or five carpet cleanings reapplication is necessary.

Padding that is installed under carpeting should be nonallergenic and nontoxic as well as the carpeting should be easy to clean and maintain. Carpeting with a dust-tight construction will prevent dirt getting through to the padding.

Rugs of untreated cotton installed upon wood floors have an appeal to persons who are environmentally sensitive. They do retain a benefit in being washable. Size and thickness and type of backing are all factors of ease or difficulty in maintenance. Wood floors treated with ecologically acceptable finishes can demand their share of continuing maintenance. They can avoid the chemical outgassing of synthetic carpeting.

For homes, offices, stores, theaters, and institutional uses the acoustic, softness, and ease of cleaning benefits of carpet for the most part outweigh most hard surface or combination of flooring materials. As a variation of flooring materials may be used within a project, cleaning, maintenance, and attendant costs are increased. How wall-to-wall or other forms of carpeting are cleaned as an ongoing process should not be neglected as a major matter of concern. A central vacuum system can avoid the dust that can filter back into the room through a bag of portable vacuum. Vacuum cleaners that perform as air-cleaning machines with HEPA, charcoal, multi-layered bags or water filtration can be a better alternative that average vacuum machines.

Periodic carpet cleaning should be done with nontoxic and nonallergenic cleaning agents. Methods that leave the carpet damp are best accomplished at a time when maximum ventilation can speed drying. Rugs can be sent out to be cleaned that are too large for in situ washing or cleaning. A client and project will benefit by interior designers who recommend a source of ecologic cleaning products and procedures. Such advice will tend to assure that a project conscientiously designed will meet ecologic concerns as originally intended.

Image Carpets, Inc. makes plastic pop bottle recycled carpeting with 100 percent face fibers of polyethylene terephtalate (PET). It is claimed to have inherent stain and soil resistance, resistance to fading, static control, and durable fiber strength. Their address is P.O. Box 5555, 112 Turkey Mountain Road NE, Armuchee, GA 30105.

Intersept carpeting, fabrics, coatings, window blinds, and other products are available from Interface Research Corporation, 100 Galleria Parkway, Suite 1875, Atlanta, GA 30309. Intersept is antibacterial, stain and soil resistant, durable, and with low water solubility. It is a high-tech rather than low-tech solution for commercial and institutional carpeting. It is described as a synergistic blend of substituted ammonium salts of alkylkated phosphoric acids mixed with free alkylated phosphoric acid. What we breathe can be more important than what we eat. It is carpeting developed as a need for hospitals, nursing homes, and other installations that have a high bacterial or mold environment. It has essentially a nylon face and synthetic latex bonding agent.

Hendrickson Naturlich Flooring, 8031 Mill Station Rd., Sebastopol, CA 95472. Natural fiber and linoleum floor coverings of seagrass, sisal, coir, wool, provide very casual to more formal textures and surfaces that avoid synthetic fibers.

No-Muv, 5801 Phillips Highway, Jacksonville, FL 32216. From Builder's Choice, this is an underlayment padding of various available weights for use with wall-to-wall commercial carpeting. The company also manufactures rug underlayments that keep them from shifting around. It is of a polypropylene and acrylic composition that is hypoallergenic, nontoxic, has a nylon reinforcement, and no formaldehyde.

Environmental Coating Systems, Inc., 3321 S. Susan St., Santa Ana, CA 92704. The makers of "All Deck" offer this 100% acrylic, VOC compliant, deck coating for exterior and interior applications over a fiberglass mat. It is waterproof and weatherproof.

Bio-Intervention

From a biologic standpoint intervention can play a major role in containment, neutralization, or as a barrier to outgassing and shedding of allergenic particulates or as an "in the works" means of attenuating or contravening anti-biologic electromagnetic fields.

Formaldehyde and other toxins within plywood and particle boards can be contained by sealants and coatings that lock in the gases. The natural chemistry to wood also outgasses to the symptomatic disturbance of some sensitive individuals. For these surfaces AFM Water Seal can be applied as a sealant as well as for reducing noxious emissions from walls, ceilings, and over painted surfaces.

A barrier to moisture penetration is AFM DynaSeal, a black coating that can be applied to waterproof foundations or other surfaces and used as a subgrade concrete floor coating as a barrier to moisture and radon gas emanating from the soil. AFM makes a Safecoat Primer, Safecoat Paint, Hard Seal for use over previously painted surfaces, and Polyuraseal as a low sheen clear finish for floors, cabinets, and woodwork as an indoor intervention for benefit of chemically sensitive and environmentally aware persons. Spraying the outer wall cavities of wood framing and inner side of exterior sheathing can reduce emissions from these materials.

Makers of paints that have low or no toxicity include: AFM Enterprises, Inc., 1140 Stacey Court, Riverside, CA 92507. A broad range of cleaners, mildew controls, coatings, finishes, paints, and sealants are available, formulated to prevent outgassing and for safe use. Livos PlantChemistry, 614 Agua Fria St., Santa Fe, NM 87501. Their products are composed mainly of plant oils and tree resins and use water or citrus thinners and earthen mineral pigments. Auro organic paints are very similar and their importer is the Sinan Company, P.O. Box 181, Suisin City, CA 94585. Both paints are imports from Germany. The "embodied energy" of imported products from an ecologic standpoint is a judgmental trade-off with biologically conscious domestic products. Commonly used solvents should be banned from use. Water-based materials or citrus thinners should take their place.

Bio-intervention can take up the slack when materials or products that have ecologic and biologic merit are too expensive, not available or manufactured, or not well suited to purpose or when no contractor may have enough experience to properly apply them.

The proper application of bio-intervention sealants, coatings, or encapsulation can be critical to fully contain gaseous and particulate escape. A reverse situation occurs when the effort is to keep airborne contamination from getting into materials.

The dryness or wetness of air can play a role in the accumulation or penetration of mold, yeast, and bacteria on surface materials that encourage microorganic growth. In the case of lumber and other materials, destruction of its composition can be seen as dry or wet rot. High humidity areas, such as indoor spas and swimming pool spaces, can be a constant aggravating problem in rapid proliferation of mold.

Within the author's experience, AFM SuperClean and AFM X158 mildew control were the most successful products for his swimming pool application to inhibit mold on walls, ceilings, and doors. Generally under conditions of none to limited ventilation and relative humidity above 90 percent, no mold was evident after a period of four months. These products appeared to have no toxicity and no odor after application. As with all bio-intervention materials, meticulous care and manufacturer's instructions for application must be followed. Crawl spaces, attics, and basements can harbor mold and bacteria. Taking protective facturer's instructions for application must be followed. Crawl spaces, attics, and basements can harbor mold and bacteria. Taking protective anti-bacterial and anti-mold measures before a problem occurs is prudent. Molecular adsorbers can be effective in improving air quality by significantly reducing mold and bacteria. To this end, Molly Aire is manufactured by Sande Corporation, 8150 Corporate Park Drive, Suite 104, Cincinnati, OH 45242. Molly Aire can be used in newly acquired or renovated old buildings to reduce odors and adsorb toxic gases. Environmentally sensitive persons within their cars as well as within the indoor environment can be relieved.

Nontoxic and nonallergenic materials (or with very low increment of toxicity) can intervene other materials that have a higher risk of toxicity.

Cross-Tuff is a tough, cross-laminated polyethylene only three mils thick that with a very low permeability factor (claimed to be 2-1/2 times less than conventional 6 to 10 mil polyfilm). It is also more resistant to physical penetration. Environmentally sensitive persons should test it before installation. It is available from Cross-Tuff Manufactured Plastics and Distribution, Inc., 2162 Market St., Denver, CO 80205. They also manufacture a radon gas barrier film.

Architecture is a form of bio-intervention. It protects us and our possessions from sun, climate, and unpredictable weather.

Insulation is an element of architectural thermal intervention. How effective it is depends upon the interactive thermal responses of the architecture and its systemic form.

Unfortunately, filters that effectively remove outdoor dust, mold, spores, pollen, and other bio-antagonistic substances from intake air are only somewhat effective with natural air flow and not at all for toxic gases.

Pressurization, ventilation, and cooling by outdoor air intake require appropriate filters to provide bio-intervention in the interest of "cleaner" indoor air. Most filtration of intake air by mechanical systems distribution is very inadequate. Attic and other exhaust fans (usually very noisy) have a notable disadvantage of increasing the introduction of unfiltered air into interior space.

HEPA or modified HEPA intake air filters are very effective in removing down to sub-micron particles, but they have no effect on airborne gases. Molecular adsorbers that act as a molecular sieve, catalytic devices, or microorganic conversion are essential for gaseous filtration.

Frequency of filter "throw away" is environmentally undesirable. HEPA filters have a very long life but become terminal waste. Cleanable filters (adequate to need) avoid disposal. Self-actuating electrostatic filters made with dissimilar plastic screens that negatively charge particles by air movement and then deposit them to a positive field are available. Cleanable filters that require no electricity include: Air Magnet (two-stage filtration) manufactured by Great American Filter Company, 2107 Lann Ave., Cincinnati, OH 45212-9899, EnviroGuard manufactured by Air Purification of Houston, 1662 W. Sam Houston Pkwy. N., Houston, TX 77043, and Allergen AirFilter Corporation, 5205 Ashbrook, Houston, TX 77081 manufacturer of electrostatic pre-charged disposable filters.

With varying levels of outdoor air pollution, prudence and judgment are required as to when or when not to ventilate, provide oxygen, and remove CO_2 from indoor space. A low-cost monitoring device is needed to alert indoor occupants to the levels and type of outdoor air pollution.

Insulation and Thermal Breaks

Insulation is one of the most problematic materials used in construction. The research into its application and performance has been long and appears endless. A new black foam board (Blackore) by Celotex with an aged R-factor of 8.7 constrains radiant heat transfer and is manufactured with reduced CFCs. But the ozone layer is only some millimeters thick. Its loss is increasing and can become catastrophic.

Some of the most effective insulations are isocyanurate and polyurethane, currently made with CFCs that have a destructive effect upon the ozone layer. As foam boards they are ideal for creating a thermal break over exterior walls and roof joists and other types of construction.

Polystyrene foam board has the advantage of being useful as an *outsulation* for exterior application of monoacrylic stucco-like coatings. It also can be used as a high density board to insulate foundations. It is available as a steam-expanded material (without CFCs or formaldehyde). It can

Certain rigid insulation boards in combustion can liberate a toxic gas. On exterior walls 1-hour fire code water-resistant gypsum board sheathing can act as an interior shield to combustible insulation and siding. Other rigid insulation boards such as wood fiber, perlite, and foam glass have lower R ratings but are well suited to certain uses.

Certainteed white fiberglass Insulsafe III without formaldehyde is not manufactured in batt form. Blowing in place with a 1/4 nylon mesh is needed to hold it in place for exterior sidewalls. Settling should be considered. It is most practical for supportive horizontal locations.

Commonly used fiberglass faced or unfaced batt insulation has formaldehyde. Installation is critical between exterior wall and roof wood frame members to secure full batt coverage, a complete fit, and means of retainage in place. Sealing around door and window framing and electrical boxes and an exterior "tight" enclosure system such as Tyvek under wood siding or monoacrylic-coated outsulation can prevent infiltration and exfiltration that downgrades the insulation R factor. High density insulation has a higher R factor but the cost benefit is lower. To avoid respiratory effects from formaldehyde, outgassing, and airborne particulates, unfaced fiberglass can be fog coated with AFM WaterSeal after it is installed in place. High density R-30 fiberglass insulation is made in particular for cathedral ceilings with 10-inch deep roof joists, allowing for a space over the joists. It is claimed to have less formaldehyde. But it can be shielded with a low perm cross-laminated polyfilm as well as with a nontoxic sealant and paint finish over plaster or gypsum board.

Air that goes through insulation can considerably decrease its insulation value. Convective "loops" within the loose fiber installation of fiberglass can depending upon heating and cooling transfer lessen insulation value. As a case in point, outside air ventilation of attics leaves in question the actual insulation value that may be derived from loose fill between and over ceiling joists.

Published R ratings tend to be higher than accomplished within the full reality of most projects. Thermal insulation breaks between sheathing and other members and thermal conductive characteristics of roof members reduce energy losses. After snow it is usually easy to detect the location of wood joists or other members that conduct heat energy more readily than the insulated portion. Rapid melting is visible along the line of members. Infrared photography is instructional in revealing the total energy losses of a home or building.

Rockwool insulation is energy intensive in its manufacture, but where fiberglass has a factor of R-19 for a six-inch outer wall application, rockwool will have a factor of R-23. It also has a greater thermal mass, less proclivity to internal convective energy loops, and can more fully correspond to the total wall cavity. It has largely been superceded by fiberglass due to the "cleaner" aspects of fiberglass and general preference by installers.

Cellulose can be noted as a recycled product. Shortcomings are that it can settle down in a wall, allowing an energy loss to occur, and its borates may lose their fire protection capability through time. It can also be an environmental anathema for sensitive persons. Several case histories indicate severe reactions. From a biologic standpoint, cellulose is made from a polyglot of paper products with inherent toxic residues and added borates and other chemicals to impart fire resistance. Inhalable toxins from very small particulates can affect occupants. There is an opportunity to make cellulose more biologically acceptable as well as for the recycled environmental benefit.

Air Krete is a magnesium oxide inorganic product extracted from Gulf of Mexico sea water. It is nontoxic, non-combustible, and when foamed in place produces no chemical gases or vapors. It has no formaldehyde or fluorocarbons and weighs two pounds per cubic foot when dry. Its R factor is 3.9 per inch. It can be retained in place during the foaming process with insect screen across exterior wall and roof members. It has been quoted as an ideal solution for environmentally sensitive persons. It does require training for proper installation. It is available from Palmer Industries, Inc., 10611 Old Annapolis Rd., Frederick, MD 21701.

Filtration

Filtration is a form of intervention. The market place abounds with air cleaning filtration machines. Machines using multiple filters with a prefilter, HEPA or modified HEPA for submicron particulate filtration, charcoal for adsorption of gases, and a final stage of negative ionization provide effectual sequential filtration. Negative ionization vitalizes the air in the last stage. Adequate capacity for space and space conditions is critical to performance.

In contrast to the filtration offered by machines of the foregoing description, common filters are crude air cleaners. Central systems lack the sophistication of multiple filter portable room air cleaning machines. Ductwork is a negative aspect in the essential need of ventilation and thermal air distribution in buildings. Cleanable filters have an extendable life. But they are ineffective in small particle removal and have no effect on gases. Throw-away filters contribute to landfill clutter.

Tobacco smoke is especially provocative from a filtration standpoint. With a vast combination of submicron particulates and gases, it quickly compromises any type of filtration. The most effective solutions are separately enclosed spaces for smoking with 30 to 50 air changes per hour with outdoor air.

Among these poor choices, a view of architecture as a bio-vitalized air and energy-sustaining system leaves much to be desired.

Heating, Ventilating, Cooling

The more that the thermodynamics of the architecture is the heating, cooling, and ventilating system, the more the need for a mechanical system can be lessened or avoided.

Thermal load dominated buildings can require cooling in cold weather. Rather than mechanical refrigeration, "economizer cycle" cool ventilation air can be used to accomplish desired temperatures. Higher ventilation rates are recommended to avoid or overcome "sick building syndrome." But the question should be asked as to how polluted with gases and particulates the outdoor air is and how good is the filtration of entering outdoor air. Molecular adsorbing or catalytic filters are needed to remove objectionable gases, mold, and bacteria. Biologic filter beds are being studied for development and foretell future possibilities of bioculture filters specific to specific air pollution conditions.

HEPA filtration is best for single pass outdoor intake air ventilation for the interception of dust and other particulates as well as that from internal space. Negative ionization can be beneficially applied at the supply end of duct systems. Ductwork is the primary and problematic method used for ventilation in commercial buildings. An air supply uniformly perforated ceiling plenum for substantial or entire area ventilation, heating, and cooling is most comfortable with uniformly spaced floor returns.

The devious tobacco industry has concocted a ventilation plan purported to protect the non-smoker in a common area with smokers. It is a deceitful and ill-conceived attempt to parry the weight of official evidence that sidestream smoke is unequivocally harmful to nonsmokers. Their system is mainly a floor plenum with ventilation supply air delivered through carpeting directly to the ceiling. If a ceiling plenum is part of the return air system, particulate filters are either too easily compromised and gas adsorbing ones too rapidly unload back into the airstream again. If the air is continually exhausted it would put a large and wasteful demand upon the removal of heated or cooled interior air. The scheme also ignores unwarranted expense and the forcing of dust, bacteria, mold, and whatever else tracked over the carpet into contaminating the breathable air.

Smoking cannot be ignored in design. It is the most pernicious and common indoor air pollutant that not only offends but also permeates the indoor air through mechanical systems and by convection from lobbies, corridors, private office, and where anyone might smoke. More ventilation, except in separately enclosed and ventilated smoking rooms, can never be adequate. All smoking is strongly anti-ecologic and anti-biologic. Seventy-nine percent of smokers want to quit. With no accommodation by design, indoor air quality can be more easily benefitted.

Solar atria and sunspaces can function as an air tempering means. Various interior spaces with various ventilation and thermal requirements can be served from central atria or sunspaces with an advantage of selective planting to absorb CO_2, provide oxygen, and act as a general air filter.

Increasing ventilation as now advocated as a prevention or remedy of "sick building syndrome" creates in most cases a greater energy demand for heating and cooling, as well as for ventilation power.

A closer look at mechanical systems is needed towards quiet, efficient vortex fans with energy-efficient motors. In contrast to older HVAC equipment, new furnaces, boilers, and in-line water heating units are greatly more efficient. Gas-fired units can have direct combustion air, automatic electric ignition, and closed damper of the exhaust vent when the unit is not in operation. Safe equipment location and effectual insulation should not be overlooked.

Where people spend most of their time in an office or other indoor environment, heating and cooling energy could be most efficiently supplied to individual spaces rather than trying to deliver a uniform level of comfort to everyone within a thermal zone irrespective of their task or need. Corridors, enclosed entries to the exterior, and certain other places in any building require no heating or refrigerated cooling. Evaporative cooling is an exception in which air discharged through any entry or opening benefits the high volume of air cooling effect and relieves the counter-effect of a buildup of indoor humidity.

In locations that have a high level of humidity or some cities in which humidity has been escalated by high-water-demand landscaping and water features, evaporative cooling performance is negated or compromised. The cross-sectional area of evaporative cooling ductwork is relatively large, requiring adequate architectural and structural clearance. Evaporative coolers and the ductwork are subject to mold and can have mild to serious bio-effects.

As in the Hotsy Corporation Office Building project (see case study pages 122-125), dark south window blinds can act as air-type solar collectors to transfer direct solar radiation to useful purpose. A suspended plenum ceiling with the heat from recessed lighting can add to the thermal gain, and the energy can be stored in a rock bin or directly used to distribute heat through a mechanical HVAC duct system to indoor spaces.

Sunspace applications have already been covered. The particularly difficult energy analysis of every home and building based on calculations alone can be inaccurate. The periodic habits and other space-use factors of people, lighting, and energy demand are influential in their effect upon system performance. Attitudes and attire can be significant as to indoor perception of comfort. Numerous years ago the author was made aware of employee discomfort in a building remodel of his design in a general office work area. Some employees would turn up the thermostat, others would turn it down. Without their knowledge the author suggested relocating the thermostat connections out of the control of the employees. The disconnected thermostat then remained open to anyone who wished to manipulate it. Complaints immediately ceased.

Residential comfort, adequate ventilation, and low utility bills appeal to homeowners. The more that HVAC systems do not exist or remain supplemental to the natural thermal comforts and ventilation of the architecture, the more that the foregoing objectives are realized.

Forced-air duct systems are not easily thermally zoned. Their popularity is more attributable to ventilation and refrigerated air space cooling. Hydronic baseboard, radiant floor panel, fan coil, or ceiling applications avoid interior effects of forced air. They provide greater heating comfort but no ventilation or cooling. They have the advantage of being thermally zoned. The more zones, the greater the cost.

Domestic hot water heating can be accomplished with in-line heaters. If they are gas fired, the BTU demand can be met if appropriate to use. Electric in-line heaters can peak the utility load (which is not desirable) when sized adequate to use. The positive aspect of the insulated hot water tank is that it can provide a ready reserve of hot water. The negative aspect is that even when insulated it can continually lose energy at its location.

Electromagnetics

We are electromagnetic beings in an electromagnetic world. For prudence and our own well-being, various electromagnetic field meters for testing the milligauss field strength give a clue to "safe" proximity. An electric clock can emit 10 milligauss. At a prudent distance of several feet away from it, the field strength is likely to be under two milligauss.

Nearly all electrical devices and equipment found in homes and buildings will generate an electromagnetic field. Sustained time in magnetic fields over one milligauss is questionable; over three milligauss may not be prudent. The electromagnetic effects as to prudent distance from light fixtures, computers, and all forms of electrical equipment should be a factor of concern and design. Places where people spend much time, such as bedrooms, in an office, or other long exposure locations, should be given consideration. Attention is paid to radioactivity and protection from it, but little to electromagnetic fields generated by various forms of medical equipment.

Some persons naturally have electromagnetic sensitivities and other persons acquire them. Field meters are available from: Bio-Physik Mersmann (Fieldmeter BPM 1003); Safe Computing Co. (The Safe Meter), 33 Williams St., Needham, MA 02194; and AlphaLab (TriField Electromagnetic Pollution Meter), 1272 Alameda Ave., Salt Lake City, UT 84102.

In addition to the new supersensitive field meter, Mersmann also has a bioelectromagnetometer for taking a profile of the earth's magnetic fields. The Baubiologie Institute of Germany has given concern to earth field geopathic vortexes as an indicated cause of human dysfunction and cancer. Bedrooms as a place of sustained exposure have been particularly singled out for evaluation. Moving a bed or otherwise avoiding a geopathic "point" of sustained exposure is advisable. Scientifically corroborated electro-dowsers were first to find the geopathic correlation with illness.

The electrophoresis effect (an interrelation between negative ionization and a positive pulse field) is being used for "clean rooms." For a biologic response in harmony with the body's 7.83 Hertz, a Schumann positive pulse field with negative ionization meets such correspondence. Pure air is basic but the electrophoresis effect is essential to vitalize the air.

Clean room and electrophoresis equipment is manufactured by American Environmental Systems, 4699 Nautilus Court South, Boulder, CO 80302.

Interior Furniture and Furnishings

Minimalism in design and "clean line" practicality in furniture are on course with an ecologic and biologic perspective. Minimal materials and minimal maintenance conserve the most of energy, time, and money. Ergometric interior design planning with optimal adaptability is an ecologic objective.

Local domestic wood furniture with contemporary or "Shaker-like" simplicity, finished with nontoxic glues, stains, clear finishes, paint, or lacquer, is a good ecologic choice. Hard plastic laminates, avoidance of formaldehyde or other toxins in

"treated" wood, minimal and simple functional design, and minimization of energy-intensive metals can also be within an ecologic/biologic choice. Long-term durability and modularization of elements, appropriate to purpose, are plus values.
In the final amortization of a material or product, one should consider how initial design can foretell final usefulness as a reclaimed resource, reconstitution for reuse, as a recycled item, or at least as productive waste.

Untreated wool, cotton, linen, and other natural fibers can avoid a biologic impact but are more likely to soil when left untreated. Leather can be naturally comfortable, but various dyes or finishes can evoke an adverse bioresponse.

Polyurethane-filled pillows and cushions can cause problems for environmentally sensitive persons. Polyester fill is likely to be less troublesome. Feathers work their way through fabrics and can trigger an allergic reaction. Environmentally sensitive individuals seem to prefer untreated cotton covers with untreated cotton fill that has no residual pesticides.

On the other hand, certain synthetics such as nylons that are fully outgassed can offer greater stain resistance, easier cleaning, and greater durability at less cost. The author has successfully used Molly Aire (a molecular adsorber) in a sunspace to outgas some very odoriferous and likely chemically-laden fabrics. Several weeks or more may be necessary to eliminate detectable chemical odors.

The unsealed wood frame or other constructive elements of seating pieces can outgas through fabrics. Nontoxic sealants can avoid this problem. With metal frames exposed or unexposed coatings are less apt to bother anyone, but being fastidious, the possibility should be checked. Plating and anodization are energy intensive and chrome for finishes, while highly desirable, is imported.

Case pieces, tables, desks, and other furniture including seating pieces tend to materially alter natural indoor air convection patterns. The effect of furniture on cross ventilation should not be disregarded. In commercial projects studies have been made on the effects of mechanical system air delivery relative to the modular systems of "office landscaping." See previous sections regarding sunspace furniture, carpeting, and window treatments for additional information.

index

Smoking, impact of, 51–52
Social responsibility questions, 19–22
Societal change, need for, 72–73
Solar applications: basics, 280–284;
    interior, 106–109
Solar energy projects, examples of, 43,
    45–46
Solar gain, 281
Solar inductive ventilation, 92
Solar lithium bromide absorption cooling,
    92
Solar skyshafts, 240
Solar systems: active solar, 43; hybrid
    solar, 42–43; passive solar, 40–42;
    solar energy projects, 43–46
Southwest Solar Adobe School, 285
Stack action ventilation, 92
State of the World 1990, 42
Steel, 37
Subdivision residence, rural, 167–171
Sun/Earth, 16
Sunspaces, 40, 42, 87, 108, 202, 219
Survival issues, 23–25

Technology: urban planning and, 74;
    versus ecologic necessity, 29–31
Tester, Jeffrey W., 46
Therapeutic uses for solar energy, 45
Thermal mass objects and furniture, 42,
    84, 281–282
Thermal protection, interior, 103–104

Urban architecture, recycled, 172–182
Urban forestation, 77–78
Urban perspective, need for, 72–73

Urban planning: bio-sensory response,
    187–188; ecologic paradigm, 185–186;
    factors to consider, 189–191;
    landscaping and land forming, 186;
    need for, 74–75, 184; vehicles and,
    188–189

Vehicles: bio-effects of pollution, 61;
    need for energy policies/action, 68–71;
    photovoltaics and, 45; pollution from,
    51, 52, 61–62; urban planning and,
    188–189
Ventilation: commercial architecture and,
    92, 221–222; guidelines, 282, 295–296;
    methods of, 53–54, 104, 105;
    residential architecture and, 201–203
Venturi ventilation, 92
Vitality: architecture and, 6, 7; of nature
    versus human, 24, 34–35

Walls, Trombe, 108
Water: attributes of, 59; conservation,
    58–60; desalinization, 45, 58; distilled,
    57–58; methods of heating, 43;
    purification, 57–58; solar projects
    using, 45; supplies, 57; systems, 57–59
Wells, Malcolm, 285
Windows, 42; commercial architecture
    and, 93, 231; coverings for, 103–104,
    105, 211, 231, 240, 283; guidelines for,
    282–283; residential architecture and,
    83–84, 86, 201, 211
Wood, guidelines for, 287–288

Zoning, 1, 90, 215